THE NEW FINANCIAL GUIDE FOR THE SELF-EMPLOYED

John Ellis

Contemporary Books, Inc.
Chicago

Library of Congress Cataloging in Publication Data

Ellis, John, 1915–
 The new financial guide for the self-employed.

 Revision of: A financial guide for the self-employed,
1972.
 Includes index.
 1. Finance, Personal. 2. Self-employed—United
States. 3. Small business—United States—Finance.
I. Title.
HG179.E44   1981   331.024   81-65179
ISBN 0-8092-5900-1   AACR2
ISBN 0-8092-5899-4 (pbk.)

For Ellen, An Understanding Wife—

The greatest aid to successful self-employment

Published by Contemporary Books, Inc.
180 North Michigan Avenue, Chicago, Illinois 60601
Manufactured in the United States of America
Library of Congress Catalog Card Number: 81-65179
International Standard Book Number: 0-8092-5900-1 (cloth)
                           0-8092-5899-4 (paper)

Published simultaneously in Canada by
Beaverbooks, Ltd.
150 Lesmill Road
Don Mills, Ontario M3B 2T5
Canada

Contents

Foreword

FOR more than thirty years, I have been using the designation "self-employed" on my income tax return. The fact that I work for myself indicates, of course, that I wish to be my own employee rather than someone else's and that I prefer to rise and fall mainly on my own efforts. My preference is reinforced when I read about life in the "executive jungle" and hear about men thrown from their jobs and unable to find others because they have passed the age of forty.

Of course, working for oneself has its own problems. Demands are made on self-employers that those who work for others usually do not face. You must take the final responsibility for your own efforts. Unless *you* produce income, you must face the consequences. No employer will pay you if you become ill or even take a few days off. It is up to you to provide protection against dozens of business hazards, including many—like the inroads of competition—against which no insurance can guard you. You must prepare for your own retirement. In the absence of a pension plan set up for you by an employer, you must establish one of your own. You must also manage your business affairs efficiently, maintain a place of business, and perhaps hire, train, and supervise employees.

In accepting the responsibilities of a self-employer, you accept the responsibility of making vital business judgments every day. In many cases, however, self-employed persons must make their business decisions in a vacuum of inexperience. While hundreds of guides have been written for the managers of large corporations, the problems of the self-employed have gone largely ignored. Until now, no guide has existed to help the self-employed person cope with many problems of which he may not even have been aware until he began operating on his own.

I know from personal experience that such a guide is needed. Only through costly trial and error over many years, for example, have I learned to relate accurately the time required to do a job with the compensation received for it; to save incredible amounts of valuable time and energy by simplifying office procedures; to understand how and where to save on taxes. From experience with other self-employers, I know that relatively few pay close attention to legitimate ways of reducing their tax liabilities and that even fewer are concerned with building an adequate pension program for themselves.

Recently, a highly successful manager of apartment properties in New York City—a man who operated from a small office with one competent secretary—announced his retirement after forty years of self-employment. I asked him where he had obtained the greatest number of useful ideas in running his business.

"From people who had the same problems as myself," he replied without hesitation. "From one I picked up a tip on taxes. From another I got an idea to save money on office management. From others, I learned of more efficient ways of handling my letters and telephone calls. Only by benefiting from the experience of others could I solve all the problems that finally landed on me."

He had to get these useful ideas the hard way, over a period of years. He had to look for expert guidance on his own. As so many self-employers have done, he longed for a book that would bring together in one place the best ideas to help him meet his special responsibilities. It is to meet this need—to help you run your affairs profitably and to handle your inevitable problems at a minimal cost in time and money—that this book was written. I earnestly hope that, in practice, it will serve the intended purpose.

John Ellis

Acknowledgments

FOR her valuable assistance in reviewing, updating, and expanding the material contained in this revised edition, I wish to thank Janet Attard. For their help in preparing some of the new material that has been included and in checking the completed manuscript, I wish to thank the writers and editors of *The Professional Report*—specifically Karen Sanders, Hilda Meilman, Amy Melman, Sally Carty, and Arlene Winton.

Chapter 1

Self-Employers Are Different

As a self-employed person, you occupy an uncommon place in our society. You are a member of a minority that makes up about 7 percent of the working nonfarm population, according to the Department of Commerce. You have a personality makeup distinctly different from average. You have more self-reliance than most persons. You have a more highly tuned sense of motivation. Even though many persons who work for others are well educated and have strong professional skills, you probably have stronger talents than most other people and have developed them to a greater degree.

In itself, the fact that you work for yourself makes you different. For, no matter how much they think they might like working for themselves, most persons truly prefer to be employees. Most times, their reasons are completely valid—for them. Some don't want to grapple with the insecurity and uncertainties that usually go with self-employment. They want to know that a paycheck will be there whether they are ill or not, whether they perform outstandingly or indifferently, whether their employer makes a profit or loss. Some don't want the responsibilities and worries that

1

might require longer work weeks and sacrificed weekends. Others might not want to risk the capital needed to start a business or profession or to take a cut in income while waiting to build it up. Others prefer a completely predictable routine. They want to think they will still have their job years from now and a comfortable pension when they retire. Perhaps some also realize that they earn more as employees than they could earn on their own.

As a self-employer, on the other hand, you give low priority to values the typical employee rates highly, and you value highly those aspects of being one's own boss that make employees uncomfortable.

While your income is not certain, neither is it limited. If you perform successfully, you see your efforts reflected in your income at once; you don't have to wait for an employer to recognize your work and reward you. The employee on a nine-to-five schedule is greatly limited in what he can do to augment his income. You can do it by working longer hours or producing more efficiently during the hours you do work. As proof of the rewards obtainable, self-employers are in the top income brackets by any measurement. Figures released by the Internal Revenue Service show, for example, that professionals in partnerships reported net profits far above the averages of employees. Self-employed individuals also are among the most respected men in the community: leading members of political and civic groups, community organizations, social clubs.

Once you build your practice, trade, or business, you are more secure than the typical employee. No one can fire you. You need not fear that your firm will be sold or merged or that a new management will move it elsewhere or bring in a new broom and sweep you out. Nor need you concern yourself with the politics and destructive one-upsmanship that is a part of so many office and factory employee relationships.

You are free to be more creative than the typical employee, to try your own ideas and test new ways of doing things. If they fail, you must be willing to shoulder the entire blame. More important, if they succeed, the credit will be yours—not something to be shared with supervisors.

Perhaps the acid test of an activity is whether those engaged in it would do so again if they could choose new careers. Several studies of self-employers have been made on this question. One survey of sixty-four college graduates who had started businesses of their own found only two who would not immediately do the same if given another chance. Another two would go into their own businesses again, but wanted more experience as employees first. Another study of ninety-three entrepreneurs, all University of Oklahoma graduates, found many who would do things somewhat differently in starting their careers anew. Twelve would make better plans before operating on their own and nine would acquire more experience. But nine would do nothing differently and fifty-three—the overwhelming majority—would go into their own business even sooner than before. Only three—one in thirty-one—would work for someone else.

WHAT IT TAKES

A booklet issued by the Department of Commerce sums up the qualities required of the self-employer:

> First and foremost, he is the leader type and gets a big kick out of being independent. He has ambition and initiative, energy and good health. He isn't afraid of hard work.
>
> He likes people and he knows how to get along with all kinds and all ages. . . .
>
> He thrives on responsibility. He takes the bad breaks and the good breaks in his stride. He has the knack of sizing up a situation accurately and making quick decisions. If his judgment is wrong he isn't sunk. Rather he swallows his medicine and determines not to make the same mistake again. . . .
>
> He is businesslike—a good manager. He watches details and knows at all times the state of his business and where it is headed.
>
> He knows when to borrow money in order to take advantage of cash discounts or quantity buys. He also knows when to expand, when to draw in, when to risk and when not to risk.

He gives his customers their money's worth in goods and services. He studies their likes and dislikes; strives to satisfy them without giving away his profits.

In other words, he keeps his eyes wide open, is smart enough to seize a good bargain and honest enough not to take an unfair advantage of anyone.

The Department of Commerce of New York state suggests a test for persons who aim to manage their own enterprise, questions that suggest what is required for the self-employed:

- Do I get along with people and inspire confidence?
- Do I like the field I want to enter so that I won't mind working long hours and making other personal sacrifices?
- Do I understand that I am engaging in a speculation, and am I willing to take the risk involved?
- Can I make decisions and can I weather wrong ones?
- Am I resourceful in emergencies?
- Am I a good organizer?

The department goes on to state,

If you can answer most of the above questions affirmatively, you can feel quite certain you have the personal aptitude you need. Some are more important than others. For instance, you will find that courtesy and understanding are important factors in handling the public. The main thing is to get along with people, understand their needs and inspire their confidence. A reputation for honesty and reliability can make the difference between success and failure. One who lacks tact in dealing with people and who does not keep his word cannot stay in business long.

Also, the department stresses the ability to make wise decisions quickly and says this quality is closely related to the ability to adjust and readjust rapidly.

Finally, it states that you must be a good organizer and administrator even if you have no employees. You must be self-disciplined and able to arrange your own time profitably. You must coordinate your activities so that you can achieve maximum efficiency. If you have assistants, you must plan their work so as to obtain the full value of their services. You must arrange to meet payments and wages on time and must maintain your credit rating, since credit can be almost as good as money in the bank—something to draw on in emergencies.

As a self-employer, the Commerce Department suggests, you will also find that your workweek does not stop at forty hours. Long after others have gone home you may have to stay in your office, getting books in order and handling countless other details.

As a self-employer, you must face a mix of business and financial problems much different from those encountered by persons in the employ of others. Unlike an employee who may draw his paycheck despite his employer's success, you must remain constantly alert to what is happening to your enterprise. You must cope with the problems of employers, deal with matters of office management, taxes, finance, insurance, collecting and paying bills, and meeting a payroll. At the same time, you are in effect an employee. You must make certain that you receive adequate compensation for your services and that your future is protected.

Not only must you face the combined problems of employer *and* employee; to a great extent you must grapple with these problems alone. On your desk might well stand the motto coined by President Truman: "The buck stops here." Even if you have advisers to suggest procedures in conducting your business affairs, *you* must accept or reject their recommendations—and take the consequences of your decisions.

It follows that you must keep yourself informed about the many questions that will be passed on to you for a final decision. Of course, you must have the particular skills required to practice your profession effectively. But professional success involves more than competence in the field of your specialty. Indeed, to be successful from the financial point of view requires business expertise—the information and judgment with which to make sound business decisions. So important is financial acumen to self-employers that when such persons get together their discussion usually turns to the business rather than the professional side of their profession.

There are great variations in the world of the self-employers. On their own, resourceful persons have made successful careers in fields that defy counting. Hundreds of professions are made up of those who, fulfilling the prescription for business success, have found a need and filled it. Some professions (such as medicine, dentistry, and law) count their practitioners by the tens of thousands. Other professions (those of specialized appraisers and consultants, for instance) may include less than a hundred full-time members. Incomes also vary widely. Some persons earn hundreds of thousands of dollars a year; others net less than $24,000.

Educational requirements, training, and professional skills also vary widely among self-employers. An accountant handling the books of an electronic concern may call on a much different set of intellectual and mechanical strengths and interests than the pediatrician who treats infants and young children. Some professions demand great manual dexterity or a physical strength totally unnecessary in others.

SHARED PROBLEMS

In one area, the interests of all self-employed persons are identical: the financial management of their businesses. Whether you are an auctioneer, one-man advertising agency, or allergist, you face basically the same practical business questions— questions concerning the legal form your operation should take; whether and when it is desirable to hire employees and whether they should be hired on a full- or part-time basis; when to hire specialists to guide you through complicated business and financial and legal problems; where to get the money to start or maintain your trade or business; how to be sure that you won't be wiped out financially by a catastrophe not of your making; how to manage your time effectively to maximize your income; how to make certain that you get paid for the work you do; how to manage paperwork, maintain records, take all the deductions the law allows, and keep your income taxes as low as possible; how to ensure yourself an adequate income in retirement.

Most self-employed persons who deal in services are not fully prepared to cope with these questions. Even when graduate schooling was required to prepare you for your profession and rigid tests were passed in order to practice it, your *financial training* probably has been inadequate. It almost always is. Yet, if you don't manage your business effectively, you risk failing professionally as well.

Year after year, studies show that the survival rate of new businesses is low. Statistics published by the American Women's Economic Development Corporation show that of all new businesses, four out of five fail within the first five years. And the failure rate for businesses started by women is even higher. Some of the eighty out of a hundred that will no longer be around will be sold to others or merged, as in a partnership. Some owners will close their doors because they have been offered better opportunities working for others. Some will quit for reasons of health or family circumstances. But in the case of most new businesses that don't survive, the organizers aren't properly equipped to make a go of it. Often they lack financial management experience.

The Dun & Bradstreet organization, which has kept tabs on the strengths and weaknesses of American businesses since 1834, says the same factors show up as causes of business failure year after year. When a new business goes under, it says, it will almost surely be due to neglect, fraud, lack of experience or unbalanced experience, incompetence, or some disaster that often could have been anticipated.

There are patterns of success as well as of failure, and what makes a business go full speed ahead usually can be identified just as readily as what makes it stop. *The Professional Report* has consulted dozens of management experts and others who have achieved notable successes with their own firms. In the judgment of these authorities, the individual who starts his own operation can sharply increase his chances of success—if not assure it—if he follows the eight rules below.

1. Know how to get the business. Many consultants consider this the most important factor of all. Unless you have clear precedents to prove you can get clients or customers for the kind of goods and services you offer, and unless you have solid ideas about how to get the business you need to survive, you may face rough sledding in your early years. A Dun & Bradstreet survey of 13,514 business failures found that 40.7 percent—two in five—resulted from "inadequate sales" that were the by-product of inexperience in the art of "getting the business."

Outstanding competence in your trade or profession may not be enough for success if you don't know the proven techniques for calling the public's attention to what you offer. The vice-president of one of the country's largest public relations firms decided to go into business for himself. His lawyer asked if he knew the procedures the firm used in attracting clients. The PR man—a genius at servicing accounts once somebody got them—admitted he didn't know. The PR man started his own firm—and closed it eight months later.

Every trade and profession has its own ways of attracting customers and clients. Some self-employers thrive on referrals—business coming their way through the recommendations of others. Others get the bulk of their income from promotional activities—advertisements, direct mail campaigns. Insurance agents, brokers, and others who offer financial services often build their clientele from those who respond to offers of free literature. Some franchise organizations search out locations for prospective franchise-holders that will virtually guarantee a flow of customers.

"One of the worst pieces of advice I ever heard is that if you build a better product, the world will beat a path to your door," says Dr. Harold Bauer, who operates a consulting service for personnel managers. "I learned long ago that a superior product isn't enough—you have to find ways of letting the public know about it and of getting them to buy it." He says most owner-managers would put "knowing how to get the business" even ahead of quality of goods or services as a factor in business success, particularly for new firms.

How can you develop skills in attracting clients or customers? "Find successful models and copy them," says Dr. Bauer. Professional men should study where referrals come from and take the necessary steps to get their share. Most persons who start their own businesses have spent time working for others. They should determine how their old employers found customers. In your own enterprise, note where each new client or customer comes from. See if there's a pattern (newspaper ads? friends from social clubs? contacts on the golf course? personal calls on prospective clients?) and then work those fields that have been most productive. Study how your most successful competitors attract business—for example, how they get the names of prospects and then turn them into clients or customers—and adapt their methods to your own purposes.

2. Keep your expenses low. The person starting out in business needs many things. He may have a whole office to furnish and much equipment to buy, and he is faced with hundreds of appealing devices designed to make his work easier. Often he has never before had to buy so much in so short a period. He suddenly gets the royal treatment from sales people with products to sell. It's a heady experience and many new self-employers can't cope with it. They can't resist the urge to play the role of the successful operator (before they achieve success). As a result, they often buy more than they can conveniently pay for.

The Dun & Bradstreet survey found that "heavy operating expenses" were the third-greatest cause of business failures overall, and the primary cause in the construction industry.

Several experienced self-employers stressed the importance of keeping fixed expenses low until you have clear indications of what income and profits you can count on. They say organizers of new businesses and professional practices often commit themselves to high rents, high salaries for employees, and expensive services of various kinds that prove difficult to carry in their early years.

"It's better to keep your fixed expenses as low as possible at first," says Charles S. Benson, who has started three different businesses in his lifetime and now owns a small electronics firm outside of Boston. "It's always easier to rent bigger and more expensive quarters when you have to, rather than move to a smaller place. Even suppose it costs you a lot to expand your operations. Because you've been successful, you'll have the money to do it and the move won't hurt you. But if it takes longer to achieve the results you want, every extra dollar of cost will hurt severely."

Mr. Benson firmly warns against hiring employees before you need them. "When I started out, I did almost everything myself," he says. "I ran my own errands and typed my own letters. Later, as business expanded, I hired part-time help on a temporary basis. I was always able to cut back on help if I had to. Only when business started coming on a regular basis did I hire a secretary—and then for only two days a week at first. I was never like one competitor who said nothing depressed him more than having to pay his employees when they had nothing to do."

Jacob Weisberg, a veteran New York customs broker, says many novices at managing a business "spend a little extra here, a little extra there, and before they know it they're up to their ears in expenses." He's also critical of "easy credit." He maintains that most persons running their own businesses would do better if they paid cash for everything. "If you don't have the money to spend, it's surprising what you can do without," he says.

Sometimes you can use borrowed money to make a great deal more than your costs of borrowing. But, Weisberg warns, "all too often newcomers in business borrow to buy things that won't produce income and are more for show than anything else."

George Glenn, an accountant with many small businesses as his clients, says a beginner should generally avoid new equipment or furniture. "You usually can buy good used items for less than half their cost when new," he says. "I shudder when I see a young fellow dressing up his office with shiny new equipment and ladling out money he'll need for his business. Sometimes I think some of them want the best-looking office that ever went into bankruptcy."

Along the same lines, "knowing how to buy" is highly regarded by many experts as a necessary quality for success. Its importance depends upon your trade or profession. Someone dealing in services probably can get ahead even if he pays excessively for the few things he needs in his work. But a retailer who is a poor buyer faces a tough struggle, because his competitors may be able to undersell him consistently. If he tries to match their prices, he may have to cut his profits so sharply that he can't survive.

3. Concentrate on your main goals. Not long ago, the author Irwin Franklin made a study of business and professional persons who had achieved outstanding successes. He found one trait in common: a single-minded concentration on objectives.

"The successful ones had a clear idea of where they wanted to go," he declares. "When they faced a business problem, they almost always asked themselves what solution would best help them achieve the goals they had set. They always kept their eyes on the doughnut and not upon the hole."

Your energy is like money. You have limited amounts of it—mental and physical. Spend it for one thing and you generally won't have it for another. In a broad sense, those who use their energy for nonprofessional purposes don't have it to use in their careers. Franklin found that persons who weren't especially smart or dynamic often achieved phenomenal successes because they poured their energy into their operation.

There is another side to this coin. Many who are outstanding in their own fields have paid a price for their accomplishments. Many ignore what happens outside their own area of expertise. Franklin noted that many successful businessmen knew little about other subjects. One nationally known surgeon didn't know the names of his senators, representative, or any member of the President's cabinet, and knew almost nothing about sports, films, music, art, or literature. He had practically no friends and no interests outside of medicine.

Others neglect their families and are virtual strangers to their wives and children. Franklin found this condition more common among corporation executives who often travel extensively on company business. Self-employers generally lead more stable lives. Even so, persons who manage their own enterprises often borrow "family time"—evenings, weekends, vacations—and use it for business purposes.

Most self-employers wouldn't want to concentrate on their business or professional affairs to the exclusion of all else. All work and no play may make jack—but it may still make Jack a dull boy. Nevertheless, many newcomers to the world of self-employment aren't ready to make the commitment in time and energy that is required for success. You must devote more of yourself to your job than if you were a mere employee. You needn't and shouldn't shut out everything else. But if you want to achieve success in your career, you will have to give your professional goals one of the top priorities in your life.

4. *Stick to what you do best.* Don't offer too many services or sell too many products. Most new owner-managers, in starting their own operation, believe they can do certain things better than they are now being done. You have a competitive advantage when you offer superior services or products. You lose your advantage when you spread out so much that you perform services or sell goods that are no better, or maybe even worse, than those of your competitors.

"Most people in business do not properly use their real talents," writes Richard R. Conarroe in his book *Bravely, Bravely in Business"* (American Management Association). "Instead of building on what they do best, they go off in other directions. That is why most people in business experience only a fraction of the success they could enjoy."

Conarroe maintains that highly successful people are generally no smarter or more skilled than others; their secret is that they use their talents to the fullest while they build experience. He says specializing doesn't mean standing still; as you accumulate experience, you broaden your scope by building on your best skills. In this way you build on your strengths, not weaknesses.

He urges a soul-searching study to determine your true talents and limitations. Then build a growth plan based squarely on the things you do best.

"Never forget your limitations," Conarroe advises. "You will find there is more than enough success to be had in the areas where you excel; it simply isn't necessary to reach for success in areas where you don't. The temptation is to grow by venturing into new areas. Up to a point this is healthy and pays off. But as you get further away from the basics you know best, the ice gets thinner."

In the final analysis, your enterprise will endure to the extent that it does a better job—offers a better product, performs a better service, sells at a more attractive price—than your competitors. Business and professional men who have been through the mill agree that, over the long term, there are no substitutes for quality. Your competence in some special area is what separates you from others and makes you distinctive. Don't weaken it.

5. *Develop workable techniques for collecting bills.* At least one in ten business operations fails because its owner is unable to collect monies rightfully due him. New self-employers are often uncertain of themselves and hesitate to press delinquent clients or customers. Every business must allow for a certain number of accounts receivable that will never be collected. But often keeping such bad accounts to a minimum enables a struggling business to remain afloat.

"There are two factors in keeping bad debts from ruining you," says R. M. Grossman, a New York tobacco wholesaler. "The first is to be extremely careful about those you extend credit to. Check them out thoroughly. Never extend them credit beyond the amount you think they'll be good for. If you're an easy mark, they may give you plenty of business, but you'll have a terrible time collecting.

"The second factor is to follow a systematic policy of collecting. Keep after them. If they haven't paid after a certain time, cut off their credit. Don't hesitate to take legal action. I've learned you have to be tough to survive."

Most experienced self-employers agree that you usually can't just send a bill and wait until it is paid. To get some customers to pay up, you will have to send a series of bills, and perhaps follow up with phone calls and personal visits. The important thing is to keep track of habitual late-payers and make sure they never owe you more than you can afford to lose.

6. *Understand how the tax laws work.* "When they begin managing a business or profession, few people understand that they're really in partnership with the government," says accountant Anthony H. Metzer. "But unless you realize that the federal and state tax laws can take half of every dollar of your profits— and unless you take advantage of every tax deduction you can— you'll find yourself on a treadmill as long as you're in business."

One poll of self-employers, asking what attributes they considered necessary for success, put "tax wisdom" at the top of the list. Almost without exception, owner-managers are keenly aware of the need to keep abreast of tax regulations. A few successful operators say their knowledge of the tax code is deficient, but that they hire the best tax lawyers or accountants they can find. Everyone says he never makes a major decision—and some say they never make even a minor decision—without considering the tax consequences.

It is vital to know not only what deductions you can take for business, but when and how you can take them for your maximum benefit. For example, there are many facets to taking deductions for business expenses. If you buy a "business meal" for a business associate, you will generally have no problems with the IRS when you deduct its cost on your tax return. Take the same man to a football game and the deductions may be disallowed. In every category of expense—use of your car, travel, meals and lodging, payment of employees, gifts to charity, purchases and sales of equipment used in your business—there are right ways (from a tax standpoint) and wrong ways of doing things.

"Some young self-employers think the tax laws are too complicated to cope with," Mr. Metzer says. "Some think they don't want to bother with the grubby details of saving $20 in taxes in one transaction and $40 in another. One thing usually convinces them that they'd better learn all they can about taxes if they want to get ahead in business. It's when they're hit with their first big tax bill, and realize it could be a great deal less if they paid more attention to the tax laws."

7. *Maintain proper records.* The typical self-employer begins his own operation not as an expert in business management, but rather as a person skilled in a trade or profession. As often as not, the bookkeeping requirements are strange to him, and he doesn't understand the importance of keeping careful, easy-to-refer-to books of accounts that reveal how well he is doing financially.

Adequate records serve several purposes for every entrepreneur. You need them to know where your income comes from and what is boosting your costs. If you have employees, you must keep full records concerning the amounts paid them, amounts deducted from their wages for Social Security, federal and state or local income taxes, as well as your own Social Security and unemployment tax payments on their behalf, and the tax deposits you have made in accordance with the law.

You also must maintain up-to-date account books detailing your income and your business expenses in order to support the figures on your income tax return.

What if you are too busy to set up and keep proper records, or if the detail work seems too much for you? You would be well advised to hire, on a full- or part-time basis, a competent book-keeper who will set up and maintain your books, file the necessary tax reports, and call your attention to accounts that are running dangerously delinquent. (Ideally, you set up your books before you open your doors for business.)

It is generally shortsighted to try to save on bookkeeping expenses. A trained bookkeeper can do the job faster and more accurately than the average self-employer and saves him considerable time, which he can use to produce income at the work he does best.

8. Try to profit from the experiences of others. Any person who starts his own enterprise runs into countless problems, large and small, for which his training has failed to provide the answers. Unless you want to learn "the hard way"—by ignoring advice and information available to you—you should be prepared to draw on the practical experience of others.

A striking characteristic of the American business and professional system, which often astonishes foreigners, is the willingness of experienced and successful persons to share their knowledge. Those who have conquered difficult operating problems or have developed more efficient ways of doing things freely discuss their discoveries with others—even with competitors. You will have no trouble finding older or more seasoned persons to give you the benefit of their experience. All you need is a willingness to look for such advice and to consider it carefully when you get it.

Where do most self-employers pick up information that helps them solve their business problems and operate more efficiently?

From others in the same profession, through trade associations and professional groups. From business organizations in the community—in the local Chamber of Commerce, Rotary club, etc. From tradesmen and suppliers, who often have wide-ranging contacts and learn of new ways of doing things that may save much time and money. From business publications and guidance services.

"Don't be afraid to ask questions," Dr. Bauer advises. "Most people are flattered when you seek their advice. If you pay attention to the answers you get, you'll often pick up other helpful pieces of information as a bonus." He advises young business and professional men to make the acquaintance of the oldest and most experienced men in their field. "It amazes me," he says, "how these older men, just for the asking, will often give advice worth hundreds and thousands of dollars."

But don't expect experts to do the hard work of making your decisions for you. Says David Rolphe, who has spent forty-two years as a real estate agent and manager:

"I have nothing against competent advisers. I use the services of accountants and lawyers regularly. But I found long ago that when somebody sets himself up as an expert in one field, he often thinks he has to be an expert on every subject his client asks about.

"Lawyers seem to suffer from an occupational obsession in this respect. I know men who are competent at uncovering hazardous aspects of a contract, but they're not willing to stop there. They think they have to tell me whether I'm making a good deal or not. They invariably base their judgment on a totally incomplete knowledge of the commercial facts in the case. Early in my career, a lawyer talked me out of taking a long-term lease in what has since become one of the most attractive sections in the city and in which offices are now worth three or four times what I would have paid under my lease. The lawyer overstepped the bounds of his expertise, and it taught me a lesson I've never forgotten.

"Many accountants and bookkeepers don't seem to feel they have to know everything, but I've known some who thought they had to make my business decisions for me and even tell me I was overpaying my employees."

Someone starting out in a business or profession naturally needs advice about many questions that may be completely new to him. For legal advice, he should consult a lawyer, and he should get an accountant to help with accounting problems. But his lawyer may not be an experienced businessman or an accountant, and his advice outside the field of his competence often may be no better than anybody else's. Don't make the mistake of thinking that just because an expert is good in one field, he knows the answers in all of them.

As might be expected, successful self-employers have a high degree of confidence in their own judgment. They need it, because they know they will have to take the responsibility whether their business decisions turn out good or bad. By and large, they are prepared to make their own decisions. That doesn't mean they don't seek information and advice. They usually hire the most competent lawyers, accountants, and other specialists they can find. But they are realistic about the help these specialists can give. They know that, if anyone gets the credit or blame for their success or failure, it will have to be themselves.

Can you ignore these rules and still succeed? Perhaps you can do well by disregarding one or two, but your chances of achieving a genuine success will be diminished if you bypass more than that number. One New Yorker who set up an advertising agency felt it was important to project a successful image from the start. He spent $35,000 on furnishing his business offices in order to impress prospective clients. His tactics worked; he is convinced he never would have gotten his agency off the ground if he had established bare headquarters in a low-rent district. Without giving much thought to the matter of attracting new business, some retailers and professional people luckily choose a location that brings clients and customers as a matter of course. Some new self-employers accidentally hit upon advisers who save them from costly and even ruinous mistakes.

Usually, it is unwise to depend on luck. If you choose to break the rules, as did the ad agent, you should have sound reasons for doing so. And if you disregard one or two elements in the above prescription for success, you had better follow the remaining ones with extraordinary care.

In general, experienced pros agree that a sharp business sense is a necessary ingredient for self-employers. They know owner-managers who are outstandingly competent in their own fields and highly respected by their fellows. Many of these persons are content to do a good job and let it go at that. From a business viewpoint, their performance may be mediocre but they don't care.

Most persons who operate their own enterprises *do* care. Solid financial progress is, for many, the main reason for setting out on their own. If you put yourself in this group, you would do well to follow as closely as possible the proven patterns of success.

Chapter 2

Some Common Concerns of the Self-Employed

REGARDLESS of the professional service you provide, you must make certain basic decisions about the management of your affairs. *You must choose a specific form of operation.* This choice may seriously affect the day-to-day conduct of your profession and your freedom to make decisions, and may also have dramatic tax and other financial consequences. *You must decide to what extent you want to set up an organization. You must decide whether to hire employees and on what basis, and you must then develop efficient employee-hiring and supervisory techniques. You must also remain alert to regulations covering your professional activities*—to submit, perhaps, to state and local licensing requirements and to conform to rules regulating the way you run your particular enterprise.

FOUR WAYS TO OPERATE

Your enterprise may take one of four forms:
• *Individual Proprietorship.* This is the most common form of organization for self-employers. Generally, no legal requirements

19

must be met to begin operating on one's own. However, you may have to obtain special licensing. (See the "Licenses" section in this chapter.)

The procedure to be followed if you plan to operate under a name other than your own varies from state to state. You may have to file a certificate with the clerk of each county in which you intend to conduct business, a precaution that will enable creditors and others to determine who actually owns the concern. For instance, in New York state a special form, obtainable at business stationery stores, must be filed. Called a "Certificate of Doing Business Under an Assumed Name," it must be made out in triplicate and signed by the person or persons conducting the business. The original is filed with the county clerk. Upon request, he will certify the other two copies. One of these is needed by the bank to open an account under the assumed name. You are expected to keep the other on display.

As an individual proprietor, you are liable for federal and state personal income taxes, just as if you were salaried. Your income will also be subject to federal old age and survivor insurance (Social Security). Some cities and states impose an unincorporated business income tax on taxable income derived within their jurisdiction.

• *Partnership.* This is commonly defined as a "form of business organization in which two or more persons formally agree to combine property or labor, or both, for a common undertaking and acquisition of a common profit."

A partnership may be formed for almost any kind of business enterprise. It is often particularly suitable for architects, lawyers, doctors, engineers, and other professionals. However, commercial and industrial firms may benefit from this form of organization as well.

Many kinds of partnerships can be formed, but the two most common types are the *general partnership* and the *limited partnership.*

The usual arrangement is the *general partnership,* in which all partners are general partners. They own the business jointly, share in its profits and losses according to an agreed-upon formula, and are personally liable for the firm's debts. According to law all partnerships must have at least one general partner who assumes liability for the partnership's activities.

A partnership is formed by an agreement between the persons involved (the principals). This agreement can be oral, but it is wiser to have the agreement put into writing. In many states, if you intend your partnership to last more than a year, the terms of the agreement (Articles of Co-ownership) must be written out.

In most states, persons organizing a *general partnership* must file a certificate of doing business as partners and file the firm's name with the county clerk of each county in which the business is conducted or transacted. You need not file the partnership agreement, but it should be prepared by a lawyer for each partner. It should clearly spell out all the details concerning the rights and duties of each partner in the enterprise.

One copy of the form used for certification should be filed with the county clerk, one copy with the firm's bank, and one or more retained by the partners. Also, the trade name must be filed unless it contains the full name of each partner.

Partners are liable for federal and state personal income taxes as well as Social Security. The partnership itself may also be liable for a state unincorporated business income tax.

A general partner has an equal voice in the partnership along with the other partners. In a two-person partnership, both partners must agree on a course of action. In larger partnerships, the majority vote usually prevails.

Since all partners can't be present for every transaction, each partner is usually authorized to act as an agent for the firm. Say one partner enters into an agreement for the purchase of new equipment. The partnership is required to honor that purchase even if the other partners are opposed to it. On the other hand, a partner may not alter an existing contract with outsiders without the OK of the other partners.

A partner has the right to use the firm's property in the conduct of its business, but not for his personal use unless authorized by the other partners.

A partner is entitled to be informed on significant developments affecting the firm. He also has the right to inspect the partnership's books at any time and satisfy himself as to the accounting procedures being followed.

In a *limited partnership,* one or more of the partners are relieved from liability beyond the amount of the capital contributed by them, under provisions of special legislation. This means that the limited partner does not become legally responsible if the enterprise runs into debt or is sued. Responsibility in such cases rests on the general partner or partners. If the business fails, a limited partner can lose all he has invested, of course, but no more than that. If the business prospers, he gets a specified share of the profits. A limited partner has no say in the management of the business.

Limited partnerships must be organized and operated according to state regulations. In New York state, for example, legislation requires persons organizing a limited partnership to file a "Certificate of Limited Partnership" instead of the "Certificate of Conducting Business as Partners." It must be notarized and, in addition to filing with the county clerk and the bank, a copy of the certificate or an abstract must be published once a week, for six successive weeks, in two of the county's newspapers designated by the county clerk. One of these papers must be published in the city or town in which the principal office is located or the nearest town if the place of business residence has no newspaper.

• *Regular Corporation.* Under certain circumstances, it may be desirable for self-employers to incorporate. When they do so they become employees of the corporation and cease to be self-employed. Legally, a corporation is defined as a body consisting of one or more persons established for a stated purpose, capable of continuing even after the withdrawal or death of the original founders, and authorized to function by an individual state or Congress.

As this definition implies, a corporation has an existence of its own. It can sue or be sued as a separate entity, apart from its owners. Your liability as the major or only shareholder of a corporation generally is limited to the amount of your particular investment; in effect, therefore, your personal possessions may be a thing apart. Another characteristic of a corporation is that it can increase or decrease the number of its owners without altering its fundamental nature.

Corporations owe their legal life solely to the states in which they are organized. No other state is required to recognize them. Although all states permit out-of-state corporations to function inside their boundaries, out-of-state corporations must always comply with special in-state obligations. These include: filing certain legal papers with the proper state officials; appointing a representative in the state to act as agent in serving process on the "foreign" corporation; and paying specified fees and taxes.

Corporations also are regulated by state laws, which vary considerably. Even when the language is similar, these laws have been interpreted differently in different places. Competent legal counsel is virtually indispensable in running any corporation and absolutely so if the normal course of business involves statutes and court decisions of a state other than where the corporation is founded.

Tax considerations may dictate the best form for you. Corporations generally are most desirable for large enterprises that need substantial amounts of capital and employ large numbers of persons, or when a self-employed person earns so much money that he can reduce his tax liability by taking some as an individual and some as a corporation, each on a lower level of the graduated tax scale. Incorporating also allows you to participate in fringe benefits.

As a sole owner, you report your "income from business or trade" with your personal income tax return.

As a partner, you receive a share of the partnership income and report it in your personal return.

As a corporation, you file a corporate report; you then file a separate personal report, listing income paid you by the corporation as its employee plus dividends and other tangible benefits received as a stockholder.

To determine the most desirable form for you, you must compare your present tax liability as an individual with what your liability would be as a corporation. If you are in a top personal tax bracket, you may be well advised to incorporate, pay yourself a lower salary, and keep the rest of the money (up to a maximum of $150,000) in the corporation.

For example, look at the example of Bob Greene, a successful small businessman. Until recently Greene had been sole proprietor of his business. He enjoyed making his own decisions and felt no need to change his organization. He listened, however, when his accountant pointed out the tax advantage he would gain by incorporating.

Last year, Greene's business made a net profit of $94,000. During the year his personal and family expenses, which were not deductible as sole owner, amounted to $28,000. Thus, he had to pay a personal income tax on the entire business profit. He reported his income on the calendar year basis and filed a joint return with his wife. He subtracted $8,000 in personal exemptions and deductions and reported $86,000 as taxable income. As a result, his tax bill for the year came to $33,738.

If his business had been a corporation that reported its income on the calendar year basis, and if he had taken a $34,000 salary ($6,000 more than the $28,000 he spent on personal and family expenses), Greene would have paid considerably less in taxes. The figures break down like this:

(1) Personal income tax on $34,000 salary (less $8,000 exemptions and deductions	$5,017
(2) Corporate taxes on the net profit (after salary) of $60,000:	
17% on the first $25,000	$4,250
20% on the next $25,000	$5,000
30% on the remaining $10,000	$3,000
(3) Total tax	$17,267

Thus, if the business had been incorporated, Greene would have saved $16,471 in taxes for last year alone. Under those circumstances, incorporation certainly seemed worthwhile. Also, the $34,000 salary for Greene would draw no objection from the Internal Revenue Service since comparable executives often get as much or more for their services in other corporations.

Could incorporation save you money in the same way? Maybe. But before you jump on the corporate bandwagon, be sure you are not going to exchange one set of tax problems for another. Owners of small corporations are often faced with the problem of how to take profits *out* of the corporation without losing too much to the tax collector through double taxation.

Your corporation is taxed on the profits left over after business expenses, depreciation costs, etc. It is permitted to accumulate a "reasonable" amount for future needs of the business. This amount is $150,000 unless you can prove a real purpose in accumulating more. You will be penalized if your corporation has an "excess" accumulation. Hence there is pressure on you to distribute profits to shareholders in the form of dividends. You are taxed on these dividend payments at your highest rate. It is possible, therefore, for a successful corporation owner to pay 70 cents or more in federal, state and local taxes on every dollar of dividends.

Can this double taxation be avoided? If your corporation is profitable, you will probably have to distribute some dividends. But you can reduce dividend income by taking profits out of your corporation in other ways. Here are some of them:

If you are approaching the upper limits of your allowable accumulation, determine whether you are paying yourself as large a salary as you could. You face a high personal tax if you increase your salary, of course, but the federal level reaches a maximum of only 50 percent and it is a tax-deductible expense for your corporation. Your overall tax on money received as salary is generally less than that received as dividends, because your corporation may not deduct dividend payments.

The IRS reserves the right to adjust a corporation owner's salary if it seems excessive. However, you generally can beat back a challenge if you can show that you are paid no more than other corporation owners in a similar business, trade, or profession with the same income. After all, you are probably the main reason for your corporation's success and you are entitled to handsome remuneration. Courts have ruled, however, that stockholders invest in corporations to share in the profits. So, when a top executive draws a higher-than-average salary, it should be accompanied by dividends or other evidence that shareholders are benefiting from the firm's prosperity, too.

When you work for your corporation, you regard yourself as its employee insofar as the tax laws are concerned. This means you are entitled to the tax-free fringe benefits available to any employee. The cost of these benefits is deducted by your corporation as a business expense and is not reported by you as taxable income. Thus you can get your corporation to buy many benefits that you would otherwise have to pay for yourself. In making these outlays, your corporation reduces its cash on hand.

To take personal advantage of fringe benefits, you must have a certain number of employees—as few as one in some states and ten in others. You must treat your employees evenhandedly when setting up these plans. Discriminating in favor of yourself or other stockholders or top executives isn't permitted. But you can gear benefits to income—for example, relate the amount of life insurance carried to a fixed percentage of each employee's wages or salary.

The cost of including a large number of employees may outweigh the amount you save by including yourself. To some extent, however, these fringe benefits can be presented to employees instead of cash wages. The argument can be made that if they bought life and health insurance and set up their own pension plans, their cost would be considerably higher. Insurance companies promoting fringe benefit plans also claim that they make for more contented workers and discourage them from switching jobs.

A popular tax-saving device involves personally owning the premises or equipment used by your corporation and leasing it to your firm at an attractive rental. The amount it pays under terms of the lease is deductible as a business expense. The amount you receive is taxable income, of course, but only after you have taken substantial deductions for depreciation.

Even more beneficial from a tax viewpoint is to give the property to your minor children, setting up a trust to manage it. They will pay little or no tax on the income due to their low tax bracket.

Leasing business space to one's corporation is done all the time. Generally, the IRS looks critically at such arrangements only when the rents paid are out of line. Remember that your corporation can pay as much rent as it would pay if the property were held by an outsider, but no more. The lease must be set up in what appears to be an "arm's length" negotiation. If challenged, you should be able to prove that landlords elsewhere charge their tenants as much per square foot as your corporation pays.

You can get money out of your corporation and avoid the high tax rates you would pay if you took the funds personally by setting up different classes of corporation stock. Many business owners think only in terms of common stock with voting privileges. Actually, you can use different kinds to solve specific tax problems.

You can set up different classes of common stock—for example, one class with special dividend or voting privileges. You also can use preferred stock of different kinds—with or without voting rights, with variable dividend privileges, with an option to convert into common stock.

Let's see how these different types can be made to fit different circumstances.

Say your salary from your corporation puts you in a top bracket, and unless it declares dividends it will face a penalty on its excess accumulated profits. You don't want to pay dividends to yourself for tax reasons. You create a class of preferred stock and give it to your children. They receive dividends regularly. Because of their tax bracket, they pay little or no tax on the proceeds. Your common stock pays you no dividends and the danger of excess profit penalties is reduced.

In setting up the preferred stock, you can stipulate that dividends may be suspended at the discretion of the board of directors. Thus you can avoid payments when the company isn't profitable.

You can make preferred stock convertible—changeable into a specified number of common shares after a named date. It may be advantageous for your dependents to retain their preferred stock now in order to get dividends taxable at lower rates. When their need for such income passes (their education has been completed, for instance) their preferred stock can be converted into common shares that pay no dividends.

You also can use preferred stock to give yourself the benefit of income after you retire. Say that you wish to turn your firm over to others, at neither loss to yourself nor cost to them. You convert your common stock into preferred stock worth as much as the company itself. You then give common stock to your employees or others. You receive a fixed income in the form of dividends on your preferred stock while they have the opportunity of working to increase the value of their own common shares. Presumably your tax bracket rate after retirement will be lower than at present. Hence the tax cost of your dividends will be lower than it would be if you sought to take out the money while still actively managing the firm and drawing a salary as well.

There are other ways of using your corporate money for the simultaneous purpose of avoiding highly taxed dividends to yourself and a penalty for excess accumulations:

For instance, you can accumulate inventories and keep your equipment up to date. In an inflationary era, almost everything you use for your business will probably cost more tomorrow than it does today. So it generally makes sense to buy now for future needs in any event.

You can also invest in property for present or future business development. One manufacturer bought a tract of land next to his factory and paved it over to provide parking for employees and visitors. The area has three times as many parking places as are now needed. The manufacturer confesses that his real purpose is to hold the land for future sale, but its present use gives him a legitimate business reason for the expenditure.

• *Subchapter S Corporation.* This is another form of organization that many owners of small businesses and professional practices find beneficial. The Subchapter S format can be advantageous when a business needs only a limited capital investment and when the shareholders are not in the highest personal tax brackets.

The main advantage of Subchapter S is that it enables you to enjoy most of the benefits of incorporation—participation in fringe benefits, limited liability, etc.—while avoiding the double taxation to which ordinary corporations are subjected. In an ordinary corporation the firm pays taxes on its profits before it distributes them as dividends to its shareholders. The shareholders, in turn, have to declare the dividends as income on their personal returns, thus paying an additional tax on the dividends. But a Subchapter S corporation (also known as a *pseudocorporation*) does not pay taxes. All of its profits are passed directly to its shareholders, who then include this income on their personal returns.

To qualify for Subchapter S status, a corporation must meet a number of special requirements. Among these are requirements that the company be a domestic corporation, that it have no more than fifteen shareholders, and that all shareholders agree to the Subchapter S election. Other regulations govern such things as sources of income and kind of stock that may be issued.

Most self-employers operate as proprietors or partners for several reasons. First, their income is not large enough to give them a tax advantage by incorporating. Second, forming a corporation involves many complications and formalities, such as holding stockholder meetings and obtaining the approval of stockholders or boards of directors before making important decisions.

A corporation is subject to many regulations. One architect who incorporated estimated that it increased his paperwork— filing of reports and returns—by four times. Some legal decisions also have whittled away at the idea of the corporation as a thing apart from its creator. When one person is the dominant stockholder, he may be held personally liable for fraud or other violations of law done in the corporation's name. Most important of all, perhaps, starting and operating a corporation requires the *continuing* advice and guidance of a competent attorney.

The partnership form generally permits greater freedom of action than the corporate form. It allows partners to maintain greater control over their affairs, affords the opportunity to expand by taking in new partners with new capital, and lets them divide income in line with the capital or services contributed.

When all partners contribute something to the firm's resources, each individual partner can operate on a larger scale than if he were on his own. A partnership allows each partner to concentrate on that phase of the business—office management, finance, or sales, for example—for which he is best equipped; it also allows each individual to retain his personal relationship with his clients or customers and generally conduct himself like a sole proprietor. Many lawyers themselves use this form.

A partnership makes possible more efficient office and plant operations than if each partner were in business separately. It offers each partner greater security by assuring continuity of operations if one is absent, sick, or disabled.

Partnerships also have greater freedom of movement than corporations. With their informal setup, they can act more quickly than a large corporation that operates through channels.

A disadvantage of partnerships is that they often lack a clear-cut definition of control. The person with strong wishes to make his own decisions may feel frustrated when he finds that he must often defer to decisions by others. If a partnership dissolves, separating the assets may be a long, involved process. A public relations counselor developed irreconcilable differences with his two partners and bowed out of the firm. "I've been divorced twice and I can tell you that breaking up a partnership is worse," he commented. Decisions made by one partner may bind all partners. You may be sued because of an act performed by your associate of which you knew nothing. Disability or death of one partner may disorganize the whole operation or force it to dissolve, unless appropriate precautions—such as insurance that helps the remaining partners continue the business—are taken. Your right to sell your interest may be restricted since a customary provision states that the other partners must approve of anyone else seeking to enter the partnership.

The setting up and management of a partnership also demands expert legal help. You need a lawyer to make certain that your rights are protected in the partnership agreement on these vital points: how much each partner will invest and how profits or losses will be allocated; how decisions concerning conduct of the partnership will be made and how deadlocked decisions will be handled; to what extent and under what circumstances partners may withdraw their capital; what happens to the organization if one partner becomes disabled or dies; what conditions cover the withdrawal of a partner and the admission of a new one; how long the partnership will last, how it can be voluntarily dissolved, how the assets will be divided upon dissolution.

A sole proprietorship offers you the most flexibility, is easier to start and manage, and involves less legal red tape than the other forms. It truly enables you to be your own boss, since you can make decisions without consulting anyone. You can operate with greater secrecy, can more easily adjust to new conditions (even changing your field of operations, if need be), and can terminate operations at will. You also reap all the profits from your own labors and may become more cost-conscious since every dollar you save adds to your own profit.

Disadvantages are that your liability is unlimited: you may be sued for *all* your personal possessions. Hence the need for complete insurance coverage, a subject discussed fully in chapter 4. If you must raise large sums of money to conduct your affairs, you will probably find many sources of commercial credit closed. Loans made to you probably will be on the strength of your personal credit rating. If you need employees to help you manage, you may find it more difficult to get and keep competent ones. Once trained, they may start their own businesses or seek employers who can promote them to a partnership or give them a share of the profits through ownership of shares of a corporation's stock.

When considering a legal structure, you should understand clearly how it influences the continuity of the business. *Single proprietorships* have no time limit by law but aren't fundamentally perpetual. Illness of the owner may derange the business; his death ends it. *Partnerships* are perishable in the same way; they are ended by the death or withdrawal of any one of the partners.

Corporations have a permanent legal structure, a separate continuous life of their own. The withdrawal, illness, or death of an official of a corporation does not mean its finish. Moreover, the certificates of stock, which represent investments in the business, may be transferred from one to another without hampering operations.

LICENSES

If you are self-employed in a profession or quasi-profession, you may be required to obtain a license from your state—and, in some cases, county, city, town, or village—in order to conduct your affairs. Often the government prohibits certain courses of action, or certain uses or ownership of property, unless a license is obtained and then attaches "regulations to the granting of such a license." The license may be accompanied by a fee and may involve some form of examination to see if the would-be licensee can qualify according to certain standards.

The *Master Index of McKinney's Consolidated Laws of New York State* contains six pages of listings of licensing provisions. Even allowing for duplication, this indicates that hundreds of licenses were issued under New York law alone.

Professional personnel are generally subject to regulation by their state. Among those usually licensed are physicians, including osteopaths and physiotherapists; dentists, including dental hygienists; podiatrists (chiropodists); chiropractors; engineers and land surveyors; lawyers; nurses (registered and practical); optometrists; ophthalmic dispensers; pharmacists, including drugstores; architects; veterinarians; certified public accountants; certified shorthand reporters; teachers in public schools. In many states, licenses must be obtained by employment agencies, private trade schools, insurance agents, brokers and brokerage companies, licensed lenders, licensed cashers of checks, dealers in securities, funeral directors, social workers, firms furnishing character information, and private investigators.

Many licensed occupations also are subject to regulation because of their relationship to public health, welfare, safety, or morals. These include auctions and auctioneers, ticket agents, and real estate brokers, and salesmen.

Federal and state constitutions, as interpreted by the courts, require that the exercise of the state police power over persons in a profession, trade, or business be reasonable. Unless the courts are satisfied that licensing is reasonably related to protecting the public health, safety, morals, and welfare, they will invalidate such legislation. If you have doubts about whether your occupation comes under the licensing requirements of your state, or if you have questions about the regulations, you probably can obtain full information from the State Commerce Department or Department of Education at your state capitol.

EMPLOYEES

Most self-employers sooner or later face the question of whether to hire someone to help handle their affairs. Sometimes, at least, you will probably feel the need for an assistant to type bills and letters, to answer the telephone and take messages, or to keep your place of business open during your absence. Self-employers have widely different opinions, however, as to whether it is preferable to hire permanent employees or, when feasible, to seek part-time workers they don't have to put on a regular payroll.

Many lawyers, doctors, and dentists say they can't function effectively without a secretary to handle appointments, type bills, and handle routine contacts with clients or patients. Other professional men prefer to use telephone answering services, professional secretaries, and freelance bookkeepers. Often there is no practical alternative to taking someone on permanently as a full-time employee. Under other circumstances, work requirements may make the addition of a regular employee economically undesirable. Sometimes it may be wise to hire one or two regular workers and to call in independent contractors when the work load requires.

In any event, the question is bound to arise. You probably can't answer it wisely unless you consider the advantages and disadvantages of having a permanent employee or employees and weigh these pros and cons in the light of your own circumstances and personality.

The latter factor may be the most important of all. A lawyer who spends most of his time with legal documents and relatively little time in face-to-face contacts with clients says he would have a secretary in his office even if he had no work for her. "I need somebody to talk to once in a while," he says. Another lawyer has tried several secretaries and now operates without one. A perfectionist, he says: "I just can't watch somebody make mistakes all day."

I recall interviewing a well-known architect for a magazine article on money-saving designs he had created for several low-cost housing developments on Long Island. As we left his office to see the houses under construction, he turned to his pretty young secretary—his only employee—and said, "Be sure to stay around the office this morning. I'm expecting a builder to leave some important specifications."

During our field trip, he frequently consulted his watch. Three times he sought out public telephones and called his office. After the third call, he commented: "That's a relief. The specifications finally arrived and my secretary has them.

"You know," he added, "I can't ever tell when she's going to call in sick, come in late, leave early, or go down the hall for half an hour, leaving the office unguarded. I'd fire her tomorrow, only I have no reason to think the next one will be better. The secretary I had before this one was even worse."

On the other hand, it is almost impossible to pay a good secretary too much.

In terms of the ordinary range of secretaries' salaries—from $190 to $265 a week—a $265-a-week secretary may be a bargain. Assuming that you get more when you pay more, the difference between what you get from a run-of-the-mill secretary and a top-notch one is far greater than this salary spread would indicate. The poorly trained, poorly motivated secretary can cost at least an hour of your time a day—explaining what you want done, correcting her mistakes, cutting your own productivity because of your nagging fear that she is fouling things up. The secretary who knows what's what and goes about her work competently can save you that hour and often much more. She can manage the office in your absence, take over routine work such as day-in, day-out correspondence, screen callers, free you for your own job. The difference between mediocrity and competence in a secretary is only about $1.90 an hour—and as one who has experienced both, I can affirm that for this $1.90 difference you can get one of the greatest bargains anywhere.

Benefits and Objections

One or more regular full-time employees offer these advantages:

- They keep your affairs going. You need not be tied to your desk or phone if you have someone sitting in for you. You may take holidays, even extended vacations, knowing that they will get in touch with you at once if something urgent requires your immediate attention.
- They automatically take care of routine matters— bookkeeping, filing, etc.—and thus permit you to concentrate on the matters that produce income.
- Once trained, they need not be instructed again.
- If you know them to be dependable, you can go about your special affairs with greater confidence.
- If you have enough work to keep them reasonably busy, they cost less per unit of work done than temporary help hired only occasionally.
- Once they know how you operate, they may "backstop" you—keep you from making costly errors due to carelessness.
- Experienced employees may take over some of your income-producing duties, enabling you to make a profit on their labor and allowing you to concentrate on even more profitable activities.

On the other hand, regular full-time employees can be burdensome. The objections are:

- Employees are a constant expense. Even when you don't have enough work for them, you must pay them and provide office space, equipment, etc. If they become ill, you probably must keep them on your payroll, at least for a time. If your income drops, it may be difficult to trim your overhead accordingly.
- They may have to be supervised constantly. Like the architect mentioned above, you may find yourself worrying about what they are doing when you are not there. This means you may have to report to your office, even when you don't want to, to make sure that they don't "goof off."
- Having employees multiplies your paperwork. You must keep records and make regular reports and payments concerning income tax withholding, Social Security contributions, unemployment taxes, etc.
- They increase your own pension costs. Under the "Keogh

plan" for the self-employed, you may not make tax-sheltered contributions to a pension fund for yourself unless you include your regular employees.

• They interfere with your privacy. Almost inevitably, employees in a small office know more about their employer's professional and personal affairs than he realizes. All the clients of a consulting engineer knew that his wife planned to divorce him even before the papers were filed. His two office workers had overheard phone conversations and spread the news of his marital troubles around town. The presence of employees may make it difficult to keep important negotiations, etc., a secret from outsiders.

TEMPORARY HELP AND OTHER SYSTEMS

If you have no employees now, you may need someone to handle clerical or other detail work during periods when you are unusually busy. If you have an employee or two, you may need someone to fill in during vacations or periods of illness. The need for competent temporary or part-time help is so great that several nationwide organizations exist to fill it.

Basically, temporary help services are contractors. They pay salaries, handle payroll deductions, supply insurance, and test workers' skills, bonding them if necessary before sending them on assignment. This means that while necessary short-term jobs are getting done, you need add no one to your payroll. And, no matter what the job, a short notice will get the help to you. Important paperwork doesn't backlog while you interview and train someone new.

Most temporary personnel do typing and clerical jobs, but management, industrial, and scientific career people are also available. There are contractors who specialize in such diversely skilled jobs as bookkeeper, market researcher, factory worker, EDP personnel, payroll expert, accountant, and so on. Some contractors offer as many as thirty skills.

Generally, you will do well to use a temporary service when you need to fill a position for only a short period of time. You may want to use service personnel to fill in when vacations, illnesses, or other emergencies create temporary vacancies in your staff. Or you may find it advantageous to hire temporary help to keep work from piling up during peak seasonal periods or at tax time. You might also want to use a temporary worker to see if there is justification for creating a new position in your company. Using a temp would answer any question you might have as to whether there is really enough work to keep someone busy on a permanent basis.

If you need help over an extended period of time, however, you should keep in mind that using a temporary service can be expensive. According to a representative from one of the largest nationwide temporary help contractors, "it is generally not cost-effective to hire a temporary worker through a service for a period longer than six weeks." Of course, if there is a skill shortage—say your secretary has left and you haven't been able to find anyone to fill the position—you probably would want to use a temporary worker until you find a competent replacement, even if it takes longer than six weeks.

The biggest benefit of using a temporary service is that, when you need it, help is quickly available. Generally, temporary help needs little or no breaking in and, with a minimum of instruction, can begin to function right away.

But before you hire a temporary, take a close look at your needs:

- Do you or your staff feel overworked much of the time?
- Does work often get backlogged?
- Do you frequently have to pay employees expensive overtime to catch up on work?
- Do you seem to need help only at certain times of the day?

If the answer to any of these questions is yes, you should probably consider hiring permanent help.

When you need some assistance in your office, but not enough to warrant a full-time employee, consider these possibilities:

- *Employee "sharing."* Several self-employers sometimes get together and hire one receptionist-secretary. They may split her salary evenly between them or get her to keep a record time sheet showing how much time she works for each. They contribute to her salary accordingly.

• *Permanent part-time help.* In many communities, the number of highly skilled women seeking part-time jobs far exceeds demand. You may have a better choice among them than if you seek full-time help. The reason: many mothers of small children, who have had top secretarial or professional experience, seek work while their youngsters are at school. Set up a work schedule during school hours—say, between 9:30 A.M., after the children have left for school, and 2:30 P.M., before they return—and you will likely have a large pool of skilled applicants from which to choose.

• *"Independent contractors."* You probably can find several secretarial, typing, or telephone answering services nearby, operated by women who prefer to be on their own but will work for you on a per-job basis. Some will do your secretarial work, then come to your office a few hours a week to keep your files up to date. Because they must cover their own overhead expenses, they usually charge more per unit of work than you would pay an employee. A consulting engineer solved this problem neatly. He rented office space to a professional secretary and paid her so much per job when he needed her. He combined the advantage of having and not having one on his payroll.

THE ART OF HIRING

Finding good help can be a time-consuming (hence expensive) task. It is perhaps more difficult for "small" employers than for large corporations; the latter may require someone to do only a specific task, but you will probably need an assistant who can do many things reasonably well. Usually the employee in a small office also must have a greater sense of responsibility and integrity.

Here are some suggestions from management experts on how to find and hire employees in the most efficient way:

1. Determine what you specifically want done in the job to be filled. Form a clear picture of the kind of person you want to do it. Write your requirements on paper.

2. Use an employment agency wherever possible. It can screen prospects and eliminate the plainly unqualified. Give the agency

the complete details you have written down: educational background that you want your employee to have, extent and kind of job experience, personal qualifications. If you need a secretary, you may want to stress good phone personality, ability to write letters on her own, etc.

3. Check applications before setting up interviews. You may decide against an applicant who has held too many jobs, has worked where he or she may have picked up sloppy job habits, or does not measure up for other reasons.

4. Interview prospective employees yourself. Better than anyone else, you know what kind of worker you want. You will have to fire the employee if he or she doesn't pan out—so why not try to prevent that at the beginning? In fairness to the applicant, conduct the interview in private—not where others can overhear. Allow enough time for both of you to clarify any points and avoid possible serious misunderstandings.

5. Prepare a checklist and refer to it. Here are some typical things to consider when interviewing a prospective employee.

SKILLS. Does he or she have the necessary skills to do the job? If you are hiring a secretary and you normally dictate a lot of letters, the person you hire should be good at stenography and spelling as well as typing.

WORK HABITS. Does he or she seem to have the ability to take on responsibility and work independently?

APPEARANCE. Will the person you hire be meeting your customers or representing your company to the public in any way? If so, you will want the person to be neat and well groomed.

PERSONALITY. Does the applicant seem to be the kind of person who will get along well with your customers and with others in the office?

LOYALTY. Will the person you hire stay after you have trained him? Obviously, a person who is looking for a job with "room for advancement" will leave your firm soon if no such opportunity arises. Likewise, a person who is overqualified for a job may soon become bored and look elsewhere for more challenging work.

6. After you interview each applicant, write a report summarizing your impressions. Write the applicant's name and also some characteristic that will enable you to remember the person

("woman with big black hat" or "man who went to school with my brother"). Unless you do this, you may find after a few interviews that you can't separate different applicants in your mind.

7. If you decide to hire a person, make sure that both of you clearly understand the terms of employment. Specify the days he or she is to work, the hours per day, how much time will be allowed for lunch, what the salary will be, how and when it will be paid (every week, on Fridays; twice a month, on the first and fifteenth, etc.). Point out that this salary is the *gross* amount before deductions for income tax, Social Security, etc. Explain what fringe benefits, if any, are included: Will you make contributions to health and hospital insurance? How many weeks of vacation do you give per year? If overtime work may be required, make sure the individual will do it—and know what you will pay. A commercial artist who had many assignments from retail stores hired a secretary in June and neglected to tell her that he often had to work on Saturdays and Sundays in November and December and would need her help at those times. When autumn came and he asked her to work on weekends, she said she had made plans to ski with her boyfriend. In another case, a youngster who was working at his first job told me his boss cheated him every week: he had been promised $160 but received a check for only $140. He thought the employer should pay income, Social Security, and unemployment taxes.

8. Final points, stressed by job counselors: Don't hold out for a perfect employee; you will often have to settle for reasonable but not outstanding competence. (Many small employers rate "cooperativeness" in employees more important than competence.) Modern workers also are more demanding than ever. They insist on considerate employers, good working conditions, time off for coffee breaks, etc. Competent employees know that they need not settle for "any" job. To get—and keep—someone who measures up to your standards, you will also have to measure up to theirs.

RENT OR LEASE A CAR

If you don't need a car regularly, consider a rental for occasions when business warrants one. There are certain advantages to doing this. Capital that would otherwise pay for an automobile may be employed more profitably in your business. You avoid fixed insurance charges and depreciation that must be faced whether a car is used a little or a lot. If you live or work in a congested urban area, you may avoid expensive garage fees.

The business of renting (when a car is taken for a short period) and leasing (when it is used for months) has become a major one throughout the country. The number of firms engaged in it totals many thousands. This intense competition means you probably can find an agency that will rent a car to fit your specific requirements. It means that many car rental bargains can be found, but also that, in their scramble for profits, some agencies practice deception and outright fraud on their customers.

Before renting or leasing a car, satisfy yourself with the answers to these questions:

- What kind of reputation does the car agency have?
- What is the car's age and condition? An advertised advantage of renting is that you largely free yourself of maintenance problems. But a car that breaks down on the road may cost you many hours of lost productivity—and income. A car showing more than 20,000 miles on the odometer may be in poor mechanical condition and still have the original but by now well-worn tires.
- What are the *exact* rental terms? The Association of Better Business Bureaus reports many complaints from consumers who thought they rented a car for a "day" but later discovered that the contract defined a "day" as running from 9:00 A.M. to 5:00 P.M. The price you pay to use the car is only one factor in its cost. Others are the mileage charge; whether or not you pay for gasoline; to what extent you are protected by insurance in case of accidents—and the price per day for complete liability coverage. When all costs are considered, the "bargain" rental may prove costlier than one that merely *seems* more expensive.
- Will the insurance remain in effect if your employees or others drive the car? Must you pay extra for coverage if the drivers are under twenty-five or twenty-one years of age?
- Will you be restricted as to where you can drive the car—out of the state, for example?
- What are the pick-up and drop-off conditions? If you save

time by having the rented car delivered to your door, this service may be worth its extra cost, if any. If you want to deliver the car in a distant city, an agency permitting you to do so without extra charge may be best, even if its per-day and per-mile rates are higher.

• Are you entitled to a discount? Some agencies freely distribute discount cards entitling business and professional men to a 10-percent reduction. If you rent a car several times a year, you probably can get a similar markdown from the published rates.

Most car leasing arrangements run six months or longer, and many run for two or three years. Because the total sum involved is significant, it is wise to get a blank contract from the leasing agency and read it carefully before you make a long-term commitment. Compare the exact costs of all services offered by the different leasing organizations. For instance, some lessors provide full maintenance, grease the car, and change the oil regularly, without extra charge. Others require you to do so at your own expense. Some lessors include a comprehensive insurance policy in the monthly price. With others, such coverage is extra. Some contracts allow you to purchase the car at a stipulated price when the lease runs out; others do not. In some cases, you may be let out of the contract ahead of the expiration date by paying a specified penalty; in other cases you must continue your lease whether you need the car or not. It is up to you to place a value on these services and options when making cost comparisons.

Chapter 3

What Specialists
Can Do for You

ONE of the obvious qualities needed by self-employers is a strong degree of self-reliance. You must be enterprising and imaginative, confident that you can achieve success in an enterprise from which most persons shrink. Successful self-employed persons of all types—professional people such as doctors, lawyers, and accountants; various kinds of agents and consultants; originators and operators of one-man businesses—invariably create the impression that they know what they are doing. To succeed as a self-employer in any business one must see a problem, analyze it, and act on it. To do this requires self-confidence. Self-doubt is of little value.

But every coin has two sides. While self-reliance is an undoubted necessity for the man on his own, there can be too much of it. In the modern complicated world, no individual, no matter how gifted, can remain aware of all the problems in a profession, trade, or business and of what others consider the most satisfactory solutions. You can't do your own work, whatever it may be, and simultaneously grapple with the intricate legal, tax, accounting, and financial questions that arise in the course of it. Of course, you should familiarize yourself with the general nature of these questions and the generally accepted solutions. When it comes to hard decision making in matters of law and taxes, accounting and finance, however, *you should get help.* In these areas, professional men have spent years acquiring specialized textbook knowledge and many more years in building on that knowledge through practical experience. When the self-employer tries to dispense with their services in hopes of saving money or with the conviction that he can solve involved problems in their fields of competence, it usually proves a mistake. In many cases it can cost thousands of dollars; in some cases it can be ruinous.

Of course, you can't run your affairs effectively if you need a lawyer or accountant at your side every time you need to make a decision. At this point, your self-confidence must assert itself. But you should not dispense with professional help when taking a major step: when buying a business, negotiating an important lease, filing an involved income tax return. For at this point your sense of reality must take over, along with the realization that in these important areas others may know more than you.

LEGAL ASSISTANCE

Legal questions exist at almost every major point in the self-employer's career. They arise when you embark on your enter-prise and must decide which form—sole proprietorship, partner-ship, or corporation—will best suit your purposes. They are intimately involved when you sign a lease on your office, in contracts with those you serve and who serve you, in your relations with employees, and possibly in obtaining licenses be-fore you may operate legally. How you conduct your affairs may be restricted by dozens of laws and regulations on local, state, and federal levels. You face legal questions regarding the taking out of insurance (you should know what error in judgment or failures in performance the law will hold you accountable for and a policy will protect you against), the payment of taxes (a legal labyrinth if ever there was one), and the planning of your future so as to maximize your income when you retire. In fact, hardly a decision you will make does not have some legal ramifications, though not all such decisions will require that you consult a lawyer.

Legal problems are so pervasive in the modern business and professional world that the question is not whether you need one lawyer, but whether one is enough; whether you might do better by dealing with one large firm with specialists in real estate, taxes, insurance, estates, etc., or with several different experts with different specialties.

Your answer to this question will depend mainly on the size of your enterprise, the legal intricacies and possibilities of damaging litigation, the availability of qualified legal counsel in your community, and comparative costs. You probably can operate effectively without constant legal advice, and seldom are your affairs so complex that you need more than one lawyer. If complicated questions arise, calling for a specialist, your lawyer should be able to tell you so and recommend one, just as your family doctor is best equipped to recognize when to call in a specialist. Moreover, by giving all your business to one lawyer you encourage him to familiarize himself with your operations and to pay close attention to developments that may affect you. An additional benefit of being loyal to one lawyer can be seen in the fact that most lawyers (and other professionals) are loyal to *their* clients (you); they often help steer business to those who steer business to them.

Of course, it is your responsibility to anticipate possible legal problems and to avoid them wherever possible. You alone must decide not to sell your services to a bad risk who will force you to sue for payment. You cannot put your head in a legal noose and then expect an attorney to get you out of it. As one lawyer put it, "If my client wants me to be at the crash landing, I'd like to be there at the takeoff." However, at certain times you should consult your lawyer *before* making your decision. Such times are:

• *When signing a lease on business premises.* The lawyer will check the fine print to make sure you are not prohibited from using equipment you want to use or from using the premises when you want to, such as nights and weekends. If you intend to use the space on Sundays, he will see that no clause could give the landlord the right to cut off heat on that day. A chiropractor found what he thought was an ideal spot for his office in an office building close to the business section of Yonkers, New York. What appealed most was a large parking space next to the building. Most of his patients came by car and he assumed that they could use it. In reading the lease, his lawyer found that no such right was given. Investigation disclosed that space in the lot was in fact rented. Realizing that his practice would suffer seriously without adequate parking space nearby, the chiropractor found a more suitable place.

• *When embarking on a major purchase or contract.* As a rule, the advantage in any contract lies with the party who draws it up. He knows from experience what contingencies to guard against and includes appropriate clauses to protect himself. If *you* prepare a contract involving a substantial amount (or one for small amounts that will be used over and over), your lawyer can make certain that your rights are protected and your demands legally enforceable. Before signing a major contract prepared by *another* party, be sure that your interests are not jeopardized. Your lawyer can do this for you, for he knows that innocent-sounding phrases may cost thousands of dollars. An author friend of mine was offered a contract by a major New York book publisher. Thinking that the contract was not negotiable because it was printed, he signed and returned it. After his book was published and the expected flood of royalties proved to be a trickle, he asked a lawyer experienced in the ways of publishing to review the contract. The latter found that almost every clause gave the author less than did contracts offered by most other publishers. One clause cut the author's royalties in half on reprints of 3,000 copies or fewer. Too late, the lawyer told the author that except for best-sellers, this publisher ordinarily reprinted *only* that number. Therefore, the author got only half the expected royalty on each book sold after the first printing.

• *When ordinary methods of collecting delinquent accounts fail.* Of course, if only a small amount is owed, it won't pay to consult an attorney. Often, however, a threatening letter from a lawyer is enough to elicit payment. (I once visited the office of a large mail-order advertiser. Along one wall was a bank of automatic typewriters, rattling off "individualized" letters to delinquent customers on the letterhead of a law firm in their employ.

"Those typewriters paid for themselves in two months," the head of the firm told me.) Your lawyer may suggest low-cost ways of suing—in some states, if the amount is less than $1,500, you can haul your debtor into a small claims court and avoid heavy legal costs. If a large sum is involved, he can give a realistic picture of what it will cost to sue, your chances of winning and, if your debtor is in shaky financial condition, of collecting enough to justify your expenditure in time and trouble. Of course, if legal action seems warranted, he will be prepared to press it or recommend a specialist in that particular kind of case.

• *When considering a major change in your way of operating.* Let's say you decide to take in a partner or associate. Is a verbal agreement and a handshake enough? In rare cases, perhaps yes; more usually disagreements arise when the terms of the agreement are not set down on paper. Such disputes, which could destroy the relationship, could be avoided with a contract, drawn up or checked out by your attorney, in which all basic aspects of your working arrangement are defined.

• *When planning important steps in your personal life.* You need a lawyer when buying or selling your home; when marrying or when your marriage is dissolved by death or divorce (in order to make changes in your will); when children are born (same purpose); when setting up a retirement program. As a self-employer, your business and personal problems are more closely related than are those of most persons. Hence the same legal adviser should handle both. Because he has a thorough understanding of your professional problems and needs, he will be able to propose the best legal steps to take as a person. And vice versa. For example, he will have a clear picture of the amounts of capital you will need for your business in the future to educate your children and to retire comfortably. He can suggest a well-rounded program, which might include giving some of your assets to your children now. When the time comes to pay college or postgraduate tuition costs, income from their holdings might be used with little or no deductions required for taxes.

As in every field, there are competent lawyers and some not so competent. There also are lawyers highly competent in one area of law but equipped by neither temperament nor training to operate effectively in another. A counselor who achieves spectacular results in a criminal court does not ordinarily perform equally well in analyzing contracts between businessmen.

The lawyer who is best equipped to serve you satisfactorily probably now serves other clients with problems like your own. Hence the man who comes recommended by your professional colleagues merits your consideration. Your banker, accountant, or insurance agent may know who is highly regarded as a legal adviser for those in your field, and your local bar association may also provide suggestions. But make sure that the man you choose is not so busy that he won't be there to help when you need him. Don't expect a jack-of-all-trades. It's better to list the areas in which competent legal representation is most important to you, then choose the man who is tops in those fields. If you want one who is strong on business contracts and estate planning, you may have to settle for weakness in, say, casualty law. An attorney who recognizes his limitations can be valuable; if a complex legal problem arises, he won't hesitate to suggest a competent specialist who can do a better job for you. You will probably need an accountant, too. If you select one who can guide you through the maze of income tax rules and regulations, it may be less important to have a lawyer who is a tax expert.

At times you may be working intimately with your lawyer. Hence it is important to choose one whose personality, if not compatible with yours, at least doesn't conflict with it. Many factors make up an effective lawyer-client relationship; the most competent man in town may be unsuitable if you can't get along with him.

ACCOUNTANTS

It is wise to consult an accountant when you first become self-employed. He can set up your books in the most efficient way and establish sound business practices from the beginning. He can show you how to conduct your affairs so as to get the maximum tax advantage and to keep records that will satisfy the IRS. He may also set up a budget, do your financial reports, and take the responsibility of regularly auditing your books, paying income and self-employment taxes, and seeing that you fulfill your financial responsibilities under the law if you have employees.

There are two types of public accountants: those who are certified and those who aren't.

Noncertified Public Accountants. Public accountants must meet license requirements in seventeen states: Alabama, Alaska, Arizona, Georgia, Indiana, Iowa, Maine, Montana, New Hampshire, New Mexico, Ohio, Oklahoma, Oregon, South Carolina, South Dakota, Tennessee, and Vermont. Standards vary widely from state to state. The thirty-three other states require no educational background or qualifying exams. Anyone can hang out a public accountant sign and begin doing business.

Public accountants usually serve professionals, small business owners, and individuals who earn between $5,000 and $20,000. They charge a little more than local and national tax services but less than CPAs.

According to the IRS, the error factor for noncertified accountants is lower than that for local and national tax services but higher than for CPAs. If your tax situation isn't too complicated, a public accountant may be exactly right for your needs.

To get a list of the members of the National Society of Public Accountants, write to the society at 1717 Pennsylvania Avenue NW, Washington, DC 20006.

Certified Public Accountants. CPAs are the elite in the tax preparation field. Most have college degrees or the equivalent in tax work experience and must pass an exam before being certified. This 2½-day exam is so difficult that only 10 percent of aspiring CPAs pass it on their first attempt. To be eligible to take the exam, the accountant must have worked under the supervision of a CPA for a specified length of time, which varies from state to state. The CPA can qualify to represent you in tax court by passing another written exam. However, few choose to do so. If you must go to court, you will need a tax lawyer.

CPAs are qualified to handle complex subjects. Most of them are steeped in tax law, and they are authorized to represent you before the IRS. CPAs generally can advise you on all your financial affairs. Their fees are the highest of all tax preparers.

The best way to find a good CPA is by word of mouth. Big

CPA firms usually specialize in large corporations, so you will probably save time by concentrating on small firms or individuals. If you select a CPA firm, ask if junior personnel will be doing your work—a common practice in even highly reputable firms. If the answer is yes, ask how much supervision they are given and if all of their work is checked by a CPA within the firm.

Like any professional confidant, your accountant can serve you best if you give him the full facts and figures about your operation. Be equally frank in discussing what you expect him to do for you and in negotiating the charges you will pay. Most accountants bill clients on an hourly basis with tax preparation treated as a separate item. You can get the services of an accountant for $20 to $100 an hour. Some accountants offer a package rate that includes year-round availability and the preparation of tax returns for a flat annual fee.

An accountant who handles your business affairs and tax reporting probably has sufficient knowledge of your affairs to help you with your personal planning as well. A man who owns seven industrial buildings in the San Fernando Valley in California told me that advice received from his accountant has enabled him to save almost $100,000 in taxes. The accountant showed him how to set up trusts for his minor children so that they would receive the rents from some of his buildings; because the income per child was low, the total taxes per year were many thousands of dollars less than if all the income was credited to their father's account. There are many twists and turns in the law concerning gifts to minor children and others; setting up trusts so as to minimize probate costs; and estate planning that can avoid taxes in some instances and keep them as low as possible in others. Your accountant should be able to provide important guidance in these areas even if your overall estate plan is handled by your lawyer.

INSURANCE AGENT

Another indispensable specialist is the insurance agent. It is virtually impossible for the *prudent* self-employer to operate without him.

First, insurance is more important than ever before for everyone; it is absolutely *imperative* for the self-employed. You must accept responsibility for yourself entirely. You must make arrangements to insure that some income continues if you are ill or disabled for a long period and that your family is financially protected if you die. There are hazards connected with ordinary living against which you must gird yourself; hence the need for insurance on your property, home, your car, your other personal possessions. As a businessman, you require protection against dozens of other contingencies.

Second, insurance is costly. The average middle-class head of a family with dependent children, owner of a home and car, can scarcely avoid a total insurance bill of around $5,000 a year if he wants adequate life, medical and hospital, automobile, and personal liability insurance. You may well pay $8,000 or more a year when your business policies are added to your personal policies.

Third, insurance is complex. About 4,800 insurance companies are in existence, with so many different kinds of policies, with vastly different protective features and wide variations in premiums, that it is impossible for the layman to sort them out intelligently. Seeking to travel through this wilderness without a professional guide, you can easily pay 25 percent more than necessary for the identical coverage.

Fourth, and most important, the consequences of mistakes can be financially ruinous. A freelance labor negotiator I know handled all his own insurance affairs, buying one policy here and another there. It didn't occur to him to carry more liability coverage on his automobile than his state required. One wintry day, his car skidded on the ice and knocked down a pedestrian on the sidewalk. Unconscious, she was taken to a hospital where she remained two weeks, claiming intense head pains. Six months later, her lawyer filed suit for $500,000. The driver of the car was insured for only $10,000. He had to hire a lawyer to defend himself against the additional claim of $490,000. His net assets totaled only about $40,000. Thus he faced the threat of bankruptcy. A competent insurance agent, conversant with the amounts that victims in accident cases are now claiming and receiving, would have warned him that his coverage was entirely inadequate and that for a few dollars more per week he could have been protected against almost any claim up to $1,000,000.

The kinds of coverage available to protect you against personal and professional catastrophes are discussed in detail in the next chapter. While it helps to be aware of the hazards that lurk in your life, it is probably more important to understand what to expect from your insurance adviser and how to go about getting it.

The most desirable agent usually is one who handles all kinds of insurance business and deals with many different companies. The agent who knows all about you—your income, family responsibilities, the nature of your special business hazards—can best formulate an overall program that puts all the pieces together. There is a considerably reduced risk of overlapping and less likelihood that you will pay in one policy for protection you have already paid for in another. Because he knows your problems, he can see that you are defended against the particular risks that could hurt you most.

You can't expect an agent to spend the time necessary to do this unless you make it worthwhile for him; and in most cases, you can't do this unless you give him all your business. When he constructs a total program for you, he need not worry about the possible loss of commission if he advises against a particular kind of policy. He knows that if he recommends term life insurance instead of twenty-payment life, the lost commission may be offset by the additional coverage you need to protect you against suits arising from the practice of your profession. Moreover, the total income from your account is large enough to motivate him to keep you a contented client.

The agent who deals with different companies (in contrast to the one who represents only one interlocked group of companies) is best situated to choose those that provide the kind of coverage you need at the most reasonable rate. Every company has its strong and weak points, and no one company is best for all kinds of coverage. An independent agent can tailor an insurance program to fit your needs; he does not have to sell what his employers offer, whether it suits your requirements or not. You need an insurance adviser most when you must press a claim, and that is when the man with his own business can act on *your* behalf. In contrast, the person who writes for only one group is its employee. His self-interest lies in keeping his job, not in getting the best settlement for you.

Just as you get more from an agent when you give him all your business, your agent can get more from the insurance companies because he provides business for them—and can, if dissatisfied, take his clients elsewhere. This factor may distinctly work in your favor if you have a marginal case, for bending of rules by insurance companies to accommodate an agent is fairly common. A syndicated newspaper columnist gave all his business to one agent and regularly bought mutual fund shares from him as well. The columnist was a careful automobile driver and had had only a few tickets for traffic violations and no major accidents in forty-five years. But now that he was sixty-seven, several underwriters labeled him a bad risk. His agent interceded on his behalf—and as a "favor" to the agent, one company agreed to take the man's policy at its regular rates. The client thus saved $150 a year.

Of course, the fact that a man is a general agent does not automatically qualify him for your use. Here are some questions you should ask before giving him your business:

• Is insurance his main occupation? The scope of this field is vast enough to challenge anyone. If he works at it only part-time, he is probably not keeping up with all the trends and developments.

• What is his reputation in your community? What do your lawyer, accountant, and broker think of him? Are his other clients successful professional men or businessmen who expect high levels of competence?

• If he has associates, could they contribute to the service he provides? For example, if he specializes in casualty insurance, are others in business with him competent to handle life or medical insurance?

• What is his background? Has he attended recognized insurance training institutes? Has he received a professional designation like CPCU (Chartered Property Casualty Underwriter) or CLU (Chartered Life Underwriter)? These designations, while not infallible guides to competence, suggest that at least he is not generally held in low esteem by fellow agents.

• Does he display definite interest in getting and holding your business? He should be ready and willing to devote several hours to obtaining your complete economic profile and to working up a program to insure adequate protection against all possible eventualities. He should be willing to explain his recommendations fully. At least once a year he should review your entire program with you—change beneficiaries in your life policies, increase your home insurance to conform to rising replacement costs, add to or discontinue policies on other members of your family, etc. You are entitled to expect more than automatic renewals each year; your agent should determine whether changing conditions dictate policy changes.

• Does he process claims promptly and willingly? His is a *service* industry, and a basic test is how well he serves you when you need him. If you have an automobile accident, for example, he should promptly send you the forms you need in making a claim and he should see that the insurance carrier gets to your claim immediately. A good agent will keep in touch with you until the case is settled.

• Above all, does he inspire your confidence? When you buy insurance, you are buying "peace of mind." You want to know that the unexpected—an illness or disablement, an accident, a mistake that injures a client—will not bring financial ruin. You must believe that you are adequately protected. Short of conducting an exhaustive and impossible investigation on your own to assure yourself of this, you must depend on your agent. Because of this dependence, "peace of mind" is possible only when you are confident that he knows what he is doing.

BANKER

It is possible, though hardly advisable, to run an enterprise without the help of a lawyer, accountant, or insurance agent, but you can't run one without a bank. You need a bank if only to process checks received or to enable you to write checks for expenditures.

So the question is how to develop a good relationship with your bank so that you can use its services most effectively: borrow money quickly if you must; get credit information on present or prospective clients; obtain up-to-date facts about developments in your community that may affect your future. A modern all-purpose bank can perform dozens of services: suggest ways for you to get the best return on your savings and to pay the lowest rate on your loan; refer you to qualified specialists (a tax lawyer, for example) to help with your financial problems; set up trusts so that your estate will benefit those you want to benefit; handle your self-employment pension fund. Properly used, it can be a source of all-around financial information and advice. Here are points to consider when selecting a bank:

• *Does it truly want your business?* Primarily, what banks sell is service, and the quality of their service to you is the basis on which to compare them. Some banks, particularly the less well-established ones in the community, are often more accommodating than those that already have plenty of business. The ideal banker is one who shows a genuine interest in your problems, makes constructive suggestions, and extends himself to work things out for you. A good banker is not the man who always knows why something can't be done; it is often the man who finds a legitimate way to do them. Even when two institutions are run by the same rules, a banker who wants your business somehow can make things easier for you than an indifferent one.

• *Is it progressive?* The bank's appearance can tell much about it. Up-to-date quarters furnished with modern equipment suggest that the bank wants customers to think it is in tune with the times. The special services it offers—installment credit for small businessmen, for example—and the way it advertises and promotes them will give strong clues as to whether it is your kind of bank. You might investigate how deeply your prospective banker is concerned with the growth and prosperity of your local community and the speed and flexibility with which decisions can be made in your local area.

• *What is its financial condition?* Bank failures are rare, but they *do* happen. Although the Federal Deposit Insurance Corporation (FDIC) insures each depositor in a bank for an amount up to $100,000, this amount applies to all your deposits in a single bank. Thus, if you keep several checking and savings accounts in the same bank and the balances total more than $100,000 the excess would be unprotected should the bank fail.

It is difficult to determine the safety of funds in a bank, since no sure measure of the safety element is available. But there are several statistical approaches to the analysis of a bank's strength. The ratio of deposits to capital funds helps to establish the margin of protection for depositors. The ratio of "risk" assets to capital suggests the extent to which a bank may sustain losses without endangering depositors' funds. But these analytical tools fail to take into account the most important factor: management. Your most reliable indication is the combination of integrity, experience, ability, and initiative in the people who run the bank. Good management will usually produce a reliable and progressive bank, as it will usually produce a healthy business.

• *How big is it?* For most ordinary purposes, it is not important whether you do business with the biggest or smallest bank in town. Sometimes size does make a difference and the biggest is not necessarily the best. You probably can develop a closer relationship with the manager of a small bank, since he, and not a group of specialists, will handle your different banking problems.

On the other hand, the overall quality of advice from one man may not be as high as that provided by specialists. Many small banks don't offer the services of a trust department, which you might need in connection with your will, with escrow arrangements, or with the management of your investments.

"Sometimes prestige also goes along with size," says a spokesman for the Small Business Administration. "After all, it may be assumed that one bank is bigger than another because more people do business with it. This may not be important to you and need not be decisive in your considerations. It may mean, however, that more contacts are available to you through your bank. At least it's a point not to be ignored."

A good banking relationship is a two-way deal. Your banker must come to certain conclusions about you, too. Your ability to get what you want from him will be greatly enhanced if you come across as a responsible citizen with a reputation to uphold. "Good character" is the first quality bankers look for in those to whom they lend money, and the second is an ability to operate successfully. If you have a good, long-established record in the community, are willing to discuss your financial problems frankly, and have no serious black marks chalked up against your credit rating anywhere, you will probably be a highly desirable customer for any bank. (If you are just starting out, it may pay to establish some kind of credit rating. I personally know one man, brought up in the tradition of old New England, who never borrowed money. At the age of fifty, his wife suddenly was hospitalized for major surgery and he sought to borrow the money to pay the medical expenses. It took five excruciating days to get the loan—the bank suspected anyone the credit agencies didn't know about.)

Give all your business to the banker of your choice. You might save a few dollars by shopping for bank bargains (your checking account here, savings account, safe deposit box somewhere else), but you would defeat yourself in the long run. A bank's services are most valuable when needed most—and they are generally needed most when hardest to get. Tight money conditions can force banks to limit loans to their regular and best customers, excluding others who give them only business from which they profit least.

Keep your personal and professional checking and savings accounts and safe deposit box at the same bank. If you must borrow under an installment contract, try to use the bank's plan. Use the bank as a trustee for your trust accounts, if any, and consider making it an executor or coexecutor of your will. If it has other services you could use (a bill-rendering and collecting service, for example), give it preference. The only exception to this rule might be if you have a considerable amount of money in savings. In this case, you might want to take advantage of the higher interest rates paid by savings and loan associations, savings banks, and money market certificates.

It also pays to stop in and see your banker occasionally so that you will be remembered personally when you approach him for a loan, other assistance, or advice. Moreover, you will probably want him to recommend you if other customers ask him for the name of someone in your profession. "Keep your banker informed on new developments in your work," suggests the SBA man, "and keep him supplied regularly with complete and current financial statements—even when you have no need for bank credit. Continuity of information enables him to handle credit inquiries intelligently, increases his confidence in you, and makes it possible for him to meet your requirements as they arise."

CONSULTANTS

If you think you need one, you might hire a management consultant to help you identify and strengthen weak spots in your methods of operating. Efficiency engineers cultivating the business of self-employers constitute only a small fraction, proportionately, of the number of management consultants to corporations. Their number appears to be growing, however. There are organizations catering to different professional groups, but more often the consultant is a member of a one-man or partnership organization. Often he has been a successful practitioner himself and has taken up consulting work as a part-time, semiretirement project—a thought for your own later years. There does not seem to be any set way for consultants to get together with self-employers in need of them. Some consultants make their availability known to trade and professional groups of which they are members. Some advertise in trade and professional journals or, if they live in a large city, in the classified telephone directory. Some solicit prospects directly. They may be able to improve your methods of turning prospects into customers, clients, or patients; set up smooth-functioning office procedures; take the bugs out of your billing processes; show you how to use work-saving materials and methods.

If you think you need some general guidance or help in solving special problems, consider asking a former colleague who is now semiretired for his advice. It is better if you know your consultant, at least by reputation, and if you can discuss matters frankly with him. Beware the fast-talking promoter who seeks you out and says he will revolutionize the way you do things. Flashy management consultants who promise much but deliver little more commonly try to sign up gullible corporation executives, but some fish for victims among self-employers. Make certain that they will save you, over a reasonable period, the amount of their fees. Above all, don't sign an expensive long-term contract with any "efficiency expert" until you have investigated him thoroughly—with your local Better Business Bureau, for example—and find former clients to assure you that his services are indeed worth what he asks for them.

PROFESSIONAL ASSOCIATIONS

An invaluable aid to almost all self-employers is the professional or trade association comprising others in the same field as themselves. Trade associations serve as clearinghouses of ideas about ways to operate one's business or profession more effectively. Many sponsor technical research that will benefit members; develop streamlined record-keeping methods; produce promotional material on which members can put their own names; compile statistics to enable members to compare costs, expenses, and profits with the industry at large; operate training courses; and run services to warn members of bad credit risks. Most remain alert to legislation affecting members' interests and frequently mount lobbying compaigns to make sure that their viewpoint is heard in federal, state, and local capitals. Many associations hold annual conventions at which equipment manufacturers display new products. Some trade groups have consultants to advise members how to solve special problems. Some have local chapters that provide frequent opportunities to meet and exchange information.

Another must for the self-employer is a subscription to one or several of the special publications dealing with his trade or profession specifically or with business conditions generally. A physician can hardly remain well-informed unless he reads several medical journals that describe the new methods of treatment and drugs in the area of his specialty. An accountant will not remain competent long unless he remains familiar with the latest tax rulings from Washington. A sales representative cannot compete effectively unless he knows what his competitors are doing, and often he can get this information only by reading the journals of his trade.

Chapter 4

You *Must* Protect Yourself with Insurance

ONE of the responsibilities you must accept is that of protecting yourself against calamity. You must make certain that you are not wiped out in the event of an accident connected with your profession or business; that you don't suffer ruinous losses due to thieves, from outside or inside your organization; that the financial resources you have built are not eroded by prolonged or expensive disease or illness.

You would have to be responsible for some insurance even if you were an employee of others. Your employer might provide life insurance and pay the costs of your hospitalization and medical care insurance, but you would still have to obtain adequate fire and theft and personal liability insurance on your home, personal possessions, and automobile.

As a self-employer, you must provide all the insurance that an employer might provide, as well as all that the ordinary employee provides for himself. You must take out policies to protect yourself against the loss of your income if you become sick or disabled and those that protect you against the hazards of your occupation.

In this chapter, aspects of insurance that specifically relate to you as a self-employer are discussed—on the assumption that there is no need to consider the basic kinds of insurance, with which everyone should be familiar.

"Buy Term and Invest the Difference"

There are differences of opinion as to whether life insurance should be of the *term* or *cash value* type. Term insurance is pure protection, of course. It expires at a certain time, after which you may have the option of renewing without another physical examination, but at a higher rate. Most term policies have no cash value: if you survive the period the policy covers, you gain nothing.

In contrast, straight or ordinary life insurance is permanent; once taken, it can be held a lifetime. Premiums remain the same; at fifty you get the same protection, without higher annual cost, as at twenty. Premiums for the young on such policies are much higher than on term policies with the same death benefits. Amounts paid in, above what is required for actual insurance, build up a cash value that you may borrow against or take as cash or income should you terminate the policy.

Whether to buy term or cash value insurance is often resolved for the individual by a consideration of his own personality and ability to discipline himself. Many experts in family finance advise: "Buy term and invest the difference." They reason that insurance companies invariably pay low interest rates on money left with them and that the individual as a rule can get a better financial return by buying common stocks, shares in mutual funds, or even bonds and debentures with money that would otherwise go into ordinary life insurance policies. As a self-employer, you might also use the extra money to build up your business.

While admitting that the "buy term and invest the rest" advice sounds good in theory, many insurance men argue that the typical individual lacks the willpower to follow it. He will spend money that would otherwise go into a cash value policy. Hence the cash value policy forces him to save; he pays certain amounts at specified periods and thinks no more of it. Meanwhile, his assets are building up.

No doubt of it, many persons *must* be forced to save. Even if what they earn on these savings is not as great as they could get elsewhere, they are better off by having to put aside a certain sum with regularity. As a person on your own, you are no "ordinary" individual, however. The fact that you are in business for yourself automatically sets you apart.

To succeed as an independent entrepreneur, you need ample amounts of self-discipline to begin with. No one tells you when to work or how to do it, what to charge for your services, or how to plan your schedules so as to achieve a profit at the end of your week. You must utilize your resources, whether time, talent, or money, so that they produce the greatest maximum return for you. If you must *pay* someone to supply discipline or willpower, you lack the quality most important for your professional success. Furthermore, if your career requires a large investment in equipment, you can hardly remain in business unless you earn more on your investment than insurance companies pay on the cash entrusted to their care.

For you, therefore, term insurance seems indicated. In fact, since you will need more protection for your dependents than the average employed person—when the latter dies, his heirs may be entitled to severance pay or various union benefits; in most cases, apart from Social Security survivors' benefits, there are no post-death benefits for survivors of the self-employed—money available for life insurance should probably go to purchase the largest feasible term policy.

Term Insurance

Term policies run for as little as one year, but the usual length is five or ten years. Get a policy that is both *renewable* and *convertible*.

The *renewable* clause allows you to continue your insurance for five- or ten-year periods without another medical examination. Premiums for each succeeding term are higher than for the preceding term, corresponding to the increased risk of death that comes with age.

Some companies won't renew your term policies after age sixty. Thus your effective protection may run out when you are sixty-five or seventy. (At that time, your need to protect your heirs probably will be less than when you were young; your children will be able, or almost able, to take care of themselves and your spouse won't need as much money for lifetime security.)

The *convertible* feature entitles you, within prescribed periods and without another medical examination, to switch to a straight life or ordinary policy in which cash values will accrue and that will continue in force throughout your lifetime. Premiums on the new policy are based on your age when you make the switch.

Worth looking into are term policies that will protect you for limited periods, when your death might be especially harmful financially. A best-selling author began writing a novel that would take three years to finish. If he died during the three-year period, with his book unfinished, his efforts would be wasted. His insurance agent advised a three-year term policy for $150,000. If the writer died within that period, his heirs would get as much as he hoped his book would earn.

The least expensive insurance usually is the kind available to groups of individuals with something in common—members of a trade or a professional organization, perhaps. Generally such insurance is term insurance without a cash value, and its premiums are low because individual selling and bookkeeping charges are eliminated. Because a wide cross section is represented in terms of age and physical condition, the likelihood of a large number of poor risks is reduced.

In most policies of this type, premium rates are computed on the average age of all members of the group. Everyone is then charged the identical rate. Older members pay less than under individual policies—sometimes only half as much. Savings under group plans are not as great for younger persons, but usually even they can obtain lower rates as group participants than as individual policy holders.

When a group is insured, there is no requirement that each person to be insured take a medical examination and be found in good health. Thus, those who might be rejected as poor risks when applying for individual policies have no difficulty in obtaining coverage under the group umbrella. The usual policy of this kind provides that a member who leaves the group may continue his insurance without a physical examination but at the higher individual rates. Once you become insured in a group policy, therefore, you may be assured of adequate protection for your lifetime regardless of your physical condition.

Don't overlook life insurance on your wife. In the past, many people concentrated insurance on the male wage earner in the family on the theory that his death would cause the greatest financial strain. But if your wife dies before you do, lack of insurance on her life could create serious financial and estate problems. Consider these circumstances.

• Your wife is employed, either in your business or with another firm. If she dies, the loss of her earnings could cause monetary problems for your family or business.

• You are starting on your own and have small children. If your wife dies, will you have to pay someone to care for them? To do so while your income is low, and cash is needed to build up your profession or trade, may make it difficult for you to carry on. A term insurance policy on her life, with a large enough benefit to pay a caretaker for at least four or five years, might be a good investment.

• Your wife owns part of your business and it has a substantial value. Insurance to pay the estate tax might be desirable. Otherwise some of the business might have to be sold.

ILLNESS AND LOSS OF INCOME INSURANCE

You will also have a need for more-than-usual *medical expense insurance*. Major medical policies are sold by private insurance companies and used by many persons for protection over and above that provided by the customary Blue Cross and Blue Shield coverage. These policies are self-descriptive—they are designed to defend you against the overwhelming expenses resulting from serious illness.

Major medical policies generally have a deductible feature. The insurance carrier agrees to pay all expenses over a certain figure—usually several hundred to a thousand dollars. Once you pay this amount (the deductible) the plan takes effect.

In a typical major medical plan, after the deductible has been met, the plan might pay 80 percent of the first $2,000 and all the covered charges above that figure. The deductible amount and percentage vary from one policy to another.

An important factor to consider in choosing a major medical plan is the lifetime maximum benefit. This is the maximum amount of benefits the insurance company will pay out for all bills during a person's life. Some individual major medical policies have a lifetime maximum of as little as $100,000. With the high cost of medical bills, this would not be enough in the event of prolonged serious injury or illness. Therefore, if your plan has a lifetime maximum, unless it is very substantial, you should consider purchasing a supplementary insurance policy to cover you for expenses beyond what the first plan pays. This supplemental policy would have as its deductible an amount equal to the lifetime maximum of your major medical plan. If the major medical plan has a lifetime maximum of $100,000, your supplemental policy would have a deductible of $100,000. Thus, when the first plan stops paying, the second takes over.

Hospital charges now run to an average of $300 a day or more, and doctors' fees may add up to thousands of dollars. Several years ago a Peekskill, New York, woman was hospitalized for a total of thirty days and underwent two operations to seal off a leaking blood vessel in her eye. The total bill for hospital and doctors' fees came to $14,583. Her Blue Cross, Blue Shield, and major medical insurance paid a total of $11,783, leaving her with out-of-pocket expenses of $2,800. This, of course, was no small sum, but it was much less than the total bill. She has since increased her major medical coverage to pick up an even greater amount of costs should she or any member of her family suffer a serious injury or illness again.

Some policies of this type are mined with booby traps, however. Many companies, among them some that advertise heavily by mail, fail to provide even a fraction of the benefits promised. Your agent should help you steer clear of policies with hidden jokers that deny you valuable privileges. Among the clauses to beware of are these:

- A clause stating that you must be confined to your home to obtain benefits. This clause means that your payments may be cut off even if you merely leave home to visit your doctor or go to the hospital for outpatient treatments. It has even been interpreted to deny policy holders the right to sit on a porch. In effect, it cuts off your payments during the convalescent stage of an illness when you are not well enough to work but need fresh air and sunshine.

• A clause giving the company the right to cancel your policy at any time. This means that it will continue your coverage only as long as you are profitable to the company. If you become seriously ill and need protection, it can be denied you.

• A clause giving the company the right not to renew your policy when it expires. This means that if you have a long or recurrent illness, the company will pay the benefits until the end of the policy year and then drop you. Some policies with this clause are renewable every quarter—and thus are renewed only as long as you remain healthy.

• A clause stating that "falsity of any statement in the application for this policy shall bar all right to recover." In practice, this means that regardless of how long you have paid premiums, benefits may be denied you at your moment of need if the company can discover a mistake, even an honest error, in your original application. Unless the false statement in the application was an obvious attempt to defraud, you might sue the insurer and collect—but a seriously ill person is in no condition to institute what could be a long legal battle. A more reasonable clause denies benefits only within two years after the policy is taken.

• A clause restricting benefits to "bodily injury sustained through accidental means." A man wanted to rearrange his office. In trying to lift a heavy desk over a carpet, he incurred a serious back injury and was hospitalized. When he sought to collect from his "bargain" health insurer, he was told that moving a desk was an intended, not an accidental, act. Hence he was not covered.

• A clause describing total disability as the "inability to engage in *any* occupation or employment." This narrow definition means that benefits may be denied even if you are completely unable to continue in your lifetime career but could work at something else, no matter how great a step down it might be. A similar clause denies benefits unless you are "wholly and continuously" disabled.

If you once get well from your condition, you lose all rights to payments even if, as often happens, a relapse occurs.

On the other hand, there are several desirable clauses to look for. A *recurrent disability* clause recognizes a relapse as a continuation of a previous condition and entitles you to receive benefits immediately, without the wait necessary with a new disability. A desirable clause defines a relapse as recurring within six months of recovery. Only if you have been fully recovered for six months or longer will a recurrence be considered a new condition. A *waiver-of-premium* clause recognizes that disability brings with it a reduction, if not total loss, of income. Once you are disabled for a certain period, often three months, you need not pay any premiums on your policy until your recovery.

Disability insurance (protection against loss of income) is another special need of self-employers. Most salaried employees are paid at least a certain number of days per year when they can't work due to illness. Employees of large firms may be carried on employers' payrolls at their regular or reduced salaries for years if they are laid up that long. However, the income of most self-employed persons ceases if they contract a long illness and can't work. This could have disastrous consequences; many successful persons in business for themselves would be in desperate circumstances if they had no income for a year and high medical bills to pay in addition to business overhead and regular living expenses. I know a commercial artist who contracted a debilitating form of hepatitis and couldn't work for eight months. His savings account went to zero, and when he was able to take up his brush again and sought work from his former clients, they had given their assignments to competitors. Broke and faced with the prospect of rebuilding his practice, he took jobs paying only a fraction of his former fees.

The chances of your being unable to work for ninety days or more between ages thirty-five and sixty-five are much greater than your chances of dying in that age period. Specifically, seven out of ten men in that group will be tied up for three months or more at least once in their lives.

You can protect yourself by buying a disability insurance policy—sometimes called sickness and accident insurance.

Don't confuse disability coverage with health insurance, which applies exclusively to hospital and medical and surgical costs. Disability insurance pays no medical bills. Instead, it pays you a monthly income whenever sickness or accident prevent you from earning your normal income.

Disability insurance is sold in three different ways: an individual policy; a trade or professional association group policy; a company-sponsored group policy.

Most group policies are limited to groups of twenty-five or more. They are less expensive than individual policies but cannot be easily "custom-made." All group policies are cancelable at the company's option—a serious flaw.

Unfortunately, it is easier to decide to buy disability insurance than it is to buy a sensible policy. This is true for two reasons:

First, disability policies come in all shapes and sizes. You pick what you need. And that's the rub. Unless you have studied the subject, you won't pick wisely—won't spot an unfair definition of disability or a renewal clause that lets the company cancel your individual policy without your permission. Moreover, since you literally buy a disability policy a la carte, it is also easy for the unknowing to buy unnecessary and costly frills.

Second, not everyone can buy disability insurance. Insurance companies are selective. Basically, they don't like sick and/or dishonest individuals and they strive to reject their applications.

Understanding those factors—the complexity of the policy and the difficulties involved in buying such protection—is the only way you can protect your family against financial catastrophe.

Each insurance company has its own disability definition and those definitions differ widely. Some insurers consider disability to be an "inability to perform any gainful occupation whatever." That's a limiting definition that might mean that if you could perform any job on the market, your policy wouldn't pay you. You couldn't collect even though you couldn't return to the work you were doing prior to your disability. Don't accept this definition.

Other companies consider disability to be an "inability to perform regular work." That's a fuzzy definition and another you should avoid.

This is the best definition: you are disabled and eligible for monthly payments whenever you can't work at your own occupation or another for which you are reasonably suited by training, education, or experience. This means that you are protected if you can no longer earn as much as you formerly could.

Your policy should also define "accident" fairly. This word is not always defined as you would expect in a disability policy. Some policies define an accidental injury as one "sustained directly or independently of all other causes." That's tricky. The insurer could deny your claim on the grounds that your accidental injury was somehow related to a medical condition.

The best definition is: "Accidental bodily injury sustained while this policy is in force."

Now consider the policy's elimination or waiting period—the days between the time the disability began and the monthly payments start. Determine how many days you want to wait—7, 14, 30, 90, 180, or 365. You may also buy the extremely expensive no-waiting policy. The longer you can wait to get payments, the lower your annual premium.

To decide wisely, base your waiting-time estimate on your savings, your accounts receivable, other short-term sources of income, the ability of your business to run profitably without you, and your Social Security benefits. You and your family may get up to $966 a month in disability Social Security benefits. First payments won't get into your hands until the fifth month of your disability, and to collect these benefits your disability must be expected to last at least twelve months. In effect, ask yourself, "How long can we get along without my working?"

When comparing one waiting period to another, scrutinize how much you will save in premiums by waiting a longer time before disability payments begin. The savings may not be much relative to the benefits you would give up—perhaps as much as $7,000— by waiting, say, ninety or more days.

Decide how much protection you will need each month. The face value of your policy (the monthly payment you will receive) can be any amount you choose up to roughly 60 percent of your pretax income.

When you own a business or professional practice, the insurance company can't call your employer to check your salary—the basis for the face value. But the insurer can—and sometimes does when the face value is quite high—ask for a CPA's statement of your earnings or a copy of your federal income tax return, supplied by the IRS to guarantee honesty.

The insurer usually does not consider your nonproductive income (space rentals, stock dividends, etc.) when computing 60 percent of your annual income to arrive at your maximum allowable monthly payments. The only exception is when nonproductive income exceeds productive earnings.

For the best coverage you can buy, get a noncancelable policy, with sickness benefits to age sixty-five and accident benefits for life—with a thirty-day waiting period.

If you have no disability insurance now, buy the noncancelable policy first, covering 60 percent of your income. Then add an association policy—one sold on a group basis by a local chamber of commerce or professional or trade group to which you belong—to cover the other 40 percent. This is a legal way to get sufficient coverage to protect 100 percent of your income. If you buy association group first, you cannot later add noncancelable coverage.

If you are self-employed, the premiums you pay on an individual disability policy are not tax-deductible; however, you pay no income taxes on any benefits you receive. If you are the head of an incorporated business, the premium payments are deductible to the corporation and any benefits you collect are taxable to you.

Insurers are reluctant to insure self-employed people or people who work in their own home. That is because the industry finds it difficult to check on the disability of a person who sets his or her own hours.

Since an insurance company stands to pay many thousands of dollars should someone it insures become disabled for years, it wants to sign up only those whose likelihood of becoming disabled is slim. Consequently, insurers have set up a screening system that considers several factors in determining whether you will get disability insurance and how much you will have to pay for it.

Factors they consider are age, occupation, state of your health, and sex. Women generally are charged more for disability insurance than men because insurers believe they are more likely to become disabled and are less likely to return to work after a disability. Laws concerning women and insurance may very well change in the next few years, however.

If you have a serious ailment—ulcers, say—some companies still will sell you a policy but will exclude that problem from protection. Thus, if you are disabled because of an auto accident or a kidney problem, you will collect. But, if that ulcer disables you, you won't.

Since you buy a policy for protection, you ought to know beforehand if it will stay in force for a reasonable length of time. You also should know if your premiums will go up over the life of the policy.

You can answer these questions decisively because the disability insurance companies have all agreed on four different renewal clauses. You select one for the duration of your policy. They are:

• *Cancelable.* The company can cancel your policy at any time by sending you a notice and a refund on the unused portion of the policy. This is the cheapest but least effective protection.

• *Optionally renewable* (also called conditionally renewable). The insurer can cancel on the policy's anniversary date or when the premium comes due for a specific but impersonal reason. Two typical reasons: The company has elected to cancel all its disability policies in your state. Or, it has chosen to cancel all policy holders over a specific age—age forty, say. This clause affords more protection than the cancelable one at a higher cost, but it is not in your best interests.

• *Guaranteed renewable.* The company gives you a continuing policy until at least age fifty—or for at least five years if you bought the policy after age forty-four. Some insurers set the age at sixty or sixty-five. During that period the company can't change the policy but it can change the premium, provided it does so for an entire class of insureds (same age group, residents of same state, etc.) This clause is more expensive than the others mentioned, but it is good coverage.

• *Noncancelable.* The company allows you the same privileges under the guaranteed renewable clause plus this benefit: the insurer can't increase the premium during the policy's life. This is the most expensive and the best protection you can get. Most policies sold today are noncancelable.

Once you have selected the best definition of disability, waiting period, renewable clause, and monthly payment, you are ready to scrutinize the policy for its exclusion clauses. Here is a rundown on the major ones:

• A house/hospital confinement clause means that you must be confined to a hospital or to your house in order to be deemed disabled. Such a limitation would mean you couldn't visit your doctor's office without jeopardizing your coverage. Don't accept this unfair clause.

• A change of occupation clause increases your premiums if you enter an occupation that is more hazardous than the one you held when you bought the policy. It's a fair request. If you are forced to accept it, do so. Many noncancelable policies do allow you to change jobs at no increase in premiums.

• An average earnings clause lowers your monthly benefit payment whenever your earnings drop below the amount you earned when you bought the policy. This is legitimate protection for the companies who do not want to pay you more in benefits that you have been earning.

Once you have coped with those clauses, try to get these two clauses inserted in your policy if they are not already there:

• A waiver of premium clause allows you to stop all premium payments on the policy once you have been disabled for a specified length of time—perhaps three or six months.

• A recurrent disability clause wipes out the waiting period when a disability you have had while the policy has been in force springs up again within six months of your last recovery. Benefits start immediately.

Virtually all disability policies contain an incontestable clause that, stripped of legal jargon, says: all misstatements of fact on the application and all medical omissions are forgiven after the policy's second anniversary. A few companies even let you off the hook after one year. And if the company catches your omission or misstatement before the second anniversary, you suffer no financial penalty. Instead, the company just cancels your policy (even the noncancelable one) and refunds all of your premium payments.

Business Interruption Insurance. During a period when you are forced to shut down all or part of your activities due to accidents and emergencies outside your control, this insurance guarantees your operating income—payroll, light, heat, telephone—as well as your customary profits until the insured property can be reasonably repaired or replaced.

According to the Insurance Information Institute, business owners who fully insure their buildings and contents often ignore protection against losses due to unexpected shutdowns beyond their control. But, it says, "In the final analysis the key to reopening the door or closing it for good may hinge on the businessman's ability to meet ongoing expenses during the period he is temporarily shut down."

That property insurance alone won't assure a business's survival after a shutdown is apparent in the results of a survey showing that 40 percent of businesses sustaining extensive fire losses never reopened—despite having adequate coverage on both buildings and contents. Less than 20 percent of the businesses could resume full-scale operations with unimpaired credit standings.

Business interruption insurance—also known as time element coverage—can also be written for a business owner whose premises are under construction, guarding against loss to the uncompleted building that would postpone your date of occupancy. It would cover loss of earnings from the date your business operations should have begun.

For businesses that must continue in operation no matter how serious the damage to their facilities, "extra expense" insurance is another time element coverage. It is designed for a service-type operation, such as a newspaper that must continue its operation at almost any cost.

In this case, the insured's concern with loss of income is actually secondary to his need for a source of funds to enable him to meet extra expenses necessary to keep the service uninterrupted. He may, for example, have to move his whole operation into temporary quarters elsewhere at a higher cost. Under these circumstances, this "extra expense" is covered.

PROFESSIONAL NEGLIGENCE INSURANCE

Liability insurance, which protects you against damage claims made on you by other persons in the course of your professional activities, is essential. The kind of insurance needed depends largely on particular circumstances. For example, a physician must carry malpractice insurance so that he won't be financially destroyed if it is successfully claimed that his treatment or prescription caused death or disability. (There has been a drastic increase in the number of malpractice suits brought against medical practitioners recently. Awards exceeding $300,000 are not uncommon. Costs of insurance to protect against such contingencies have also risen drastically. They are a significant factor in "rising medical cost," about which little is written.) Other professionals must be protected against nuisance suits by customers who allegedly suffer injury at their hands or on their premises. Suits of this type also have increased greatly in recent years.

Who may be charged with professional negligence? John W. Wade, professor of law at Vanderbilt University, says the term includes negligent conduct by doctors, lawyers, ministers, and teachers and by members of "callings which come within a broader definition of the word profession. Herein are noted abstractors, accountants, architects, engineers, hospitals, insurance agents, pharmacists, and undertakers," Wade says. "And it includes other occupations like those of barbers and beauticians, carpenters, cleaners and launderers, electricians, repairmen, and plumbers." Negligence often involves performing a physical act in a negligent way, but it also has been held to involve the giving of erroneous information or bad advice—"negligent misrepresentation." So broad is the interpretation that anyone holding himself out to the public as having a superior knowledge or skill may find himself on the defensive side of a liability suit. Perhaps the most extreme example occurred in Colombia, South America, when a farmer filed suit against local church officials on the grounds that they had predicted the world would come to an end, causing him to squander all his money.

The major special characteristic of such suits, Professor Wade states, "involves the statement of the standard of care to which the defendant is held. As a follower of a profession or a vocation, he holds himself out to the public as having the requisite skill to practice it. He must therefore possess and exercise this skill. The word 'skill' includes not just manual dexterity but also knowledge and training suitable for the particular profession. In cases going to juries, judgments often are sought because the defendant allegedly did not use the reason, prudence, or skill of the average member of his profession."

You also must make sure that you are protected by insurance against the failure of equipment that might cause injury. Bernard D. Hirsch, an attorney in the law division of the American Medical Association, cites the case of a patient who had visited a chiropodist for the treatment of a foot ailment. The chiropodist told her to sit in a metal hydraulic chair designed for the occupancy of patients. He neglected to "lock" the chair. It rotated suddenly as she tried to get into it, throwing her to the floor and injuring her.

Contending that it was not liable for the amount of a judgment obtained against the chiropodist by the patient, the insurer claimed that the policy was strictly limited to injuries arising out of the actual rendition of professional services. However, the court held that the injury arose "out of the practice of the insured's profession" and was within the coverage of the insured's professional liability policy. The court stated that maintaining the treatment chair in a proper and safe condition for the accommodation of patients was a service or duty directly connected with the practice of the insured in his profession as a chiropodist.

In choosing a company to underwrite professional negligence insurance, you should consider its stability, present and future, above all else. It should be a well-established company with reserves that have *always* proved adequate in the past. There should not be the least possible doubt of its ability to keep going in the distant future.

A basic factor to be considered when buying negligence insurance is that *your present carrier may be required to defend you twenty or more years from now.* For example, a medical doctor who treats a child today may be held liable when the minor reaches his majority. In some states, the statute of limitations regarding alleged injuries to adults is virtually without end.

You should go over your policy with your insurance agent point by point. Most professional negligence policies have many exclusions and conditions with which you should thoroughly familiarize yourself. Typical exclusions state that coverage will *not* apply if injuries result from performance of a criminal act by the insured; if the insured is under the influence of alcohol or drugs; if the injuries result from the actions of an employee or someone else under the insured's jurisdiction. A list of exclusions in medical negligence policies compiled by the law department of the American Medical Association includes: shock therapy, contact lenses, plastic surgery for cosmetic reasons, nonpathological sterilization, hand fluoroscopy, acts performed by a surgeon without the patient's knowledge and consent, acts of an anesthesiologist who is not a licensed medical doctor, etc.

AUTO LIABILITY INSURANCE

In view of your special need to continue your operations in spite of almost any contingency, you need insurance against claims of damage done by your automobiles or other vehicles. You must meet the requirements of the financial or safety responsibility law of your state and of the compulsory law in states that have enacted such measures. Safety or financial responsibility laws generally require that you show evidence that you are capable of paying for death, injury, or property damages caused by the vehicles you own. The amount you must show yourself capable of providing varies according to the state. It ranges from $5,000 to $25,000 to be paid to one person for bodily injury or death, from $10,000 to an unlimited amount if more than one person is injured or killed in the same accident, and from $1,000 to $10,000 for damage to the property of another.

These figures are minimal; in most cases they do not equal the amounts often sought and won by accident victims. It is not uncommon for awards to run to six or even seven figures. After a truck driver was killed in an intersection accident by a taxicab that passed a red light, his widow was awarded $250,000. In each case, amounts awarded are based on many factors such as the income of the victim, life expectancy, and number of dependents.

In cases of injury, the severity and length of the disability are taken into consideration. A person with liability "protection" of $20,000 against whom a six-figure award is granted has no protection at all; such an award could wipe him out.

Your only prudent approach, therefore, is to protect yourself to the maximum extent possible. Commonly obtainable are automobile liability policies covering you up to $100,000 for bodily injury per person, up to $300,000 for bodily injury per accident, and up to $10,000 for property damage per accident. Additionally, you can obtain a so-called executive or umbrella policy that provides $1,000,000 in coverage over and above the coverages cited above. This added coverage, designed to protect you against the catastrophic accident that is unlikely but could ruin you if it did happen, is generally available for no more than a few hundred dollars a year.

In view of insurance costs that are rising all over the country, but most particularly in urban areas vulnerable to crime, riots, and other disturbances, you might question whether you should obtain *comprehensive* and *collision* insurance for your vehicles.

Comprehensive insurance will compensate you directly if a vehicle is stolen or damaged by fire, floods, or most other causes excluding collision or upset. *Collision insurance* entitles you to all but a specified amount (usually $100 or $200) of your repair bills if your vehicle is damaged in an accident even if the driver of your vehicle was at fault.

In some places, costs of such insurance are so high relative to the maximum benefits that will be paid that you might be better off assuming the risks yourself. To determine whether such policies will work out to your advantage, you must consider four factors: cost of such policies in your locality; number of vehicles you own; value of the vehicles; your income tax bracket.

A sales agent who lives in New York City and owns three cars (one business and two family vehicles) might not want to insure his cars against fire, theft, and collision unless they are new. Because of the high rates and the insurance companies' policy of paying no more than the current book value of a vehicle—even if it is demolished—it might be cheaper to use his own funds to repair or replace an older car than it would to pay the premiums for comprehensive and collision insurance. Furthermore, if only one of the three cars was used for business, only the premiums for that car would be deductible as a business expense. On the other hand, repair costs or losses exceeding $100 in any accident would be deductible as a casualty loss, whether or not the car involved was used for business.

LIFE INSURANCE FOR YOUR BUSINESS

What would happen to your enterprise if you died before you could make plans for its orderly continuation or disposal? Would the structure collapse, leaving your survivors with the job of trying to salvage the wreckage? To prevent this from occurring, and to save yourself great expense and trouble in case of the death of a partner or an employee you now depend on greatly, consider these three kinds of insurance.

Proprietorship insurance. Most states provide that when a sole proprietor dies, his business becomes part of his estate, to be passed to the heirs as quickly as possible unless other provisions have been made.

Thus, the heirs face the possibility of severe loss unless a plan is set up in advance of death. If the proprietor dies, the business can be left to a child or children, a widow, or other heirs. It can be sold to employees or outsiders or continued by the executors or trustees. Or it can be liquidated and its equipment sold.

The American Council of Life Insurance warns that each of these procedures, unless set up under a carefully drawn plan, raises problems for the heirs. The sale of the business might be forced by cash needs or the demands of the heirs, and a forced sale could result in a sharp loss. Says the council:

> Whatever the disposition of the business, funds will be needed. Debts, taxes, and administrative costs must be met. Income for the family must be provided.
>
> If the family is continuing the business, someone will probably have to be hired to manage it. Working capital will be needed, at least for a period of readjustment.
>
> If employees are to take over, funds for their purchase have to be made available, at least in part.

If the business is sold outright, working capital will be needed for the transition period. Funds may also be needed to meet the probable discounting of assets accompanying such a sale.

Most of these funds are needed quickly. The tax needs are urgent and cannot be avoided or postponed. Credit needs are likely to be even more urgent. In some types of business, there is likely to be an immediate need for working capital. Many enterprises built around professional training or expertise could conceivably find no buyer. The income-producing value would vanish overnight.

To meet these problems, the proprietor needs to set up a well-planned program in case of his death. It should include:

1. A will covering disposition of his assets.

2. A purchase-and-sale agreement or a plan for disposal or continuation of the business or its equipment.

3. An estimate of the funds required to carry out details of the plan.

Since a will, a trust agreement, possibly a purchase-and-sale agreement, and a life-insurance program are to be written, consultation between the insurance agent, the accountants, the trust officer, and the attorney of the proprietor is advisable. These experts can determine what is needed and draw up a plan to meet the legal technicalities and financial needs involved.

The details of the plan will not necessarily follow any set pattern. Business life insurance for a sole proprietorship, even more than for any other type of business, must be tailored to the particular case. A suitable insurance program can:

1. Assure immediate funds to meet taxes, debts and administrative expenses.

2. Provide income for the heirs.

3. Equitably distribute the property value to the heirs.

4. Enable the trustee to dispose of the business to best advantage, if the heirs are not taking it over.

5. Put the heirs on sound financial footing, if they are assuming direction of the business.

6. Stabilize the credit of the business.

7. Maintain good employee relations by eliminating uncertainties and hazards.

Sole-proprietorship life insurance is so closely linked with the whole program of personal insurance and personal finances of the proprietor that it should be frequently checked. Such a check helps him make certain that his insurance program is in keeping with the requirements of personal and business relations at all times.

This check should be made at least once a year. It is not enough to set up such a plan and then file away the papers unseen for a longer period. The plan, left unchecked, might prove not only inadequate, but a handicap to proper handling of affairs at the proprietor's death.

Partnership insurance. Since a partnership is dissolved by the death of a partner, such a death seriously endangers the continuity of a business. It also involves a hazard to the interests of the surviving partner or partners and the heirs of the deceased partner.

On the death of a partner, the surviving partners become "liquidating trustees." They cannot do any new business but must wind up the affairs of the partnership. If they continue the business, they may become personally liable for all losses or, in some states, for losses in excess of the value of the partnership assets.

Nor can the heirs legally take over the business. But they can demand an accounting and a cash settlement of their share of the firm's net worth.

Controversy over the valuation of this interest could lead to prolonged legal difficulties. This can be avoided through an adequately insured buy-and-sell agreement establishing the valuation in advance. Through such a plan, the business can be continued despite death of a partner. The deceased partner's heirs also can be assured full and immediate payment for his share of the business.

The major purpose of partnership insurance is liquidation of the interest of any partner at death. It establishes a precise plan of action to become effective on the death of the partner. If liquidation is planned, which is not often the case, the process can be effected smoothly. If the aim is to continue the business, practically the only way this can be guaranteed is through such a plan. Each partner can be assured that his heirs will receive his full share of the partnership, at a valuation he himself has approved. Controversy over valuation is avoided, and a primary source of contention is removed. Creditors and banking circles can be assured that no lapse in the firm's credit standing will result from the death.

There are various partnership insurance plans. One plan involves the purchase by each partner of policies on the lives of the other partners. Where there are three or more partners another plan has the firm buy a policy on the life of each partner.

Questions of how much premium each partner should pay, the amount of insurance needed, beneficiary arrangements, tax effects, and the policy assignments necessary are a few of the many questions involved. Hence all business, legal, financial, and insurance needs and facilities should be checked by experts: insurance agent, lawyer, banker, and accountant.

Valuation of the partnership is probably the most complex of all the details involved, and the one on which there is most difficulty in reaching an agreement. The American Council of Life Insurance explains:

> An attempt is made to set up a formula under which full value is to be paid the deceased partner's heirs at some future time. The formula must satisfy all partners or it could cause a long-running controversy. And yet, difficult as it may be to agree on the valuation basis today, the difficulty would be greater if the determination were put off until one partner is dead and his heirs are possibly battling for an inflated valuation of his share.
>
> There are many bases of valuation. Simplest is one that sets an arbitrary value on each partner's interest in advance. Such a plan avoids later argument, but makes no provision for a possibly rapid shift in value.
>
> If this type of plan is used, the formula for settlement could be a fixed valuation for goodwill plus net book value (the

readily determined current value of assets less liabilities). Since goodwill is a difficult element to measure, that is where controversy is most apt to develop. Often the plan provides that the partners will agree, at various intervals, on a revised valuation.

Another possibility is to leave the valuation to a trustee or to arbitration under a specific arbitration plan. The arrangement best suited to a firm will be determined by its specific needs.

Like proprietorship policies, partnership insurance should be checked at least annually, and for the same reasons.

Keyman Insurance. For self-employers, this is often keywoman insurance, a policy on the life of an employee whose death would seriously disrupt operations and cause heavy monetary loss. A private investigator from New Hampshire relied heavily on the woman who had managed his office for sixteen years and relieved him of such detail work as collecting and paying bills, keeping his books, even preparing his income tax statements. When she contracted pneumonia and died, the investigator had to drop his own work for three months while he sought and trained a replacement (after he reacquainted himself with office procedures he had forgotten long ago). Because of his office manager's death, his income dropped $9,600 that year.

Keyman insurance is intended to prevent such a financial drain. It is worth considering if the death of someone in your employ would cripple your operations or set you back substantially until you found a replacement. The cost to you of the employee's death may determine whether this kind of policy should be taken and its amount. If you reach a figure of a few thousand dollars or more, insurance is probably indicated; a policy in that amount will give you the resources to find and train a successor and to cushion your loss of income in the meantime.

CRIME INSURANCE

Almost all persons in professions, trades, or businesses dealing with the public report a sharp upsurge in shoplifting in recent years. Some large department stores reportedly have closed because "inventory shrinkage" has turned a profitable enterprise into a losing one. More and more professional people report thefts of equipment and other items by visitors to their offices. Contrary to a widely held notion, there is no identifiable shoplifter "type." It may be the well-dressed wife of a corporation executive who has no real need for the things she steals and cannot explain why she takes them, and not much is gained simply by putting yourself on the defensive against certain types—"respectable" callers at your place of business may be the worst offenders.

Whenever possible, don't leave your premises unlocked or unguarded during business hours. A young woman asked a psychiatrist in Chevy Chase, Maryland, for an appointment to discuss a serious problem that had arisen in her marriage. She said she could see him only at 1:00 P.M. When the interview was concluded, and the doctor's time was taken up with another patient, the young woman walked off with an electric typewriter worth $1,000 from the outer office; she had timed the appointment to coincide with the psychiatrist's secretary's lunch hour.

You probably need crime insurance, and there are a variety of policies available to protect your business from thieves. Theft policies cover missing goods and damaged property and help protect you against two types of crime: burglary (theft of property from a building by forced entry) and robbery (theft of property from a person by force or threat of violence). Depending on your needs, a policy can be written to cover property when it is inside a building, while it is being moved from one location to another, or both. You can also buy additional coverage (called endorsements) to protect you against such things as embezzlement, misappropriation, willful obstruction, willful misapplication, and mysterious disappearance of property.

Comprehensive contracts cover dishonesty, disappearance of property, and destruction of property. These comprehensive policies (often called 3-D policies) protect against a variety of losses such as those caused by dishonest officers or employees, theft on or off the premises, accidental acceptance of counterfeit money, and check and credit card forgeries. Extortion coverage may also be added.

ALL-RISK POLICIES

Most people are familiar with multi-peril insurance—insurance that covers certain properties for several kinds of losses such as fire, theft, windstorm, etc. But in recent years, multiple-line or *all-risk* policies have become widely available to business owners. These multiple-line policies are package deals that combine a number of traditional, multi-peril lines of insurance. They include both property and liability insurance against a wide range of potential losses and are designed to meet virtually all the insurance needs of a typical business. The two most common types of multiple-line insurance for businesses are the Business Owners' Policy and the Special Multi-Peril Policy (SMP).

The Business Owners' Policy limits eligibility to businesses whose physical space requirements are small: apartment buildings of six stories or less with no more than sixty units; mercantile operations housed in a single building no larger than 7,500 square feet or two or more buildings totaling no more than 10,000 square feet; office buildings no more than three stories high or 10,000 square feet in floor space.

Several different lines of insurance are included in these business policies. If you run a small operation and purchase a standard Business Owners' Policy, your business can be covered for certain named perils, or if you purchase a special form policy, for all risks. In either case the building and business personal property are covered at full *replacement cost value*. Built into these policies is an automatic 2 percent increase in insurance every three months to allow for inflation. Protection against theft, vandalism, and boiler pressure and air-conditioning malfunction are options you can purchase.

Other features in a Business Owners' Policy are coverage for loss of profits, extra expense resulting from damage or interruption of business, and comprehensive liability and medical payments for nonemployees. This comprehensive liability and medical insurance includes protection against:

1. personal injury other than physical injury that protects you against such things as false arrest, slander, defamation of character;
2. host liquor liability that covers you if you have served liquor

at a business function and someone is injured—say, in an automobile accident—as a result;

3. fire legal liability that protects you if fire destroys someone else's property that was in your custody or if someone's property is damaged by a fire that originated on your business premises.

If you have a seasonal business, you can also get peak seasonal coverage that automatically increases your coverage by 25 percent during your peak seasons, provided your property is insured for at least 100 percent of the average monthly value of stock for the preceding year. This is particularly valuable if you keep larger-than-normal inventories on hand at certain times of the year.

SMP policies, the other common form of multiple-line business insurance, are primarily tailored for larger, more complex businesses and institutions. There is no limitation on the space a business occupies, and all businesses, except farms, motor vehicle businesses, bowling alleys, and small apartment houses, are eligible for SMP coverage.

There are eight basic SMP programs for different types of businesses: mercantile, office, apartment house, processing or service, institutional, motel and hotel, industrial, and construction. Coverage under any of the eight programs is flexible and can be modified to meet your particular needs. (If, for instance, you own a motel complex that includes a restaurant, you would have different insurance requirements than a person who owns a motel that offers only sleeping accommodations.) Also, with SMP all major risks except workers' compensation, auto and surety bond coverage are insured or can be insured by endorsement.

An SMP, like a Business Owners' Policy, is a package deal that includes four major areas of coverage: property, general liability, crime, and boiler and machinery protection. The property insurance differs from the Business Owners' Policy in that it is usually written on a cash value basis, but you can buy an endorsement for replacement value coverage. The other major difference is that an SMP generally does not include the automatic increase for inflation that is part of the Business Owners' Policy. Options that can be added to an SMP package include insurance for business interruption, extra expense, water damage, earthquake damage, and other perils.

There are many reasons why you should consider multiple-line policies such as the Business Owners' Policy or an SMP package when you buy insurance. In his Small Business Administration publication, *Insurance and Risk Management,* Mark R. Greene, cites these advantages of all-risk policies:

1. You know that you are covered for all perils not specifically excluded. You thus avoid unintentional gaps in coverage. In "named-peril" policies, your losses are covered only when they are caused by a peril specifically listed in the contract. All-risk policies should allay possible uncertainty about the adequacy of your insurance.

2. You are less likely to duplicate your coverage—always costly to you. In purchasing several different named-peril policies, it is often hard to avoid overlapping coverage.

3. With an all-risk policy, you can more easily avoid the conflicts that sometimes result from having many separate policies. When you have more than one policy covering a single loss, settlement of loss claims is often complicated—especially if the policies' wording concerning loss settlements is not identical. For example, one policy may cover all your property, but another may cover only specific property. If loss to the specific property occurs, conflict may arise over how much each policy is to contribute. This situation, known as nonconcurrency, usually causes complicated adjustment problems and delays.

4. You are more likely to receive better agency service if you have all-risk coverage because only one agent will handle your business. Many small businessmen spread their insurance purchases among several agents, and thus no one agent feels responsible for the entire program of protection. Also, the larger commission on an all-risk policy provides the agent greater incentive to give good service.

5. Your total premium on an all-risk policy is usually smaller than on the same coverage purchased separately. Larger unit sales cut down on the insurer's overhead per policy—a saving that is passed on to you. And your time spent in supervising your insurance program is reduced because you handle all coverage in one action.

PROTECTION FROM EMPLOYEES

According to Greene, thefts by employees each year probably amount to several times the loss from burglary, robbery, and larceny. Embezzlers often steal small sums over a period of years, eventually draining enormous sums from their employers. Only about 20 percent of such loss is insured. If you have employees, consider the use of fidelity bonds to protect yourself against this hazard. Requiring your employee or employees to be bonded often discourages stealing that might otherwise occur, and the character investigation conducted by the bonding company sometimes discloses unfavorable facts about an employee's honesty, enabling you to take steps to prevent potential losses.

Fidelity bonds cover money and other property, real or personal, that is owned by the employer or for which the employer is responsible. Losses covered by such bonds must be the result of dishonesty on the part of the bonded employee, not omission or error.

There are three kinds of fidelity bonds: individual, schedule, and blanket. Individual bonds name a specific person; schedule bonds list all names or positions to be covered; blanket bonds cover all employees but don't identify them by name or position. A limit of liability, called the penalty of the bond, is always included. It represents the maximum sum payable if loss is discovered. Usually the loss must *occur* while the bond is in force and must be *discovered* while the bond is in force or within a stated period, often two years, after it is canceled.

Fidelity bonds usually are written for a period of one or three years. The premium is based on the insurance company's estimate of the probability of loss (as in fire insurance). Its underwriters look at the opportunities for dishonesty inherent in the business. In a retail store where most transactions are in cash, the risk is higher than in a professional office where almost everything is paid by check. (But this doesn't mean there is no risk in the latter case.) Also, the more employees that are covered and the more frequent the turnover among employees, the higher the rates will be.

One trouble with individual or schedule bonds is that coverage tends to be limited to obvious areas of potential loss, while losses can easily come from an unexpected source. Norman Jaspan, president of a New York business security firm that bears his name, says the majority of employees covered in individual or schedule bonding plans deal with cash. Those who handle only merchandise tend to be excluded. But loss through theft of goods, supplies, equipment, and tools is far greater than through embezzlement of cash.

"It's not uncommon," says Jaspan, "to find a firm's treasurer, a man who never stole a penny, to be covered by honesty insurance, while thirty other employees, none of them bonded, are systematically stealing $3,000 a week in merchandise."

The most effective coverage is blanket coverage, which bonds all the employees in the firm. This is particularly true of the small firm. You don't have to guess in advance which person or job is most susceptible to stealing. And you don't have to worry about implying that Smith is a potential thief while Jones is above suspicion.

Blanket plans offer two types of coverage:

(1) Primary commercial bonds. These reimburse you up to an established dollar limit, regardless of the number of employees involved in the theft. If four people—working together or separately—steal $60,000 worth of equipment from you and your primary commercial bond has a limit of $25,000, you can't recover $35,000 of your loss.

(2) Position bonds. These cover you—up to a limit—for the theft carried out by each employee. If the limit is $15,000 per position, you can recover the total amount of a $60,000 theft committed by four dishonest workers.

A bond goes into effect on the date specified in the policy. In a blanket policy, new employees are covered the moment they join the company.

But employee theft is insidious; it may have been going on undetected, long before you take out coverage. So bonding that provides only current coverage can fall far short of what you need, especially if you are finally resorting to honesty insurance because you suspect you have been victimized for years. By starting coverage with the date of the policy, you may be locking the barn door long after the horse has galloped off.

You can avoid this by arranging for a discovery bond. This type of bond is retroactive, covering an employee from the time he starts working for you, not from the effective policy date. Say you find out that your purchasing agent has been billing you for payments to a dummy firm (set up by himself) for five years before you obtained the policy. Under a discovery bond you are entitled to recover because the loss was discovered while the bond was in force.

At first glance, a discovery policy appears to put the bonding company at the mercy of a clever business owner. For example, an owner who is sure he is losing money through internal theft might think he could obtain a discovery policy and be compensated for a loss he already knows about. However, bonding companies are highly sophisticated about this sort of deception. They recognize their potential areas of vulnerability and require that business owners who obtain fidelity bonds sign written assurances that they have no prior knowledge of theft at the time they take out the policy. Those who try to fool the insurer are likely to find it doesn't work.

The need to level with the bonding company extends to other areas, including how you describe potential losses. For example, the president of a wholesale firm whose salespeople carried watches and jewelry was asked by the bonding company (as a routine procedure) the value of the merchandise they customarily carried. The reply was that the salespeople carried about $20,000 worth of samples in each case.

After the policy was in effect, a sales rep absconded with $60,000 worth of goods, and the company put in a claim for the actual amount. However, the insurance company's investigation found that the dishonest sales rep had gotten away with just one case—not three—and that his $60,000 take was indeed the average value of a case's contents. The company obviously had understated the risk to keep the premium low, so the insurance company refused to pay anything. The court ruled in its favor, deciding that misrepresentation of risk relieved the insurer of the obligation to pay anything.

Claims under a fidelity bond are subject to rigorous investigation. In addition, you can't expect a fidelity bond to act as automatic insurance against all shrinkage. You must be able to prove that the shortage is caused by the dishonesty of one or more employees. An inventory count or a profit and loss statement won't be accepted as proof as a matter of course. The bond must have a clause to this effect.

Identification of the thieves is crucial when you are trying to recover under a blanket position bond. The advantage of this bond is that you are reimbursed according to what each dishonest employee steals, rather than according to a fixed overall limit. However, you must know who the thieves are.

When you make a claim, be prepared to prove that you have lived up to all terms of the agreement. For example, bond applications ask for the number of employees whose regular duties require them to handle money, securities, or merchandise. These people are classified as Class 1 employees. The premium you pay is based in part on the number of such people. Keep your Class 1 list accurate and up to date.

Is bonding an employee tantamount to saying you don't trust him? Apparently many business owners think so, and that's one reason they never obtain fidelity bonds. This feeling is particularly strong in small companies, whose owners are reluctant to endanger rapport with key people.

A second reason is that they often assume a valued employee, who has been around for years and is fully trusted, simply isn't capable of theft. The unhappy fact is that the employee everyone trusts can often be the one stealing the most.

The best way to overcome the touchiness of the situation is to treat it matter-of-factly. Let your employees know that you're taking out this policy as a common-sense precaution, since theft is a fact of business life, not because you suspect any of them.

The easiest way to convince employees of your attitude is to bond everyone under a blanket policy. Then no one is singled out.

Explain to your staff that they will be required to fill out a questionnaire, and their backgrounds will be subject to investigation. You can point out that the insurer is basically only verifying what everyone originally put down on the job application. This implies that you believe each person has told the truth in applying for the position.

Actually, this investigative service is invaluable. The Insurance Information Institute says that it alone is often worth the cost of the protection, since potential problem people are uncovered.

If inconsistencies turn up, the employee isn't grilled by people from the insurance company. Information is passed along to the owner, who calls the worker in for a chat. Ordinarily, you can clear up such things in a few minutes. If not, there is good reason to investigate further.

When employees are bonded, they are essentially placed on notice that the company takes dishonesty seriously. One reason bonding companies can keep premiums low is that they know the act of bonding itself often deters theft. For the same reason, they are not exceptionally stubborn about paying claims—unless they think the business owner has lied to them.

If a dishonest employee is unmasked during the course of an investigation, your bonding company will try to recover the stolen funds from him. Employees actually are forewarned about this procedure because they must promise on their application to reimburse the insurer for all losses it pays on their behalf. This acts as another deterrent. The knowledge that a company bonds its workers is so effective, in fact, one expert says it is a good idea to have employees fill out the application and think they are bonded—even if the proprietor decides not to carry fidelity bonding.

There is no rule of thumb in deciding how much coverage to get. Much depends on the nature of your operation and the amount of cash handled.

The best way to reach an estimate is to think of a trusted employee whose dishonesty would be "unthinkable," and then imagine how much he could get away with before you found out. Ordinarily, the maximum that could be stolen wouldn't exceed a third of a year's gross receipts over an extended period.

If your business is at all vulnerable to dishonesty—and how many aren't?—you should give serious consideration to fidelity bonding. It not only will enable you to recover your loss; it will also deter theft. In fact, bonding may be the biggest favor you could do for a susceptible subordinate if it reduces or eliminates his temptation to steal.

Chapter 5

Where to Borrow Money When You Need It

"FOR financial peace of mind, avoid borrowing money for your business if you can." This advice was often given to entrepreneurs in the past. It was based on memories of the many persons wiped out during the Depression when their incomes dropped sharply and they no longer could pay the interest on their loans. During the boom years of the 1960s, the advice was largely ignored and the opposite advocated: "Borrow money if you can profit on it." The theory then was that the entrepreneur who could earn, say, 12 percent on borrowed money would reap substantial gains if he paid only 6 percent interest on it. But in recent years, with soaring interest costs, some borrowers have discovered that "leverage" works both ways and that losses can be acute when borrowed money earns less than the interest paid on it.

WHEN TO BORROW

As a general principle, it is probably wise to avoid *unnecessary* borrowing at any time, if only to avoid becoming so extended that you won't be able to borrow when and if you must do so. But there are times, for most if not all self-employers, when a loan may be necessary:

To establish oneself in a profession. When Arnold Drake graduated from dental school and wanted his own practice, he had three options: working with an established dentist and paying a certain percentage of his income for use of the older man's office and equipment; buying the practice of a seventy-year-old man who wanted to retire and live in Fort Lauderdale, Florida; or establishing a practice of his own. He preferred the second option, but the expectant retiree wanted a $20,000 down payment and $60,000 more paid over a five-year period. After paying for his education, Dr. Drake's parents couldn't dig up more than $10,000. He went to his neighborhood bank, where his father had had an account for twenty-five years, and in five minutes arranged a loan for $10,000 more. Many banks make loans to enable qualified persons to start or buy professional practices. Doctors and dentists are especially favored, but most professionals and quasi-professionals can get "going into business" loans. Apart from profiting from the loan itself, the bank stands to gain from the borrower's regular business.

To finance work in progress. A self-employed author, commercial artist, advertising or publicity agent may work on an assignment that will produce thousands of dollars in income when completed but that pays little or nothing until then. Most self-employers need capital to support themselves at least for a short period between the time they do a piece of work and when they get paid for it.

To take advantage of business opportunities. In many fields, merchandise and equipment are often available at bargain prices—if the buyer will pay cash. Each year inflation drives up the price of machinery and equipment; thus a loan to finance such purchases may prove worthwhile, even after interest costs on the loan are deducted.

GETTING A LOAN

Your ability to borrow money can determine the success or

failure of your business or practice. If your operation desperately needs funds, or your continued growth depends on borrowing capital for expansion, you can't afford to be turned down. To improve your chances of getting a "yes" from your banker, it is crucial to develop techniques that will convince him of your desirability as a loan candidate.

Successful borrowing doesn't require in-depth training or a financier's expertise. It does require knowing: (1) what your banker considers to be a desirable loan prospect, and (2) how to construct a presentation showing you and your business in this light. Besides presenting a positive financial statement, you must establish credibility with your prospective lender. This means you must project an image of dependability and ambition, and that, like all good salespeople, you must control the interview.

The better prepared you are to answer the banker's many questions, the more successfully you will establish yourself as a capable business person. You will need current information about your financial status at your fingertips, including: your assets and liabilities, particularly accounts receivable and payable; value of business real estate, machinery, and equipment you own outright (potential as collateral); value of inventory (subject to the lender's verification since it also may be used as security); a balance statement less than sixty days old; a current profit and loss statement; business insurance coverage; and outstanding loans.

Formulating an accurate picture of your financial situation will help you assess the exact amount you need to borrow. Since this information is required on your loan application, you will be ahead of the game by preparing it in advance.

When you are being investigated for a bank loan, there is no such thing as "getting too personal." The prospective lender will probe your personal life as well as your business history for hints of immaturity and instability, so don't be surprised by queries about your standard of living and life-style.

In order to prepare the most favorable answers to both business and personal questions it is a good idea to put yourself in the lender's shoes. What would you ask someone who wanted to borrow money from you? Adopt a banker's point of view, which typically goes as follows:

Bankers tend to prefer conservatism in their borrowers. You can live well and enjoy expensive pursuits, but tossing money around makes bankers uneasy. They also become suspicious if you appear to be living higher than the income on your application would suggest.

They look for stability and maturity. They will want to know your marital status, number of children, how often you move, and the number of friends and business associates with whom you maintain contact. If you have been divorced, expect questions about remarriage, alimony, child custody and child support, where your children live, and even their life-styles.

Your health is of major importance. They are interested in knowing whether you have had serious illnesses or accidents, how your health is now, and if you take medications. You will be questioned about the status of your business, should you become disabled or die. For example, a banker will want to know if you have life insurance to cover all your outstanding debts and if your employees are capable of effectively carrying on your business in case you become incapacitated for a long period. Lenders expect you have prepared for contingencies and will consider you short-sighted and unrealistic if you haven't.

Bankers like individuals who set goals with time limits for themselves. They will be interested in your special triumphs in your business or personal life, your future goals, and where you plan to be five years from now.

Bankers like businesspeople who keep up with the times. If you don't show you are in step with our fast-paced world, your banker may decide you aren't adaptable and that your business ideas could quickly become obsolete.

Community involvement gets a high rating. It indicates maturity, organizational skills, adaptability, and a willingness to take on responsibilities. Participation in community organizations and activities tells a lender you can carry out long-term commitments and that you have a personal stake in the community's development.

Write down answers to the questions you would ask yourself if you were the banker and study them from the banker's perspective. Ask yourself: "Would I lend money to this person?" When you are satisfied you can offer satisfactory answers to all the questions you have thought of, you are ready to apply for the loan.

A quick way to be turned down for a loan is to walk into a bank and approach the first individual in the loan department. Not only isn't this businesslike, but you will also create a nonprofessional image that may be impossible to overcome.

The best procedure is to find out as much as you can about the bank where you plan to apply for your loan, compare it to other banks in your area, and then arrange for a screening interview. This assertive technique protects you from misinformation and psychologically sets you up for a successful encounter.

Since many banks specialize in different types of loans, call the bank first to make sure that it handles your type of transaction. Ask about its current interest rate for this kind of loan. Rates vary, as do the points that banks charge for making a loan. The general criteria for acceptance can also vary: amount of required collateral, repayment method, allotment for repayment, etc. If you foresee difficulty in meeting any of the bank's criteria, prepare an especially strong case to persuade it to negotiate with you or look into the possibility of using another bank. If you can't do either, your chances of getting the loan are minimal.

Find out all you can about the various individuals who interview prospective borrowers. Possibly some of your business associates can help you here. Inquire about each interviewer's personality and behavior patterns and choose someone who sounds compatible. It is to your advantage to make an appointment for the interview. It is the professional thing to do, saves you time, and guarantees the availability of the person you wish to see. Most important, you are grabbing the offensive, even though you are the one asking for money.

When you make the appointment, state that you would like to discuss the preliminaries for a loan application, asking for only a few minutes of his time.

When you go for your initial interview, dress appropriately to make a good first impression. After you have introduced yourself, briefly explain what type of loan you are requesting and ask for an application to take with you. This invites the lender to give you pointers on filling it out and tells him you are planning to devote time to doing it properly and in detail. He will probably be glad to answer questions, but don't take up too much of his time. Tell him you will call for another appointment when you are prepared to submit and discuss the loan application.

From your first contact with the interviewer to the final handshake, you should be aware of one particular word. It is so vital that your ability to exploit its power can be your barometer of success. That word is "want": you *want* a loan; you don't *need* a loan. "Want" implies that you are growing, expanding, renovating, updating—all positive reasons and indications of prompt repayment. "Need" means trouble; it implies financial difficulties, poor business management, and the chance that the money won't be repaid.

Sometimes you have to work to put things positively. The number one reason that banks grant loans to small businesses is growth. If you can substantiate this reason for requesting a loan, do so. But what if you can't? Even if you are threatened with bankruptcy, all need not be lost.

Concentrate on developing a presentation to convince your banker that his loan will turn the tables for you. Stress the factors that may sway him in your favor: for instance, your company's success will have a positive effect on your community; the more successful your community, the more successful the bank, etc. Emphasize the position you expect your company to be in five years from now, using current figures as the base for your growth projections. Outline changes you are planning to ensure success. Include cost increases and inflation in your projection; this will show the lender that you are a realist. If you anticipate the need for another loan within the projected period, include it in your presentation, reiterating the positive benefits. Above all, show your banker how you plan to increase profits. It is your expected profit, not your sales projection, that helps to determine your ability to repay.

How you fill out your loan application will affect all your future loan transactions with a lending institution. Most banks require you to fill out a loan application only once, then file it for all future references.

Always be truthful. Banks check out statements. Lies will damage your chances of getting the loan.

Don't try to cover up negative factors in your credit rating or personal life, but do explain any extenuating circumstances. If there is a reasonable explanation, the lender will consider it.

Answer each question on the application fully. It is your banker's business to deal with confidential information, and you can trust him. It is better to reveal more information than not enough. Scanty answers suggest you are hiding something.

Leave nothing blank on the application. This will give the impression that you don't understand the question or don't know the answer. (Either way, it implies you aren't well prepared.) If a question doesn't apply to you, write NA—not applicable.

There is never enough room on a loan application form to present yourself and your business properly or to explain adequately why you want a loan. A well-written proposal and financial statement attached to your application can do this job admirably. You will impress the lender with your professionalism and answer in advance many of the questions he intends to ask during your interview. It will also make communication easier. The most you will have to do is elaborate on some points.

The Federal Reserve Bank of New York recommends a prepared form, CR-107, available at stationery stores, to help you keep your presentation short and simple. Or you can draft a professional and concise proposal using the following guidelines:

1. Brief introduction. In no more than one page explain why you want the loan, describe your company, and list some major customers and important prospective customers.

2. Personal income statement. Use one page to list your total personal income from all sources, plus your spouse's income.

3. Investments. Include a statement of all business and personal investments.

4. Loan proposal. Be specific. State how much you want, the terms that best suit your business, and a repayment schedule. If the loan is for a major purchase, report the amount you are prepared to invest personally. List the collateral you can offer. Develop the proposal to your advantage, but don't be unreasonable.

5. Arguments in your favor. On another page, explain all the reasons why you should receive this loan. Emphasize how the bank will profit, too.

6. Company history. Outline this completely from original concept through growth and achievement. Include successful advertising campaigns, major promotions, new designs, new products or services, and building renovations. Describe your management, organizational structure, marketing programs, strategy, employees, and customers.

7. Balance sheet. List all current assets (cash, inventory, accounts receivable), fixed assets (real estate and equipment, minus depreciation), liabilities (including notes payable and long-term debts), and capital. Formulate a one-year projection.

8. Business income statement. List sales, cost of sales, operating expenses, gross income, income taxes, and net income before and after taxes for the previous year. Project next year's income.

9. Company future. On this final page, describe in realistic terms where your company is headed. Project a rosy picture, but don't overdo it; lenders are experienced in spotting a fast sell. Note any potential stumbling blocks and how you plan to avoid or overcome them.

10. Cover letter on your company letterhead. Keep it short, stating your purpose in three or four lines. It goes on top of your formal proposal.

Have your proposal typed on a good-grade bond paper and make at least one copy for yourself. Place the original in a conservative press binder. Never punch holes in the paper, submit carbons or photocopies, or place the proposal in a clear plastic folder.

Now you are ready to make your formal appointment. Not any day or time will do. The best days are from the fourth working day of the month through the fourteenth, and from the sixteenth through the twenty-ninth. The best times are before 11:30 A.M. and after 1:30 P.M. so as not to interfere with lunch hours. Avoid the following busy bank days: the first three business days of the month; the day before any holiday; and the fifteenth and thirtieth or thirty-first of each month.

When the bank offers to grant your loan request, you don't

automatically have to accept its terms. If its rate is higher than the norm for your area, try to negotiate. Banks are usually flexible and will try to establish terms suitable both to you and to them. You can make any reasonable suggestions to reduce the amount of interest, down payment or collateral, and the time period for repayment.

But suppose the bank turns you down. "No" isn't the end of the road. It even can be a step toward hearing "yes." Ask why you have been refused and what you can do to change the "no" to a "yes."

Accept the refusal as an indicator that there is room for improvement and set about making the necessary changes. When you have done so, the same bank may reevaluate your request and grant you the loan. If not, you will be better equipped to bargain for a loan with another bank.

COST OF LOANS

Inseparable from the question of whether to borrow are considerations of the cost and availability of loans. A young clerk who answered the phone at a New York City bank at the end of 1980 made her feelings about high interest rates very clear. I had explained only that I wanted to talk to someone who could give me up-to-date information about business loans.

"The loan officer's busy right now; he'll have to call you back," she said, snapping her gum into the receiver. "But if you want my advice, you'd better get your loan right now, or don't get it at all. The rates are going up again and then borrowing money from the bank is going to be like borrowing from a loan shark!"

Although the clerk was overreacting to a projected increase in the ceiling rate on loans, her remarks weren't too far off base. When money is tight, a loan—if you can get one—can be a very costly proposition.

The manager of a busy branch office of a different bank explained why loans are hard to get when money is tight.

"At one time, anyone could walk in and apply for a loan. It didn't matter if the person was a regular customer or not; we'd make sure he got a check for the loan before he walked out of the office that day.

"Now things are different; they change on a day-to-day basis. The money market was so chaotic at one point that there were days when we couldn't even set a rate. The maximum interest we were allowed to charge on an installment loan was 13 percent and we were being charged 16 percent. A bank can't make money that way."

When the money markets are unstable, most banks are willing to accommodate only people with exceptionally good credit ratings who have been customers for many years.

Owners or prospective owners of small businesses—persons who must borrow from banks to get a small business started—feel the pinch of hard-to-get, high-interest-rate money. Surveys of key areas show that the person seeking a loan to finance part of his restaurant, print shop, or other small enterprise is the one who gets turned down most often by his local banker. Companies with established credit ratings and a record of operating a profitable business for a few years have an easier time of it.

Edward T. Watson, credit analyst in New York, says it may be a "disguised blessing" that many prospective business owners can't borrow at excessively high rates. "Few businesses could survive if most of their money must be borrowed at such rates," he says. "Few businesses earn 18 percent on their invested capital, least of all small businesses struggling to get off the ground. Banks may be doing the would-be entrepreneur a favor by not lending the money he wants at those high prices."

Since most *commercial* lending operations exist to meet the needs of corporations and businesses with at least several employees, you may find it more convenient to take out a loan available to you as an individual.

Starting with the lowest-cost ones and working up the interest scale, loans ordinarily made to the self-employed are as follows.

Passbook loans. These are available at the savings institution where you have a regular savings account. You may borrow as much as you have in your account simply by showing your passbook. Although banks sometimes advertise "actual" interest rates as low as 2½ percent on passbook loans, the real interest rate you pay is considerably higher. Banks figure this "actual" interest rate by subtracting the interest rate your savings account earns from the rate they charge for the loan. For example, if your savings account earns 5½ percent interest and the bank charges 8-percent interest for a passbook loan, the so-called actual interest rate would equal 2½ percent.

The problem with this type of loan is that it ties up the cash in your account for the period of the loan: under the terms of the loan your savings account balance must always be sufficient to cover what you still owe on the loan. In effect, then, taking out a passbook loan is like borrowing your own money and paying the bank for the privilege of doing so. In most cases you would be better off paying cash and paying yourself back month by month.

Loans on life insurance policies. Most policies, except the term kind, carry cash surrender values: the amount due you if you discontinued them. Such policies give you the option of borrowing against the cash value at a stipulated rate of interest, usually no more than 8 percent. Assigning your policy as security, you may be permitted to borrow up to 95 percent of cash value. Meanwhile cash invested in the policy continues to draw dividends.

Home mortgages. In many places, a legal maximum is placed on the interest rate that lenders may charge on such mortgages. Common types of mortgage loans may be made for as long as thirty years against the usual less-than-five-year repayment requirement of most installment loans. (You pay off a small amount of the principal each month, along with interest on the amount outstanding.) Some money management experts say that a full mortgage may even cost little or nothing over the long term. With built-in inflation, the value of a house may well rise more per year than the amount of mortgage interest paid.

Mortgage loans were especially desirable when interest rates were historically low. Because of the long-term aspects, many ordinary individuals with 7 percent mortgages found themselves paying little more than half the interest rate that blue chip corporations such as American Telephone and Telegraph Company had to pay when borrowing money in the late '70s. Mortgage rates are now considerably higher and such loans are considerably less attractive than they were.

Collateral loans. Most commercial banks stand ready to lend substantial sums against property they could readily turn into cash in case you defaulted on the loan. Generally acceptable collateral includes insurance policies, savings pass books, stocks, and bonds. Collateral loans may be made for three- or six-month periods, when they are usually renewable, or on a demand basis, when they run as long as the bank cares to let them. In some cases the bank may ask you to pay off a certain amount every month or quarter. If it intends to terminate a demand loan, it would probably give a few weeks' notice to enable you to make another loan elsewhere. Interest rates on collateral loans are charged on a flat annual basis. They are generally geared to the prime rate, which is the rate charged the most creditworthy customers, generally large corporations. Ordinary borrowers often pay one percentage point per year above the prime rate.

Strong speculative aspects attach to collateral loans made with stocks and bonds, which may sharply fluctuate in price. The man who needs money and has 1,000 shares of X Corporation worth $10 a share could sell some of his holdings, of course. By submitting them to a bank against a $5,000 loan he speculates in effect that their price will rise or remain the same. If he sold 500 shares to get the $5,000 and the price per share moves to $12, he would make $1,000. If he submitted his shares as collateral, he would make $2,000. On the other hand, of course, he—not the bank— must take the loss if the shares drop in price. If they dropped so low that the bank's $5,000 loan seemed imperiled, it might order him to repay the loan or sell his stock at the deflated price.

Term loans. An advance to help you buy or start a professional practice or other enterprise might fall into this category. Term loans, also called intermediate-term loans, run from one year to five or, in unusual cases, ten years. They may also be set up to enable you to buy expensive equipment; to provide working capital so that you can finance your operations from the time you do your work until you are paid for it; or to consolidate or replace other debts that may carry a higher interest rate or require burdensome installment payments.

These loans may be either secured—that is, you may be prohibited from selling your equipment while the loan is in effect—or unsecured. You may have to abide by certain other restrictions as to how you manage your affairs. The bank may request periodic statements that reveal how well you are doing. Repayment terms can be equally flexible. You may have to make monthly, quarterly, semiannual or annual payments. In some cases, the periodic installments are low, with most of the loan schedule to be repaid at the expiration date. This large final payment is known as a balloon payment. Or the installments may be paid off in equal amounts so that the last payment is no greater than the first one.

Rates on term loans depend on several factors, not the least of which is how much money the bank has to lend and the number trying to borrow it. Usually, the rate will be higher than that on a straight collateral note and lower than that on a personal installment loan.

Small Business Administration loans. If your banker can't or won't make the loan you require, you might qualify for assistance from the Small Business Administration, an independent agency set up by the U.S. Congress to advise and help small entrepreneurs. The SBA has about a hundred field offices in the United States at which you can find specialists who will advise you, without charge, on a broad range of financial problems. They may help you get a loan from another bank or from private sources. They will also tell you whether you might qualify for a loan for which the SBA provides all the funds or guarantees repayment of monies advanced by a bank or other private institution.

To get an SBA loan, you must prove that you have failed to get a loan elsewhere on reasonable terms. Such proof generally consists of a letter from one or two banks rejecting your application for a loan. You must fit the SBA's definition of a small business, one independently owned and operated and not dominant in its field. And you must meet the following requirements:

- You must be of good character.
- There must be evidence that you have the ability to operate your enterprise successfully.
- You must have enough capital or prospects so that, with the SBA loan, you will be able to operate on a sound financial basis.
- The record and prospects must indicate ability to repay the loan out of income.

The SBA will not make loans to a few types of businesses nor for certain purposes, for example, to gambling enterprises or for the purpose of speculation in real or personal property. At times, it also lacks the money to make the loans it was set up to make.

Accounts-receivable loans. If you have a number of bills outstanding, you *may* be able to use them as collateral for a bank loan. Several bankers told me they consider such loans to self-employers; however, they want to assure themselves that there is a strong likelihood that the bills will be paid. They said they would favor a few large bills owed by solvent customers over a large number of small ones owed by a diverse group. One banker said he had recently loaned $5,000 to a business broker who was in the final stages of negotiating a merger between two companies. The broker had done considerable work but needed funds to carry him for a month until the deal was completed and he would get a substantial payment.

When you obtain an accounts-receivable loan, you usually must pledge or assign all or part of your accounts receivable as security. The loan agreement specifies what percentage of this volume of receivables will be loaned. A bank loan will usually be from 75 to 80 percent of sound receivables. The charges may include both interest and service charges and depend on money market conditions.

Revolving-credit loans. Many commercial banks have plans whereby you automatically borrow money when you overdraw your checking account. Also known as "ready reserve," "instant credit," and "convenience credit," these plans are available in most communities. A typical arrangement allows you to overdraw your account in units of $100 up to a predetermined limit—in the case of reasonably good credit risks, $5,000. Each month, the amount you overdraw is added up. Interest is charged on your total unpaid balance at the rate of 1½ or 2 percent per month. You are expected to pay at least 1/24 of this balance each month, but you may do so by overdrawing your account still more. Whenever you wish, you may pay the full amount owed and the interest stops at once.

Such a plan offers many advantages. Once a bank approves your application and sets the limit of your line of credit, you have easy access to emergency funds whenever you need them. Inasmuch as interest charges do not begin until your check, which triggers the loan, is presented to your bank for payment, the period for which interest is charged is shorter than if you had to deposit the borrowed money before writing the check. The plan also enables you to keep a low balance in your regular checking account, since you need not provide a constant cushion to insure that no checks are returned for nonpayment. On the other hand, if you do not use your "instant credit" with discretion, you may find yourself in the middle of an installment plan type of loan requiring substantial monthly payments.

Personal bank loans. When banks are eager to lend money these are often advertised as available for "any worthwhile purpose"—and almost any purpose is considered worthwhile. The stated purpose may be to buy a car, take a vacation, or improve one's home. But when money is hard to get, banks often restrict loans to their regular customers, charging the maximum interest rates permitted by law.

With a personal loan, you pay a stipulated amount each month over a specified time period. Under federal law, the bank must give you a written copy of the loan agreement. The agreement must state clearly and conspicuously the annual percentage rate (APR) and the total finance charge on your loan. It must also show the total amount you must repay, your monthly payments, due date, and any penalty charges that may be levied for late payments. A description of additional costs such as life insurance must also be included.

Consumer Finance Company loans. These companies specialize in making loans to middle- and lower-income families. They provide personal loans in amounts ranging from $500 up to $5,000 or $10,000, depending on state regulations. They also provide second mortgage loans. Rates on second mortgage loans, as of this writing, average at or below 18 percent annual percentage rate, and personal loans are running at 20 to 23 percent APR.

Personal "loan shark" loans. Probably all but a few self-employed persons are financially sophisticated enough to steer clear of money lenders who may charge 20 percent interest per week—you borrow $500 today and pay back $600 a week from now. Obviously, it is virtually impossible to survive in business while paying such rates. Nevertheless, some businessmen fall into the clutches of such sharks. Many get out only after paying four or five times the original debt.

The Senate's Select Committee on Small Business once heard testimony from a man wearing a black hood and identified only as "John Doe." He had been in the food business and had been having financial difficulties. A loan shark learned of his plight and offered to lend $1,000, to be repaid in thirteen weekly installments of $100 each. Sometimes Doe could not make the payments and sometimes the lender did not appear to collect them. The uncollected amounts were added to the loan at the same interest rate. Doe later needed $900 more, including $500 for an operation for his wife. After paying $10,000, he thought he had paid enough. The lender produced a newspaper clipping describing the discovery of the body of a man encased in concrete in a nearby bay. He said: "If you don't pay, that's where you'll wind up." At the time of the testimony, Doe had paid $14,500 and the shark said he still owed $5,800—still three times more than the total borrowed.

AVOID CASH FLOW PROBLEMS

There are times when it may be difficult or inadvisable to get a loan. In times of recession, for instance, business owners often find that collections slow down and bank loans, even at high interest rates, are hard to get.

If you run a successful business, you may be able to avoid cash flow problems at such times—and hence avoid the need for a costly loan—by making your business more profitable and by making the most of your financial assets.

Cash flow is the money you have available to operate your business; the more cash you have to work with, the less likely your need to borrow to finance day-to-day operations or even expansion. When money is tight there are a number of ways to increase your cash supply.

Cut Costs

Reducing operating expenses is one major factor in increasing your cash flow. Examine every part of your operation and reassess expenses with an eye toward trimming excesses. Pay particular attention to the following factors.

1. Payroll. Study each job position on the basis of its contribution to your business, the responsibility and skill it requires, and worker-hours necessary for effective performance. Some of your forty-hour-per-week positions may require only twenty-five to thirty hours.

Realign jobs to use all your employees effectively for all the hours for which you are paying them. Perhaps you can consolidate some positions, cutting down the need for new employees or replacing others who leave. Eliminate jobs that are becoming obsolete. But don't cut so deeply that you overburden productive employees.

Consider seasonal help for your busy periods rather than carrying year-round employees who must perform at peak productivity only part of the time. You can hire supplemental workers for just the number of hours you need them, and you don't have to include them in your benefit packages.

2. Comparison shop. It's easy to become complacent about doing business with the same suppliers and service people over a long period of time. Check around for the best deals and make sure you aren't spending more than absolutely necessary.

3. Eliminate waste. Without tight controls and effective management, you can easily lose money. For example:

- Expense account abuses can drain your cash.
- Telephone bills can soar when employee usage isn't restricted and long distance calls aren't carefully monitored.
- A lax security system permits heavy losses from external and internal theft.
- Poorly supervised employees may waste time and money.
- Inadequately trained employees are usually inefficient.
- Uncontrolled energy consumption raises bills unnecessarily.

4. Hold off on speculative ventures. This is no time for unnecessary risk. Be sure that any new venture is on solid footing and will increase your cash supply, not deplete it, before you plunge ahead.

5. Reevaluate your insurance programs. While insurance is a necessary expense, your needs can change. Check to be sure you aren't overinsured for this particular time and that you are getting the best deal for your money. Review all your insurance coverage periodically.

Liquidate Unnecessary Facilities and Equipment

Check your business for surpluses. Your supply rooms and warehouses may have materials that are useless to you but that you could sell for cash to someone else. Also, if you sell at your convenience instead of in an emergency situation, you are likely to get a higher price. If you must sell for less than you can recoup through a depreciation gain, apply the loss to your current income tax.

Pay special attention to your space. Are you fully utilizing all your facilities? Could you consolidate some areas for more effective operation? You may be able to cut down on your rental needs. If you own your building, you may be able to lease part for a steady income source.

Consider Leasing Instead of Buying

If you need equipment requiring a large cash outlay, consider leasing instead of buying it. You can rent almost anything you need to operate a business, including cars, trucks, plant equipment, office machinery, and even furniture. Leasing has several advantages for a business feeling a financial squeeze:

• You can take a full tax deduction against current income for the amount you pay out each month. In contrast, when you buy outright you are entitled to only a 10 percent investment credit applicable on depreciable business assets and a tax reduction based on depreciation of the property acquired. Most pieces of office furniture, fixtures, machines, and equipment have an asset depreciation range of from eight to twelve years.

• You minimize your immediate cash outlay. If the equipment produces income or saves expenses for you, its earning power may provide you with the money to pay its monthly cost to some extent.

• You are generally assured of good service on the equipment.

The lessors have a stake in maintaining its good condition so as to increase its ultimate retail value if it must be sold later. You can withhold payments if the promised service is not forthcoming and thus have a wedge to use in bargaining.

A big plus for leasing, in the opinion of many, is that it preserves credit capacity. If you borrow from a bank to buy equipment, the amount is deducted from whatever maximum amount the bank thinks it is safe to lend you. It may not consider a lease obligation in the same light and may keep your borrowing capacity undisturbed.

Another important point is that if your credit lines are already extended, it is generally easier to lease equipment than to borrow the money to buy it. Leasing companies retain title to the equipment and need not worry about other creditors grabbing it as payment for your debts to them.

Many leases give the lessee the right to buy the equipment outright at the end of the leasing period. According to one survey most persons don't consider this privilege worth much. On the other hand, the survey stated, "A large number considered that transferring to the lessor the problem of disposing of idle and obsolete equipment is an advantage of leasing. They felt that the lessor is better equipped to dispose of equipment in the used-equipment market."

Insurance considerations often cause an equipment user to opt for leasing. One reason for the boom in automobile leasing is that motorists who find it difficult or impossible—or financially prohibitive—to get individual insurance policies because of accident records or other factors, often can lease insured cars without trouble because the leasing firms hold huge umbrella policies.

All factors considered, when is leasing advantageous for you? It is probably worth considering when two or more of these factors exist:

• When you are low on cash and would have to borrow the money to pay for the equipment anyway.

• When you are at or near the limit of your ability to borrow from a bank and want to keep a certain amount of borrowing ability in reserve.

• When you are in a high tax bracket and thus able to get the greatest benefit from deducting your leasing payments.

• When the equipment has a high rate of actual or potential obsolescence. By leasing you avoid the likelihood that you will be the owner of suddenly outmoded items with a sharply reduced value. However, lessors of such equipment often charge higher rates during the early period of the lease to protect themselves against the obsolescence hazard.

• When you can put your money to work elsewhere where it will give you a higher return than you pay as a result of leasing.

• When there is a strong possibility that changing circumstances will make it desirable for you to shift to other equipment and your leasing contract enables you to discontinue present arrangements without excessive penalty.

On the other hand, not much can be gained from leasing if:

• You have enough cash to pay for the equipment outright.

• You are getting less interest on your cash than the interest charges you would have to pay when you lease.

• The equipment has a long life and you are likely to keep it until it is pretty much worn out.

• You are now in a relatively low tax bracket and wouldn't gain substantially from a deduction for the leasing payments. Or, you are likely to be in a higher bracket in later years, when deductions for depreciation will keep more money in your pocket.

In some cases, you may face lots of work with pencil and paper before determining whether it is better to buy or lease. To arrive at the real costs of buying, you have to put down the actual sales price, what that money will earn for you over the time span you are comparing, what you estimate it will cost to service the equipment for that period, and what your insurance costs will be. Add these figures and subtract the estimated value of the equipment at the end of the period under consideration. Next make allowance for tax factors: Subtract the taxes on what your money would earn. Also subtract the actual tax reduction you obtain from depreciation and from your insurance payments. What you now have is your actual dollar cost of buying the item in question.

To get a realistic picture of leasing costs, add your monthly payments for the period plus service costs, if any. Add any insurance costs that you must pay directly. Subtract your tax saving. Say you are in a 35 percent tax bracket and you pay

$6,000 for three years. Your tax saving is $2,100. Next subtract whatever extra value you might get by exercising the option to buy the equipment at the end of the leasing period. If you can buy it for $400 and sell it for $600, you have a $200 asset (less any applicable taxes). You now have a bottom-line figure to compare with the comparable figure showing the actual cost of a purchase.

As the foregoing indicates, the question can become quite complicated. But you can take the word of experts who have slide-ruled the question that leasing generally is more expensive than its alternatives. If you decide to lease on the basis of noncost factors, the burden of proof is on you to prove you are making a wise choice.

Use Credit Buying and Cash Discounts

Buying on credit helps you keep your cash longer. The longer it's in your hands, the longer it can work productively for you. But don't hang on to it too long. Meet your due dates and don't endanger your credit rating.

It generally pays to take cash discounts available when you pay bills within a designated time. To be sure, calculate your savings compared to the interest amount you can accumulate by holding your money for a few extra weeks. Then go in the direction that most benefits your cash supply.

If cash discounts are the answer for you, set up your accounts payable to take advantage of this money-saving procedure. Pay several times a month instead of only one day a month. Heed all discount offers and beat the deadlines.

Reduce Your Inventory and Its Overhead

The larger the inventory you maintain, the more it costs you. For every $100 of inventory, you pay $15 to $20 per year to cover storage facilities and their expenses, taxes, insurance, handling and inventory control, losses due to obsolescence, and deterioration.

Study your records carefully to see if you need to maintain your inventory at its current level. Your stock department should be in constant flux, with newly received goods quickly moved on to shipping. Goods that linger on your shelves can become liabilities.

If you stockpile three-month inventories of materials that you can easily take delivery on within a week to ten days, you may be using space unproductively. Double-check quantity discounts. If buying in quantity costs you more in storage and overhead than you save, you are wasting money.

Clear out nonmoving products and materials through special promotions. "Factory close-outs" and "special purchase" sales can turn excess inventory into cash.

Be Aggressive About Collecting

Overdue accounts represent money your customers are using interest-free for their benefit and to your disadvantage. If it results in your being short of cash, you may have to borrow money and pay interest. This also costs you in terms of time and aggravation.

You can minimize your overdue receivables if you establish a strong collection program based on well-defined procedures. Then make sure both you and the employee in charge of your accounts receivable adhere firmly to those rules.

To encourage faster payments and cut out collection problems before they arise, you can take either of two steps: offer cash discounts for promptness or impose a finance charge for lateness. Before you make the discount offer, look carefully at the amount of money that won't be coming in. You must offer the same discount to all your customers, so you will have to be certain the sum you realize from the slow-paying customers who will be motivated to speed up will offset the total cost of the discount to you.

A good time to initiate your cash discount is when you must raise your prices. Your customer will see your price increase in context with the cash discount and the blow of the increase will be softened by the discount proposal.

A finance charge can also motivate chronically slow-paying customers to pay on time. You must notify your customers about a finance charge at the time of their purchase and print it on your invoice. An acceptable rate is 1 to 1½ percent per month on invoices outstanding after thirty days.

If you are in a highly competitive business, this penalty may move your customer to a competitor who doesn't charge for slow payment. On the other hand, if you have few competitors and your customer is dependent on you, a finance charge may encourage him to pay on time. For more information on collecting overdue bills, see chapter 8.

Sell Receivables for Quick Cash

Selling off receivables appears to be a developing trend in business communities when consumption goes down and credit is tightened.

Selling your receivables is simply selling off money that others owe you. They are bought by businesses that have more money than they currently need and by financial institutions. Both regard purchasing of receivables as an easy way to increase profits. They simply buy due bills and wait for the checks to come in.

Note that most receivable sales contracts include a clause that holds the seller responsible for a default rate higher than 5 or 10 percent of the receivables sold.

Minimize Your Tax Liabilities

Check carefully on your allowable deductions and tax credits. Make sure your tax preparer takes every deduction to which you are entitled. Have him pay special attention to rapid depreciation allowances.

Time your purchases to gain the maximum advantage in tax credits. Make necessary large purchases of depreciable property toward the end of your tax year. The tax credit, which can go as high as 10 percent, applies to the entire year. (Depreciable property must have a useful life of three years or more. Land purchases for business use don't qualify for this credit.)

Learn to Manage Money

Most persons who manage their own enterprises are adept at

producing a good income for themselves. A lesser number are equally sharp in controlling costs so that their profits are as large as they could be. A still smaller number put their profits to effective work after they earn them.

"Asset management"—using money to save or earn other money—is, in the opinion of many consultants, one of the weakest spots in the typical business or professional operation. They say many self-employers consider the game to be over when income is earned and don't care much what happens after that. For example, physicians earn the highest incomes of any professional class. Yet, as a group, they are constantly victimized by ill-conceived schemes that drain away their assets. Among other self-employed groups, an "easy go" attitude often prevails.

In a case that is by no means unusual, a small manufacturer fights tooth and nail to keep his prices up and his costs down. He resists his employees whenever they seek wage increases or fringe benefits. He drives a last-inch bargain with suppliers and customers. Yet he hoards his corporation's assets in bank accounts that pay less than half the interest rate he could obtain elsewhere.

In these days of sky-high interest rates, "asset management" has become a vital function of almost every large corporation. Some firms with nationwide customer lists have set up regional bank accounts. Time saved in processing customer's payments immediately—instead of waiting for checks to travel across country and to clear at distant banks—adds up to hundreds of thousands of dollars a year for many concerns.

Steps like these obviously aren't suitable for the small-business owner. However, they illustrate the point that good asset management can save or earn important amounts for almost everyone. If you tighten up your cash management so that you use $10,000 more productively—by reducing amounts in nonproductive checking and savings accounts, by taking advantage of cash discounts, by borrowing only money that you really need and at the lowest available interest rates—you can easily increase your overall income significantly.

Letting cash lie stagnant is perhaps the principal way in which owner-managers practice poor asset management. Money in most business checking accounts generally draws little or no interest at all, and the intricate formulas many commercial banks use to determine checking account charges (relating them to amounts on deposit) often give cash an effective value of 2 percent a year. Keeping large balances on hand to offset bank charges on commercial accounts generally won't do as much for you as keeping a minimum balance and putting your cash to work earning interest elsewhere. (In the case of personal checking accounts, the story may be different. For example, some banks charge $3 per month if your balance falls below a certain amount—say, $300. Hence a $300 margin in such an account is worth 12 percent a year in bank charges saved.)

The following rundown of nine commonly available short-term investments will show you the major options you have for putting your cash to work more profitably. Consider them in relation to your own circumstances, check the specific rates of interest and then, whenever you have cash on hand, choose the one that best meets your needs.

SAVINGS ACCOUNTS. The simplest and fastest investment you can make is to shift your money from a checking account that pays no interest to a savings account, which always pays interest. New banking rules that became effective November 1, 1978, have simplified the reverse of this procedure by allowing automatic funds transfer (AFT) checking. You may now keep all your funds in a savings account and authorize your bank in advance to transfer funds from the savings account to your checking account to cover checks as they are presented for payment. This means you keep earning interest on all your money until the checks you write reach your bank.

AFT checking represents a nationwide expansion of negotiable order of withdrawal (NOW) accounts, which have been available in the last few years in New England. Otherwise exactly like checking accounts, NOW accounts pay interest that is only .5 percent less than savings accounts. They are available from both savings and commercial banks and offer customers the convenience of shifting funds from savings to checking by means of a telephone call.

Since interest rates may vary from state to state, as well as from commercial bank to savings bank to savings and loan association, you should investigate rates at several banks. Equally important, investigate the way interest is compounded and calculated. Interest from day of deposit to day of withdrawal usually gives the best results, while "low balance" interest, calculated on the basis of your lowest balance during the period, gives the smallest return.

In addition to interest rates and methods of calculation, investigate each bank's requirements for whatever special accounts and services it offers. These vary considerably: some banks impose service charges while others don't, and some require higher minimum balances than others.

The above factors may not be decisive; you may prefer to remain with the bank where you have built up a relationship or that specializes in your industry. But if you are thinking about opening an additional account, they may make a substantial difference.

All these accounts offer the greatest possible safety, liquidity, and convenience, but conventional savings accounts, in addition, require no minimum balance to earn the regular rate of interest.

TIME DEPOSITS. Also known as bank certificates of deposit (CDs) and savings certificates, time deposits are specific sums of money deposited for specific periods of time. They offer the safety of savings accounts at higher rates of interest—at present, perhaps as much as 4 percent higher than regular savings accounts—but they impose some restrictions.

As a rule, to get the benefits you must deposit at least $500 and leave it in the account for a minimum of three months. Liquidity is high in that you may get your money back anytime you need it. The price of early withdrawal is also high: you earn a much lower rate of interest and pay a penalty.

Time deposits may run as long as seven years, with the interest rate climbing as the term lengthens. There is no upper limit on deposits, but there is a limit of $100,000 on the amount insured. You can make a time deposit at almost any bank or savings and loan association, but commercial banks often pay slightly lower rates. Interest is paid on maturity. Like savings account interest, it is taxed on an annual basis.

NEGOTIABLE CERTIFICATES OF DEPOSIT. Negotiable certificates of deposit, similar to time deposits, offer a few significant differences. First, negotiable CDs pay higher interest while requiring much higher minimum amounts. Instead of $500, as in a time deposit, $100,000 is the minimum amount for a negotiable CD. To broaden the market, some banks permit several investors to share ownership of one certificate.

The second difference is in the "negotiable" factor. While time deposits are subject to reduced interest and penalties if withdrawn early, negotiable CDs may be resold before maturing without any loss of benefits. However, high liquidity isn't guaranteed. Liquidity may be impaired by conditions in the money market, by terms of sharing, or by the financial position of the bank that issued the certificate. Under some circumstances, negotiable CDs issued by small banks may be more difficult to resell than those issued by large banks.

For safety and usually high liquidity at high interest, a negotiable CD may be a good investment for you if you have enough cash on hand or can join a pool to share ownership.

COMMERCIAL PAPER. Commercial paper—promissory notes of major industrial or finance companies—is designed to meet the issuers' short-term cash needs. Usually discounted rather than interest paying (the interest yield is precomputed in the purchase price), commercial paper is issued for periods as short as five days by finance companies and thirty days by industrial corporations. The maximum period is usually six to nine months.

As little as $1,000 can buy some commercial paper, but in most cases $25,000 is the minimum. Sources include commercial banks, specialized dealers, and giant companies like General Motors Acceptance Corp. Interest rates are often higher than those paid by time deposits, approaching those of negotiable CDs.

Since the safety of commercial paper depends entirely on the solvency of the issuing company, if you choose your company carefully, you can keep the risk low. Liquidity is another matter. If you need your money before the maturity date, you may have a hard time selling.

Despite such drawbacks, commercial paper is worth considering for the choice you have in timing. Frequently you can choose both the date of issuance of the note and its date of maturity. This allows you to invest your money for only the period in which you don't need it and to have it returned in time to meet your commitments.

MONEY MARKET FUNDS. Some mutual funds buy government securities, commercial paper, and negotiable CDs rather than stock. These money market funds offer the opportunity to earn the high interest rates paid by these instruments while avoiding some of their restrictions. For example, the minimum investment may be only $500 or $1,000 rather than the $100,000 for negotiable CDs or the $25,000 for commercial paper. There is no required holding time; you can sell your shares when you need your money. In addition to liquidity, these funds offer convenience: professional money managers research the markets and buy in areas where returns seem greatest.

In a money market fund investment, however, you may sacrifice safety. Like mutual funds, money market funds don't always perform well; sometimes their managers make mistakes. Also, interest rates paid by the funds aren't always as high as you could get elsewhere. When interest rates are rising, a fund that has invested heavily in long-term instruments may provide no greater interest than a savings account, and with less safety.

You can minimize some of the disadvantages by investigating several funds before selecting one and by keeping a watchful eye on the money markets while your money is in the fund. If you are also prepared to accept less than top safety, a money market fund may serve your short-term purposes.

TREASURY BILLS AND CERTIFICATES. As safe as savings accounts and time deposits, treasury bills offer two advantages over both of these investments. First, they yield interest; second, they are exempt from state and local taxes. Interest on treasury bills is taxed only at the federal level, under the agreement between Washington and state and local governments not to tax each other's debt obligations.

Available for minimum investments of $10,000, treasury bills may be bought for three, six, nine, or twelve months, with the interest rate rising as the period lengthens. The interest is paid in the form of a discount on the face value.

You can buy treasury bills from commercial banks or brokers or directly from the Federal Reserve Bank at its weekly auction (while saving a fee). A new kind of treasury bill, a six-month savings certificate, first offered on June 1, 1978, can be purchased from savings and loan associations. Its advantage is an interest rate .25 percent higher than that paid by regular six-month treasury bills.

If you have at least $10,000 in cash and you won't need it for at least three months, treasury bills may be your best short-term investment.

U.S. AGENCY NOTES. Also exempt from state and local taxes, U.S. agency short-term notes pay higher interest than treasury bills while offering virtually equal safety and liquidity. These notes are offered monthly. Minimum investment is $5,000, and the holding period may be as short as three months. Commercial banks and brokers, the Federal Reserve Bank, and some underwriters handle the notes. Among agencies offering notes are the Federal Home Loan Bank System, Federal Land Bank, and Tennessee Valley Authority. The Federal National Mortgage Association is another issuing agency, but its notes lack the tax-exempt feature.

On all three counts of safety, liquidity, and convenience, U.S. Agency short-term notes are excellent short-term investments if the minimum amount and holding period aren't stumbling blocks.

MUNICIPAL NOTES. Municipal short-term notes have traditionally been a favorite investment for individuals and companies with cash they don't need for at least one month. Requiring a minimum of $5,000 and usually trading in lots of $25,000, these notes pay only a low rate of interest (often much lower than regular savings accounts). However, they offer the special feature of tax exemption. These notes are exempt not only from federal taxes but, if bought in your home state, usually from state and local taxes, too. If you are in a high personal tax bracket, the exemptions may give you a better return than a higher-interest investment.

Extremely safe, municipal notes may also offer good liquidity, but only if the financial condition of the issuing municipality is good. These notes are available from commercial banks and brokers.

PROJECT NOTES. A variation of municipal notes, project notes are issued by local agencies and usually offer the same tax advantages with even greater safety and liquidity, since they are backed by the U.S. government. Commercial banks and brokers may sell these notes for as little as $1,000, though $25,000 is the usual minimum. The holding period ranges from three months to one year, with the notes easily resold before maturity.

The major disadvantage of project notes, as compared with municipal notes, is the rate of interest. Project notes pay an even lower rate in return for their increased safety and liquidity. In addition, the state tax exemption feature varies and must be checked in each case. However, if there is a chance that you will have to call on your cash reserves in two or three weeks, project notes may be a better short-term investment for you than municipal short-term notes.

Whether you select just one or a combination of the above short-term investment possibilities, whether your first priority is safety and liquidity or high interest rates, be sure you opt for the best use of your cash on hand. Few of us can afford not to take advantage of today's excellent opportunities to make our idle money grow.

Chapter 6

How to Find Customers and Make Sales

MANY factors contribute to the success of a business. The most important is to provide a product or service the public wants. But every experienced business owner soon learns there is little or nothing to the idea that if you build a better mousetrap the world will beat a path to your door. Providing a better product or service won't do much good unless you can call the public's attention to it in some consistent way. A satisfied customer may be your best advertisement, but you must attract your customer before you can satisfy him.

GETTING THE BUSINESS

Perhaps the foremost characteristic of the successful operator is that he knows, generally from the beginning, where he will derive his income. He has a clear understanding of how his customers or clients can be obtained. This seems like a basic principle. Yet surprising numbers of new business operators don't heed it. They often have what seems like a good idea, but they never come to grips with the hard question of how they will promote it, call public attention to it, and build a lasting trade for it.

122

The successful operator often has had specific experience in attracting customers for what he has to offer. Perhaps, as an employee, he has seen how his employer has successfully won customers. Perhaps he has been a salesperson and has developed techniques for bringing in customers. Salesmen often make the most successful business owners, provided they can master the art of producing the materials they are adroit at selling. For this reason, some management experts believe a person with solid sales experience often has the best chance to make it as an entrepreneur.

Many successful businesses have first conducted extensive marketing surveys to determine if a demand exists for their goods or services. Sometimes proof of this demand is evident in the fact that similar establishments have succeeded in many other places. In other cases, the business owners have questioned potential prospects and found that they would probably become customers. Many top franchise organizations make studies to determine if the potential business exists for a franchise outlet before they set up a franchise holder in one.

So important is the art of getting customers that persons who may be expert in all other business areas fail for the lack of it. "Many valuable products are going unused by the American public just because their manufacturers don't know how to market them," says Harold Dennison, a consultant to small factory owners. "I've seen outstanding technicians make a mess of a business while sales-oriented individuals with considerably less technical skill forge ahead."

It's easy to see how successful owners have developed methods of getting and holding customers, but less easy to set down business-getting rules that apply to different businesses, trades, and professions.

Most of them have different ways of building trade. A subcontractor in the construction trade may depend entirely on contacts with major contractors who know his work. Another contractor may give building supply dealers a commission on customers they refer to him. A successful insurance and mutual fund salesman moved from Hartford to San Diego and set up a business there without initial customers. His ace card was his knowledge that ads offering free booklets on financial questions could attract enough business to give him a good living. Another financial adviser gives free talks to women's groups—and almost every talk produces a customer for her services. A travel agent employee developed a successful way of setting up charter flights for large organizations. Before long she established her own business—and took the customers with her.

The point is that in every business, trade, or profession, certain proved techniques produce the business. The individual setting up his own organization who fails to understand what those techniques are, or who lacks the know-how to produce sales and win customers, is taking enormous risks.

Of course, getting the business is only half the battle. You must provide goods or services that satisfy your customers or clients. But it is impossible to prove to the public that you offer outstanding goods or services unless you can persuade them to try you.

Location

Depending on the kind of business you operate, location could be a key factor in getting customers. Says management consultant Harold Grable: "The world is most likely to beat a path to the mousetrap maker who happens to be near bus and transit lines and has adequate parking space." For many enterprises, location is more crucial than anything else. Some fast food franchisers spend thousands of dollars in studies of traffic patterns before selecting a site for a hamburger stand or pizza parlor. Often the location they choose will be a corner where busy roads intersect and motorists will see the food outlet as they stop for a traffic light.

Thousands of retailers—and even doctors and dentists—have assured their success by wisely choosing a business location. Others, equally competent in other ways, have failed because they weren't in the right place. A printing firm in New York saw profits running down the drain because of the excessive costs involved in moving paper through clogged streets to and from its plant. It moved to a location near a superhighway and got into the black without making any pricing changes. For many manufacturers, a location near sources of supply and ultimate consumers makes the difference between profit and loss.

Making efficient use of the space you have, regardless of where it is, is almost equally important. With costs of labor and business space at all-time highs, it makes good business sense to get the most production from the fewest workers in the smallest possible space.

Advertising

Most self-employed persons find advertising in one way or another essential for their survival.

In a broad sense, advertising is more than an announcement printed in a newspaper or broadcast over the air. It is anything that tells the public about yourself and the services or goods you offer. It might be the sign outside your shop or office, your letterheads, the packages in which your products are wrapped and sold, or how you answer your telephone. Inasmuch as you give some impression about your goods or services in any contact with the public, you may be engaged in advertising activities all day, every day.

In a narrower sense, advertising consists of a conscious effort to influence others in all ways except through person-to-person contacts. Direct persuasion is salesmanship.

Some small business owners consider advertising a waste of money. They may have run some advertising and failed to see concrete results from it and have concluded that it is not worth the time, effort, and expense.

No doubt, much advertising money is wasted. Ads may be poorly presented, directed to the wrong people, or placed in the wrong medium. But the best evidence that advertising can be productive is that few businesses in the country have grown large without it, and almost all large businesses advertise on a consistent basis.

Advertising can do many different things for you. Some will benefit you over the long run but won't result in an immediate upsurge of sales:

• Through the use of low-priced specials, it can draw the public to your place of business and give you the opportunity to make steady customers.

• It can let the public know of your existence and make it

aware of the goods and services you offer. A consumer exposed to your ad today may do nothing about it until he needs what you sell and remembers you months later.

• It can reduce your sales expense by preselling customers who already know what they want when they reach your place of business.

• It can get your message through to people who might refuse to see a salesperson who calls on them.

• It can give you the image of an established enterprise and help eliminate suspicions some people feel about patronizing new enterprises. All consumers are more confident when dealing with a known establishment.

• It can help you protect your position against competitors and give you the opportunity to tell your competitors' customers why your goods or services are superior.

Advertising takes many forms. To be effective, you should first clarify in your mind the ideas you want to convey about yourself to the public. Then fashion your advertising approaches accordingly.

One man opened a discount store featuring extremely low-priced goods, seconds of suits and dresses with slight imperfections, and odd lots of household goods that other shops couldn't sell. He advertises in his local paper in an entirely different way from the Main Street boutique that carries the latest fashions. Illustrations, typefaces, and style of language in the two ads differ vastly. In one, the entire impression cries "low-priced bargains"; in the other, "elegant, fashionable, and high-priced styling."

The message you aim to convey also affects your choice of advertising media. The appliance dealer featuring low-priced electronic calculators will advertise his wares in newspapers that reach everybody or mail circulars to every address in town. The dealer in high-priced stereo systems sponsors a classical musical program on radio that attracts only potential customers for his goods.

The effectiveness of any advertising depends on what you say and to whom you say it. A good ad addressed to the wrong people will usually achieve poorer results than a bad ad that reaches persons likely to be interested in the goods or services you sell.

Your choice of a medium in which to advertise should depend largely on your answer to this question: which one will get to the kinds of people you want to reach at the lowest cost? Sometimes you may ask a second question: which medium will help reinforce the image you wish to convey to the public?

If your goods or services could be used by a high percentage of persons in your community, you should probably use a mass medium such as the local newspaper, shopping paper, radio or television station. A downtown department store, for example, usually seeks to appeal to everyone. However, department store owners and other merchants (supermarket operators, appliance dealers, etc.) may find it is cheaper to use direct mail addressed to every occupant in certain sections.

If your clients or customers come from only a small segment of the community, you would use a more specialized medium. The operator of a discotheque, whose clientele consists almost entirely of teenagers, sponsors a rock radio program that speaks to them exclusively. A distributor of supplies to doctors knows that most newspaper readers or radio listeners wouldn't respond to his product, so his advertising consists entirely of circulars mailed to the physicians in his market area. An office supply firm advertises in business publications read only by persons who might buy its products. A motel chain believes its best results come from outdoor signs a few miles outside of town when they will be seen by motorists seeking a place to stay.

"Image" advertising takes many forms. Also known as "goodwill" or "institutional" advertising, it serves to give the public a general impression rather than selling a particular product or service. The owner of a dry cleaning firm pays all the costs of a Little League team because, he says, "I want people to know I care about their kids' welfare." There is no direct way of determining whether this expense pays off in added patronage, but he believes it builds his reputation. Another merchant runs ads in his community's black newspaper solely, he says, to let blacks know they will be treated courteously in his shop. A radio and TV repair shop sponsors a consumer program on a local radio station and announces that it welcomes an examination of its prices and policies by consumer groups.

The choice of the correct medium usually doesn't pose a problem. It often suggests itself once you decide what segment of the population you wish to reach and what you will say when you reach it.

Although advertising experts know in a general way what kinds of ads produce the best results, probably none of them would suggest a large-scale campaign without testing the different approaches. Changing a few words in a headline can alter the response to a newspaper ad by as much as 100 percent, for example.

The amounts you spend on advertising probably don't justify extensive (and expensive) testing of different ads. But every consistent advertiser can try different approaches until he discovers one that clicks. The owner of a new restaurant offered newspaper readers two meals for the price of one if they presented a copy of his ad. Results were disappointing. Then he promised free wine with meals if diners presented the ad. Patronage jumped 60 percent. A laundromat owner advertised that customers could put one load in his new dry cleaning equipment free to see for themselves how well it performed. He had only a few takers. Next he offered a $1 discount off his regular price when they used his equipment. Although customers now paid more, the number of responses tripled.

As these examples suggest, the most effective ads are not necessarily those that offer the most. So many factors go into a customer's decision to buy that it is a rare individual who can consistently predict which of two well-prepared ads will outdraw the other. One of the least reliable indicators, ad men insist, is whether the advertiser likes a certain ad. What looks prettiest or sounds best may often prove less attractive than an approach that strikes the public's fancy for unknown reasons. The only way to be sure is to test.

You can get help from many sources in preparing your ads. Salesmen for any medium you deal with—newspaper, radio, television, etc.—will show you how to prepare advertising and may even write the ad copy for you. All advertising media have access to syndicated material that can be used by local advertisers. Newspapers subscribe to art and mat services that supply text and illustrations you can use. Ads for all kinds of businesses are already prepared. You need only insert your own name, address, phone number, and hours. Radio and TV stations also have access to standard commercial copy. Often only your name and address need be added. Printing shops specializing in direct mail are usually ready to help their customers with ad copy and layout and will often handle an entire campaign, including the mailing. If unusual treatment is required—you want special artwork, for example—they generally can recommend experts who can do the job.

You may want to consider using an advertising agency to handle your advertising. If you advertise a lot, the cost of the agency's services may be largely absorbed by commissions the agency collects from the advertising media. Equally important, the agency removes from your shoulders the heavy burden of planning and coordinating the campaign, preparing ads, dealing with the ad media, and taking care of accounting details.

After determining how it can help increase your sales, an agency will recommend the ad approach to take. It may suggest radio, newspapers, direct mail, etc., or a combination of these as the best way to get your message to your public. After you approve a plan, staff members or freelancers employed by the agency create ads tailored to a particular medium (newspapers, TV, radio, etc.). The agency acts as an independent contractor, handling all the details involved.

The agency later checks invoices and evidence that the advertising has been run. This is done with tearsheets from publications and affidavits from radio or TV stations. The agency also examines and approves bills from suppliers of services or materials connected with the ad preparation.

Agencies are paid through commissions from ad media (generally 15 percent of the ad's cost), fees from the client, service charges on materials and services used to make up the ads, and charges for noncommission ads, such as direct mail.

Most small businesses don't generate enough commissions to cover their agencies' expenses, so the agencies often charge an additional amount. But an agency that builds extra business for you with its ads may be worth far more than its cost.

While commissions provide most of its income, it is often not enough to cover the agency's cost of handling the advertising. For example, the cost of a one-time ad in one medium may be only a fraction of that in another. Only by running the same ad a number of times does the ratio of commission to agency costs improve substantially.

In addition, most ad media have two rates, national and local. National rates are higher but include agency commissions. (The ad medium in effect pays the agency.) When local rates apply, the agencies can't always collect them. This is the main reason why most manufacturers employ agencies. They use national advertising, and the agency commission covers a large part of their costs. On the other hand, most retailers and local businesses pay the lower local rate and must also pay agencies an additional amount.

These are some of the fee plans used by agencies:

• The advertiser pays the agency a monthly amount based on estimated work and commissions. This fee stays the same regardless of commissions received in any one month.

• The amount of the fee is reduced by the amount of commissions the agency collects. If the commissions exceed the fee amount, the agency often may keep the surplus or credit it to the advertiser in a month when commissions are less than the fee.

• The agency charges the advertiser for layouts or copywriting on a fixed-fee or hourly basis. It uses its commission revenues to pay it for work where charges are less easily determined, such as for planning and meetings with the client.

• The agency adds a service charge to invoices for materials or services used in preparing ads. Such outside purchases include typesetting, printing, photographs, etc. Say the agency receives a supplier's bill for $1,000. It typically adds 17.65 percent, or $176.50, and bills the client for $1,176.50, of which 15 percent is $176.50.

• The agency charges in different ways for advertising and promotion items like direct-mail material and sales literature, which rarely involve commissions. One way is to estimate the cost of each job and quote a price. Another is to have a price schedule, to which the agency adds its 17.65 percent service charge.

TIPS ON SELECTING AN AGENCY. Choosing an ad agency is an important process, since much of your income may depend on how well it serves you.

Most agencies have a diversified clientele and prepare ads for many media. But some are better at advertising for manufacturers while others are stronger in working for retail or other local concerns.

An agency's size and location are other preliminary factors to consider. Perhaps a smaller agency located nearby will give you more attention. But see that the people you will be working with are competent enough and will give enough attention to the job. Don't eliminate an agency solely because it is too small or too large, but recognize that the smaller agency will probably give you more personalized attention.

You can get names of agencies from several places. You may have letters from agencies that have solicited your account. You can look in the Yellow Pages of your telephone directory. Business papers and trade journals often have indices telling which agencies were responsible for which ads; you can then judge their work. You might consult a copy of the *Standard Directory of Advertising Agencies* (Agency List) at your local public library. You might ask business associates or your local chamber of commerce for recommendations.

When you have a list of possibilities, tell the agencies you will soon choose one and ask for information about their work. Tell them about your business, advertising goals, and how much advertising you expect to do.

Some business owners have effectively used questionnaires to solicit information. Many agencies dislike them, and some may consider them too time-consuming to fill out if the prospective account is small. But with a questionnaire, all agencies supply information in the same way, making comparisons easier. You are also more likely to get the facts and figures you seek.

However you get the information, some of it should be in writing, even though a few agencies may prefer to make an oral presentation. The agency should tell you:

- Length of time in business.
- A history of past and present accounts, including the kinds of businesses and their size. Agencies usually don't accept accounts that compete with others they already have.
- Amount of total billings to clients for several recent years.

This amount should be growing annually—a sign that the agency is able to do satisfactory work and retain clients. If it isn't doing so, try to find out why.

• Media strength. The media the agency has more experience with—newspapers, radio, etc.—and the amount of billings to each medium.

• Media association recognition. This is based on the agency's financial capacity to meet that medium's credit standards, the amount of business placed with the medium, and how many agency employees have solid experience in dealing with the medium. An agency serving you only on a local basis—in community newspapers and radio stations, say—may not have or may not need media recognition. If you are considering a bigger agency, see that it is recognized by the national associations of the media you may advertise in.

• What Dun & Bradstreet or other credit bureaus say about the agency's financial strength.

• Full-time employees, including number and types (executive and professional or clerical).

• Background, qualifications, and functions of the personnel who would work on your account. These are the people you will be dealing with most frequently.

• Agency policies concerning billing, overtime, testing ads, and extra services such as research and public relations.

If the size of your business doesn't warrant hiring an agency, consider hiring a part-time ad manager. He or she could be a moonlighter who has a regular job with an agency, is an ad manager for a large advertiser, or works for a local newspaper or radio or TV station. This person would probably know more about advertising than you or another employee could learn in the amount of time you can spare from other duties.

Another way you can reduce your advertising costs is by taking advantage of cooperative offers. These offers usually are made by manufacturers, generally promote a nationally known product, and feature the name of the local outlet where it can be purchased. Much advertising of cars, television sets, and other big-ticket items is of the cooperative type.

A common arrangement calls for the manufacturer to pay half the cost of the ad while the distributors pay the other half.

CREATING ADS THAT SELL. No matter who prepares your advertising, your aim should be to make people choose your product or service rather than your competitor's. However, when you advertise, most of your costs are fixed. For example, you pay the same price for a newspaper ad whether you make a completely ineffective appeal for your goods or services or tell your strongest story possible.

Time and money spent to create advertisements are often only a small part of the total cost of the ads. Hence it is usually worthwhile to go all out to produce effective selling copy. These tips, based on recommendations by advertising experts, will improve the pulling power of your promotion.

1. Appeal to a specific need or want, starting with the headline. How-to headlines and those including specific information or helpful suggestions encourage reading the whole ad. Try to suggest a quick, easy way for the reader to get what he wants. Most successful copywriters consider the headline by far the most important ingredient in an ad.

2. Write your ads from the readers' point of view. Talk to them in their language about what interests them. Don't try to be too clever. Headlines and copy are generally more effective when they are straightforward. Many people distrust slick advertising or misunderstand tricky copy. Make your words, sentences, and paragraphs short. Address your ad to the reader by using "you" and "your."

3. Be specific at all times. Fact-filled copy that concentrates on your product or service convinces consumers. Ineffective copy consists of generalities, clever phrases, and unsupported claims. It attracts attention to itself—not to what it is selling. Provide all the information your reader needs to make the decision to buy.

4. Make your copy believable. Your statements and claims should agree with your reader's ordinary past experience. Back up other claims with concrete proof. Start off with a basic statement of fact that the reader can easily accept. This puts him in a receptive mood for later statements that may be less evident. Inspire his confidence.

5. Use testimony to support claims and statements. Present statements by users of your product or service; authorities in the field; results of tests; government reports; bulletins; local, na-

tional, or international medals; awards or citations, etc.

6. Emphasize a main idea and restate it. This constantly focuses the reader's attention on your basic selling point and makes the ad easier to understand, interpret, and act on. Summarize your sales story somewhere in the ad, preferably as a slogan.

7. Use copy that sells *your* product, not someone else's. Say you own a stereo equipment store. If you run an ad that tells only about the beauty of stereo sound, you will help your competitors sell their products, too. Show how your product, or the service backing it up, is unique.

8. Urge your readers to buy immediately. Give them a sound reason for doing so, such as "limited supply," "price is going up," or "three days only." Spell out your credit and layaway plans. Time payments may encourage undecided consumers to act.

9. When possible, include prices or price range, even if they are high. Dollar figures attract attention. Readers often overestimate prices not mentioned in an ad. If your price is high, explain why the product is worth it, such as high-quality craftsmanship or materials or unusual extras. When your price is low, explain the circumstances, such as a clearance or special purchase.

10. Offer money-back guarantees. Many ad experts say such guarantees do more than anything else to win consumer confidence and attract interested customers. They say that if your product is good, few customers will want their money back.

11. If practical, use photographs or drawings instead of straight copy to attract attention and provide information. Use a picture of the product or of people using it, so the reader can visualize it in action.

12. Make your ads easily recognizable. Ads different in some way—those using distinctive art, layout, or typeface, for example—generally attract more readers. When you find a unique and effective way to present your message, stick with it. Readers, and especially your customers, will recognize your ads right away.

13. Use a simple, uncrowded layout. It should easily carry the reader's eye through your message in proper sequence, without distraction. White space makes your headline, illustration, and, copy stick out. A cluttered ad, with many different type faces or overly decorative borders, is distracting. It reduces the number of readers who receive and remember your message.

14. Study the advertisements of others that are constantly repeated. They are usually successful; otherwise they would not be run over and over. Determine what makes them successful and try to transfer that element to your ads. Catalogs of large mail-order companies such as Sears, Roebuck and Co. and J. C. Penney advertise a broad range of products, using fully proved ad techniques.

15. Test your ads whenever possible to determine the most effective ones. Then use the most successful appeal in all your advertising, whether in newspapers, through direct mail, radio, TV, or elsewhere. What works in one advertising medium generally works in all.

SELLING YOUR PRODUCT OR SERVICE

A good location and good advertising will attract potential customers to your business. But to turn potential customers into paying customers you have to know how to sell your product or service.

Selling is an essential part of every trade, business, or profession operated for profit. In some fields it is the most important part, and the most successful operators are not necessarily those who perform the best services or sell the highest-quality products, but rather those with the most effective sales techniques. Providing top-quality goods or services plus good sales practices is generally an unbeatable combination. This is true whether the services are legal, medical, or dental (professions in which aggressive sales practices are frowned on) or whether the goods are commercial products.

Millions of words have been written on effective salesmanship. In books, lectures, and interviews thousands of experts have told what it takes to influence a human being so that he or she becomes a satisfied user of your goods or services. Almost all agree on certain fundamental principles. Below are basic points that will help everyone who must depend on others as customers, clients, or patients.

Sales problems obviously differ greatly, depending on the type of enterprise. A physician may not have "sales" problems as such, but he must develop procedures for getting and holding patients, and how he does so will have an important effect on the growth of his practice. A retailer like a variety store operator may not seem to be selling either—his customers state what they want and may even serve themselves—but whether they feel satisfied with his goods and services will often determine whether they continue as his patrons. The advertising agent may have steady clients, but he must continue to sell them on his competence lest they drop him when his contract expires. The person selling one item at a time (office equipment, machinery, automobiles) must approach prospects differently from the sales representative calling on retailers for repeat orders.

Business owners often face different selling situations at the same time. You may have steady patrons as well as those you are dealing with the first time; those who come to you and others you must seek; some who buy goods on a one-time basis primarily on price and others who want continued service and must assure themselves of your integrity.

Your success, therefore, may depend on your being an all-around salesman. Even though your problems may be concentrated heavily in one area of selling, they will inevitably overlap into other areas. In this broad sense, regardless of the nature of your operation, you will find it profitable to develop selling techniques for any and all circumstances.

Selling, it is generally agreed, consists of more than merely persuading someone to hand over money on a one-time basis. In the broad view, it covers everything that could influence prospects. For this reason, your specific sales efforts should harmonize with the general impression you try to convey. The owner of a business or practice who wishes to stress reliability and responsibility will deal with his or her public with dignity—an approach at the opposite end of the pole from the folksy one. The approach must harmonize with the product. The sales effort for a Rolls Royce must differ from that for a Jeep. The overall sales effort—advertising, publicity, design, and decoration of your place of business, appearance and attitude of sales persons—must appeal to the clientele you hope to attract.

Effective selling encompasses many different things, summed up in two slogans: "know your customer" and "know your product."

It is a rock-bottom principle of ethical salesmanship that you should never sell a product that is wrong for your customer; for instance, a suit he likes but that will never fit him properly. Applying this principle means you must size up your prospect and determine what is appropriate for him. Knowing his purposes, you are better able to recommend goods or services to help him achieve them.

Knowing your product often takes much learning about its capabilities, advantages; and disadvantages. Today's public is better equipped than ever to spot phonies—persons who pretend to knowledge they lack. If a prospect suspects you don't know as much about your product as you should, chances of making the sale begin to drop. If you don't know the answer to questions, it is better to say you don't know and will get the correct answer than to try bluffing. All too often the customer detects it—and the sales person loses credibility.

"Know your customer" and "know your product" are embodied in another slogan: "serve." Put yourself in your prospect's place, consider his needs from his point of view, and give him the attention and service he requires to be satisfied with his purchase.

Whether a customer, client, or patient decides to start or continue using your goods or services depends on the total image you project. For this reason, every contact is a sales contact. Every visit, request for information or appointment, complaint, or written communication has some effect on how your operation is regarded.

Bottom-line selling is almost always the most profitable. This involves a thorough knowledge of cost and profit ratios so that you can concentrate on those items that will produce the greatest net profit—the bottom-line figure. Even when all goods or services carry identical markups, they don't produce the same profit margins or same dollar profits. Such factors as the following must be considered.

• Whether you can sell more of Item X, which may produce a lower dollar profit per unit than Item Y, but that—because of the volume sold—will give you a greater total profit. This price comparison may be crucial if you have facilities that will go unused if you charge a higher price. Many operators of movie theaters earn greater profits with a $1.50 admission price than when they charge $3.00.

• Whether you can do better by selling for cash or credit. Many business owners increase sales substantially by selling on credit, but their overall profits may be reduced by collection costs and bad debts. Sometimes credit card selling, with the credit card company charging a commission but also guaranteeing payment, produces the highest profits.

• Whether Item A, with a lower initial profit but few if any returns or refunds, may not produce a better result than Item B, which gives a higher initial profit but continuing headaches (and costs) later in the form of returns and calls for repairs or maintenance. More times than not, salespersons underestimate how much service must be provided when guarantees are attached to mechanical devices.

• Whether it requires too much time, relative to profit, to sell Item C rather than Item D. Experienced sales managers are often suspicious of new items that require "missionary" efforts—a great deal of explaining and demonstrating to convince prospects of their value. To justify the time involved, such items should have high profit margins and should promise repeat business for supplies or maintenance if not for more of the same items.

• Whether you are spending your time with accounts that produce, or could produce, the greatest profits. Some customers demand greater time per dollar of sales and profits. Some may be costlier to call on and service—they may be on the outer limits of your sales territory, for example—and may even be unprofitable when all factors are considered. Some veteran salesmen spend years on accounts that give them no business at present because they know that if they get an order it will make all their calls worthwhile. On the other hand, you have to make a cold analysis of whether the time spent in hopes of a big sale has a good chance of paying off.

Can you succeed in business, building a list of steady customers, without a firm price policy? Most top sales experts doubt it. They say that, if you want to continue doing business with the same person or firm, you must get across to them that you won't engage in price haggling each time an order is placed. Depending on circumstances, you may have to cut prices on an initial order—grant a discount, for example, to meet competition—but you will find it increasingly unprofitable to argue over price thereafter.

Your own attitudes may be responsible if your customers try to drive you down. You must come across firmly as one who asks a fair price for his goods or services—not someone in desperate need of "favors." An effective way of discouraging haggling is to display printed price lists. Few customers will seriously bargain for lower prices if you convince them that your charges are the same for everyone.

Regardless of what product or service you sell, one thing always holds greater interest for the prospect—himself or herself. In most cases, you get and hold a prospect's interest in direct relationship to the extent to which you can personalize your sales presentation.

• Know your customer's name and pronounce and spell it correctly. To the individual, his or her name is the sweetest sound in the world. Use it often.

• Engage in a conversation, not a monologue. Ask questions to draw out the prospect's opinions and to learn his or her special problems. Avoid canned sales talks and tailor your comments to the prospect's interests.

• Bring up points you learned about your prospect in previous contacts. Audrey Taylor, a top New York travel agent dealing mainly with vacationers, maintains files on all her customers with notations about where they have been and what they liked and disliked on their trips. She gets this information by phoning them after each trip and inquiring about their experiences. She knows whether they enjoy museum hopping, seeing historical sights, nightclubbing. Whenever she talks to them she mentions their earlier trips and avoids errors like that of another travel agent who tried to sell a London-Paris vacation to clients who just returned from a $3,000 London-Paris vacation he had arranged for them.

• Emphasize what your goods or services will do for your prospect. He is interested in benefits he himself will derive. As a rule, he wants to know details of your product only insofar as they affect him. "This car will give you twenty-five miles to the gallon" is a more effective sale-maker for most persons than a discussion of the engine's technical details. Says sales management consultant Howard S. Lowell: "Sell the effect, not the cause."

• Personalize your mail contacts. A short note accompanying a requested catalog or price list, addressed to the prospect by name, conveys the message that you care about his business—that he is not just one in a hundred.

• Answer inquiries with personalized letters. Luther Brock, PhD, who writes a marketing column for *Direct Marketing* magazine, says that personal replies consistently produce better results than routine ones. (He also says that obvious form letters are better than filled-in letters in which the salutation doesn't match the letter's typeface.) A handwritten note of a few lines, accompanying printed material, also provides a personal touch.

• Answer inquiries promptly. Quick replies show that you want the business—and they are likely to reach your prospect while he is still thinking about your product.

Even business owners who have no way of knowing customers' names can effectively use a personalized approach to build sales income. Few persons really want to be anonymous. The owner of a tavern near the Stamford, Connecticut, railroad station serves many commuters on their way home from New York City. He recognizes regular patrons by remembering their favorite drinks— a sign that he considers them "special." Southern business owners are justly famed for their courteous, individualized treatment of customers—even those just passing through. The owner of a crowded small restaurant in Macon, Georgia, commented, "I greet every customer as I would like to be greeted." His is a valuable point for everyone in contact with the public: analyze what you like and dislike in the way salespeople deal with you; recognize that most people basically respond in the same ways and that what appeals to you will appeal to others as well; in dealing with others, use approaches you find most effective with yourself.

"If you're trying to build a loyal clientele, begin working on your next order as soon as you write up the present one." This advice comes from Malcolm Wadsworth, a top representative for several midwestern manufacturers in the North Atlantic states. It's another way of saying that it won't work to ignore customers except when you are trying to make a commission on them.

Wadsworth says that in his line it generally takes years to build customer confidence. Many buyers place small orders at first and carefully note how they are handled. So Wadsworth checks up constantly, makes sure goods are delivered when promised, checks with the customer to see that they arrived in satisfactory condition, and between orders provides information about trade conditions that he thinks will interest the customer. When he next seeks an order he is not a stranger.

A standard complaint of "steady customers" (and a frequent reason why they stop being steady) is that salesmen spend more time courting new customers than they do taking care of those they already have. Wadsworth thinks it is essential to give existing customers at least the same kind of attention you would devote to prospects—and the same kind of attention they would get from your competitors seeking their patronage.

In formulating a sales appeal you should identify the hurdles that must be overcome—and concentrate on the first hurdles first. In order, these are questions the consumer wants answered before making a purchase:

• Will the item be of use to me? If you introduce the prospect to goods or services with which he is unfamiliar, you may first have to show him what your product does. Before selling electronic calculators to business owners, sales agents first had to demonstrate the many shortcuts in ordinary business computations the devices make possible. Many executives don't use calculators today because their usefulness hasn't been clearly demonstrated to them.

• How will the item serve me better? Someone already using a calculator and convinced of its value will have to be sold on an "improved" model. Salesmen for units that print computations on tape stress the advantage of having all figures before you so that you can be sure you have pressed the right keys.

• Is the item of suitable quality? This question arises only when the previous ones have been answered to the prospect's satisfaction. Many salesmen err in stressing quality to prospects who haven't been convinced they can use the item offered. "You can't sell the best bicycle in the world to a man without legs" is the way it was put by Peter Bradley, a writer of sales manuals. It may also be an error to stress highest quality when an item of lower quality would serve as well. Questions of quality of service may arise if the item will require maintenance or repairs.

• How does the price of your item compare with that of items offered by competitors? Price is often the final hurdle. If your price is higher, you will probably have to convince the prospect that he is not comparing equal items—that yours is superior in one or more respects. A salesman for a high-priced printing firm stresses its twenty-four-hour service; a sales representative for a high-priced washing machine cites its freedom from mechanical breakdowns; a woman demonstrating margarine in a supermarket emphasizes its fresh natural taste.

Learn to identify and appeal to the decision maker. You waste lots of time if you direct your sales approach to those who aren't in a position to influence the buying decision. In a business organization, "non–decision makers" may be secretaries or other assistants who have to refer every question to a higher-up; among consumers, the decision maker may be a husband or wife and the other partner may just be along for company.

Arthur Handrew, a veteran Chicago automobile salesman, says years of experience have taught him to listen carefully to husbands and wives when they look over a new car. Many telltale signs indicate who will make the ultimate decision. He plays up to this partner, making sure to answer fully every objection that is raised. "In many cases," he says, "car salesmen do a great selling job on male prospects. But as soon as the prospects leave the showroom, their wives talk them out of the deal."

Harry M. Fuller, who sells printing machinery, says most assistants have only the power to say "no"; rarely can they say "yes" without consulting others. "Most assistants think their job consists of keeping salesmen away from the boss," he says. "Four times out of five, they'll turn you down because it's easier that way." Wherever possible, he delivers his sales message only to the person with buying authority. If asked to talk to someone on a lower level, he will make a low-key presentation and leave without any decision. His purpose is to avoid a definite outcome, so that he can try for another contact with the decision maker. "It's always tough to go over the head of an assistant who has turned you down," he says.

Fuller says it is important to develop reasons for getting and keeping in touch with the individual with the buying power. He keeps a card file noting each prospect's special interests. He flips through his file regularly to determine whether new developments—introduction of a new model, for example— justify making another call. "The idea is to try for a one-to-one relationship, so that people in his firm take it for granted that the head man is the one you're in contact with," he says.

Benson P. Shapiro, associate professor of business administration at the Harvard Business School, says personal selling should be used only in situations where a strong impact is desired and it is important to discover the customer's objections in order to answer them. Robert Margolis, New York sales management consultant, says personal sales calls may be counterproductive— when, for example, a customer is price-conscious. He says many customers know that salesmen must be paid out of the sales they make, and that an item sold personally is likely to cost more than one in which no personal selling is involved. Hence, he says, personal selling should be confined to high-priced items, should often be the missionary type—calling attention to useful services or products the customer might not know about—or should involve products that may require continued services or maintenance.

Edgar A. Watterson has sold millions of dollars worth of industrial products. He sums up fifty years of selling experience in this way:

"A sales presentation is like an airplane trip. An air trip meets disaster if the plane can't get off the ground safely and come in for a safe landing. A sales presentation won't get anywhere if you can't grab your prospect's attention at the beginning and if you can't bring your presentation to a close. Every successful salesman I have ever met has developed a specific method of closing the sale—sometimes even to the point of putting a pen in the customer's hand over an order form. Every sales call should aim at getting some commitment from your prospect, even if it's only his promise to consider your offer and to be willing to talk when you call again."

Handling Complaints

To some business owners, the customer with a complaint is at best a nuisance and at worst a thief, and they deal with him accordingly. They often feel they can afford to lose some customers because there are plenty more. However, when you ignore a complaint or otherwise treat a customer unfairly, it costs more than you think. Several studies have shown that the typical dissatisfied customer doesn't keep his grievance to himself. He tells his story, on an average, to eleven other people, according to one survey. Several of those people may be actual or potential customers. By contrast, concludes the survey report, when you please the average customer, he relates his good treatment to only three other people.

Not all dissatisfied customers with complaints go elsewhere. A product or service may be too important to them. But they have ways of getting back. "If we offend a customer," says an Arizona manufacturer, "we hurt ourselves. When we introduce a new product, he's less willing than previously to take a chance on it and waits until consumer demand forces him to order it. If our sales department has an exciting new promotion, he's not interested. Some of our products may not move very fast, and he'll abruptly decide not to keep them in stock. Or he'll slow down his payments, and we'll have to mail him one reminder after another."

Then there are the reprisals that aren't so subtle. A Cleveland distributor says, "Recently a customer was dissatisfied with the way we handled a complaint. He canceled a $15,000 order that was ready to be shipped. It really hurt. It hurt still more when we learned he'd placed an equivalent order with a competitor."

The way you handle your customer complaints helps determine whether you finish your year in the red or the black. If you apply these thoughts on dealing with complaints, you will not only lose fewer customers, but you will likely gain some, too.

Let customers know to whom they should complain. You will find it more profitable to cooperate with the inevitable than to resist it.

Consumer complaints are often a valuable source of information about your business. The complaining customer can give you feedback that can guide you in correcting defects. He may also make you start thinking about producing a better product and give you valuable ideas about its features.

If a customer calls with a problem and doesn't know with whom to discuss it, he may be switched around before he finally gets the person who can help him. This not only ties up your telephone line, but wastes the customer's time and makes him feel he is getting the runaround. The time of various people in your organization is also wasted. You will keep old friends—or turn potential enemies into friends—if you make it easier for customers to complain or obtain assistance with their problems. Virtually all big successful companies do so.

Even if customers know to whom they should complain, most don't bother, especially if the price of the purchase isn't high. If the product is more expensive, a dissatisfied customer is more likely to request an adjustment. Retailers are most likely to receive complaints. If you are a manufacturer, only a fraction of consumers who are dissatisfied with your product will contact you. The number of complaints that will reach you, according to recent studies, will be only 2 out of 100. Thus, for a reasonably accurate number of dissatisfied consumers, multiply by 50 the amount of complaints that come in.

Complaints from commercial customers offer a more reliable yardstick as to what's wrong. Still, only one-fifth of these dissatisfied customers bother to complain. To get a realistic idea of the total, multiply the number of complaints received by five.

When you get a complaint, the story you hear may be inaccurate. For example, it may come to you thirdhand, relayed by a salesperson, who heard from a retail merchant, who got it from a customer. Messages usually get garbled as each person adds his own interpretation. In the end you may discover that the solution you have come up with doesn't solve anything since the customer's problem was misrepresented to you.

When a complaint involves a costly adjustment, it is usually advisable to double-check the problem. Call the original complainant and ask him to give you a rundown of the difficulty. He will also be able to answer questions that will help resolve the problem. You will also get a more accurate picture of why he is complaining.

Complaints are often based on misunderstandings by customers. For example, the owner of an automatic oven repeatedly had trouble with the timer and complained to the vendor that it should be repaired under the guarantee. Questioning revealed that she hadn't read the operating instructions but was using the new oven the same way she had used her old one.

When a customer complains about a product, don't assume he knows the exact nature of the problem. With a complicated piece of equipment, don't take any major action before you are satisfied that a reported malfunction is real and not a result of improper use. Sometimes you can determine the cause of the trouble by asking detailed questions on the telephone; at other times it may be necessary to have the equipment examined.

Sometimes a customer's poor understanding of business practices and policies leads to friction. For instance, a consumer may return a purchase to you and fail to include his name, address, and invoice or account number. Naturally he will become irate if he doesn't hear from you or receive a refund. Your only recourse is constantly to inform your customers of the proper way to make returns.

It costs money to investigate complaints. When a customer complains that an item is defective or was damaged when received, it is possible he himself was responsible. But it is usually difficult to prove it. To have the customer return the product means that one of you must bear the cost of shipping. Just processing a complaint, with correspondence back and forth, may require considerable time on your part.

Experience has shown that most customers are honest and that their complaints are justified. Many businesses, within certain price limits, automatically accept the customer's complaint and make an adjustment—repair, replacement, or refund.

"We formerly investigated complaints or asked the customer to return damaged merchandise," says the customer service manager of a New Jersey mail-order concern. "But in 90 out of 100 cases, we were able to determine that the purchaser had not caused the problem. So if the price of an item is below $20, we routinely make an adjustment. It saves us time and our customers are pleased with our fast service."

When a customer comes in or calls with a complaint, it is important to treat him politely. Assume he is upset; after all, he has bought something that is not working and he isn't sure of the treatment he will receive. He will be relieved if you show him at once that his problem is yours and that you will do what you can to solve it. If you treat his complaint indifferently, he may conclude that you were interested in him only until he made his purchase.

Not all customer complaints can be resolved quickly and smoothly. If you have given the customer a date when a repair will be completed and then can't meet it, don't assume he will automatically understand what has happened if he doesn't hear from you. A two-minute telephone call will reassure him that you haven't forgotten him.

In dealing with complaints, do your best to be objective, especially when the complaint involves physical injury. You need a clearly defined procedure for processing such problems. For example, employees who have personal contact with these complainants should never express any opinion about the product involved or mention similar occurrences just because they feel sorry for the injured person.

It is also important not to react when a dissatisfied customer loses his temper. The complainant may be so carried away that he makes insulting remarks about you personally as well as about your product or service. To solve a problem you must keep a clear head without becoming emotionally involved. Try to calm the customer. Assure him that you want to help but that you can't unless you are given just the facts.

A customer should have recourse if he is displeased with how his complaint has been handled by one of your employees. His grievance shouldn't be ignored but should be passed on to you or someone else with authority. Often a company official is more successful than a clerk in making the client understand why the complaint has been dealt with as it has or else can offer a satisfactory adjustment.

Chapter 7

Time Management: The Key to Getting Things Done

MOST commentators, in discussing the self-employed, distinguish between those who deal in goods and those who deal in services. True, the problems of the dealer in goods, the typical "small businessman," differ in many ways from those of the dealer in services, the tradesman or professional man. But this distinction overlooks a fundamental fact: all self-employers deal essentially in the same commodity. It is a limited commodity, and you must make a profit on it if you are to survive and succeed. This commodity is your *time*.

The idea that "time is money" is not new. It goes back at least as far as Benjamin Franklin, who is said to have coined the phrase while advising a young tradesman in 1748. Yet surprisingly often the idea is overlooked. A number of years ago, I was with a group of freelance magazine article writers. One was accepting compliments for an article just published in *The New York Times Magazine*. He told of two meetings he had had with the editors concerning the idea for the article, of three weeks he spent in intensive research, of two weeks more in writing and rewriting it, and then of two days in obtaining clarifying material that the editors had requested. The writer is justly proud (the magazine is one of the country's finest), but another writer pointed out that he *actually lost money on his work.* He received $750 for what amounted to almost six weeks' effort, little better than $125 a week. This writer's annual income was about $15,000, equal to $300 a week. If he had spent the same time writing for his usual markets, lesser-known women's magazines that often paid $1,000 for about three weeks' work, he might have been $1,250 ahead. Perhaps the author thinks the prestige of appearing in the *Times* is worth it, but when he undertook this assignment I am sure he did not calculate how much time—and money—it would cost him.

This writer is not unique. I have asked accountants to what extent the professional people and businesspeople among their clients are aware that "time is money" and consciously try to utilize it in the most profitable ways. The consensus: It is the rare one who manages time even 50 percent efficiently. Most persons do not consciously connect the ticking of the clock with their overall performance. They realize that time must be used to produce income but seldom do they try to get as much from every sixty minutes as they might.

What Is an Hour Worth?

You are selling time. Regard it as merchandise. Just as a washing machine or a suit of clothes must be sold to the customer at a higher price than the retailer pays for it, you too must sell your time for more than it costs. Any work you perform takes up your time, of course. Unless you make a profit on it, you cannot stay self-employed any more than the retailer can survive by repeatedly selling below cost. To sell your time with greatest effectiveness, you must know three things: what it now costs; how to get it for less; how to sell it for more.

How much does your time cost you? To answer this question, find out what you must make per hour to break even. You do this by adding *all* your overhead expenses for the year, including costs of rent, heat, utilities, total salary cost of employees, fees to specialists such as accountants, interest charges on business loans, and so on. Say this figure comes to $24,000. Now divide the figure by the total number of weeks you operate each year. For most persons, this figure is not fifty-two but forty-eight, allowing three weeks for vacations and one week for holidays and other days off. In this hypothetical case, your operating costs alone are $500 a week. Figuring forty hours to the week, this equals $12.50 an hour—almost 21¢ a minute.

If you produced no more than this, of course, you would work for nothing. Hence you must also compute your own income needs before taxes. Say they are $40,000 a year. Assuming the same working year of forty-eight weeks with forty hours a week, you have 1,920 working hours in your year. To meet your own needs, you therefore must earn an additional $20.83 per hour. Adding the overhead cost of $12.50 per hour, your receipts must average $33.33 an hour—$266.64 a day and 56¢ a minute—to achieve your objective. If you do not use your time to produce that much, you are likely to face a deficit at the end of the year. If you work a thirty-five-hour week (eight hours per day less one hour for lunch), your operating costs in this example would be $14.28 an hour. Your total pretax income must be $38.08 per hour—64¢ per minute—to cover these costs and maintain your standard of living.

Many self-employers will find this example of cost per minute on the low side. One study of independent consultants showed that overhead expenses—for office rental, equipment, utilities, employees' salaries—came to 50 percent of total income. Thus a man must take in $80,000 in order to have $40,000 for himself at the end of the year. Using the same forty-eight working weeks of forty hours each, he has 115,200 minutes a year in which to do it. This works out to a shade less than 70¢ *per minute*. Another survey shows that overhead expenses of physicians in general practice total 42 percent of gross income. Thus the physician who figures fees on the basis of $60 per hour gets only $34.80 for himself.

Work out your own cost per minute by dividing your gross annual income (before any expenses) by 115,200. You probably will be shocked to discover what one minute of the usual work week is worth. "I did something like this when I started thirty years ago," a highly successful orthopedic surgeon told me. "It has kept me from frittering away my time ever since."

Also figure out what your assistants' time is worth. Let us say your secretary works a thirty-five-hour week, 2,100 minutes per week. Divide this figure into her weekly salary plus the cost of fringe benefits and taxes. You will find that, even if her overall cost to you is only $190 a week, the cost amounts to 11.4¢ per minute and $6.85 per hour.

BENEFITS FROM TIME STUDIES

Knowing your per-hour and per-minute costs can help you function more effectively in many different ways:

It encourages the time-motion-study approach. You become more conscious of the need for efficiency, and you begin to search for faster, better ways of doing things. You become more aware of leakages in your use of time. One man started thinking of his costs per minute. He soon discarded the golf equipment he used for putting on his office rug whenever he found the chance. You develop a crisp, no-nonsense approach that most people generally admire. Because you consciously try to save your own time, you also save their time.

It enables you to put a realistic price on your services. Coupled with your knowledge of how long it takes to perform certain tasks, you have a clear idea of how much you must ask to achieve the per-hour income you need.

You can consciously establish priorities. In every operation, some projects pay better than others. You are probably better equipped than your competitors to do certain kinds of work quickly and competently and in this specialty you can get a higher income per hour than your average. By cultivating work on which you get the best return, you can raise your income substantially. At the other extreme, some tasks may take so much of your time that you cannot get an average return from them. If you can feasibly cut down on such jobs (without alienating clients, for example), you can consciously strive to eliminate lower-paying tasks in favor of more lucrative ones. Or you might consider hiring an assistant to do lesser-paying work if you can profit from his or her labors.

Establishing this priority does not necessarily mean that you refuse poor-paying jobs. Let us say you are a young lawyer striving to build your practice. Often you will have nothing to do. A client paying a minimum fee might be welcomed. You might even want to answer your own phone and do your own typing, because the $6.85 per hour you save is better than nothing. (But you will have to decide whether your image will be tarnished when prospective clients realize that you don't have enough work to keep you busy.)

It helps you avoid uneconomic use of time. When you realize that you must produce $40 in income per hour, you will not use that time to save a dollar. One man I know uses a lot of stationery. There is a printer-stationer in his office building whose prices are a bit higher than those prevailing elsewhere. So my acquaintance personally gets three bids from other printers on each order of letterheads and envelopes. Whenever he buys 1,000 of each, he saves about $5. But he uses an hour searching for the low price, plus $2 in phone calls. He is convinced he is a smart operator, but would soon be out of business if he netted no more than the $3 he gained from this hour's work. Another man regularly visits a client on the other side of town. He could drive his car there, but it would cost $2 to park. He could take a taxicab, but a round trip would cost $6. So he takes a bus. Total cost: $1. "A penny saved is a penny earned," he says. But he loses an hour's time—and $5 saved is $35 *not* earned.

You also will stop wasting employees' time. You will cut needless trips by your secretary to the bank or post office when you realize that it costs $2 or more every time she leaves the office. You will realize that you are not saving money when you send her to the luncheonette for a sandwich to avoid giving 50¢ to a delivery boy.

It gives you deadlines to meet. You know that you must produce work within a certain period in order to maintain or increase your average income. You have a continuing measurement of productivity, and you are less likely to procrastinate or dawdle when each task constitutes a separate challenge. Knowing how much time you have to complete a job introduces an element of gamesmanship into your work. If you finish it ahead of the allotted time, you have won a victory; if it takes longer than expected, you have suffered a loss. You develop the art of working under pressure and engage in a self-imposed search for improved techniques. You discover that Parkinson's Law works two ways. If "work expands to fill the time available for its completion," it also contracts when you allow less time in which to do it.

ORGANIZING TIME

With disciplined work habits, you can accomplish more per day than you may think possible. The following suggestions from time management consultants, if adhered to faithfully, can help you get as much as 50 percent more work done per hour—and accomplish more easily those things you consider most important:

Set up a "work priority schedule" every day. When you arrive at your office, list in order of importance the things you want to do. If possible, tackle the big jobs first, then other jobs in descending order. This may mean that for one day, or even a few days, much of your mail will go unopened and unanswered. Such delays rarely harm anyone.

Also list some fill-in jobs. If you finish early or it is impossible to complete a major job for various reasons, you should have additional work to fall back on.

If some jobs must be completed by the end of the week and you don't know how long they will take, get started early in the week. This is especially important if you will need the help or approval of someone else—a client, say—as the work progresses.

Leave some time free on your daily schedule to give yourself leeway for a sudden emergency or for tasks that require more than you thought they would. If you end up with free time, fill in with one of the extra tasks at the end of your schedule.

When you are working to meet a deadline, plan to be finished well beforehand. On almost any job you can expect to encounter snags, holdups, interruptions.

Choose for each job a time slot that matches the kind of energy you will have available. If you are like most people, your energy peaks during the morning hours. It begins to run down as noon approaches. Between the hours of 2:00 and 4:00 P.M., you reach a secondary energy peak. After that your energy curve turns down rapidly. Choose your peak energy hours for the most demanding tasks and assign the more routine jobs to low-energy times. For example, if you have to see salesmen, you might schedule their visits for the late afternoon when they are not likely to take much out of you.

Stick to your schedule. Do not allow yourself to be disturbed while concentrating on major problems. Refuse to take phone calls or see visitors unless they involve matters more serious than those with which you are dealing.

What if you can't escape interruptions and diversions?

"Whenever I try to concentrate on a job for a few hours my secretary asks how to do something," a designer complained to a management consultant. "Next thing, I'm helping her. Then I work all night to get my own work done. Any ideas?"

"Yes," came the reply. "Fire her. Get somebody to do the work without needing you to hold her hand."

Other self-employers constantly interfere with employees and discourage them from developing the self-reliance to work on their own. Remember that an office routine is not adequate unless it can function without you. If your office constantly draws you from your main tasks, find out why—and make changes. Your work, the work that produces the income for everyone, must always come first. If anything must suffer, let it be that which is less important to your success.

Keep track of how you spend each quarter-hour. Make up a time sheet divided into fifteen-minute segments. Write down everything you do in those time periods. Like the couple who record their expenditures to learn where their money goes, you may discover huge leakages of which you were not fully aware: prolonged phone conversations; more minutes spent chatting than you realized; excessive wastage doing tasks that others could do as well; too much time spent on jobs in proportion to income produced; excessive time on personal matters; drawn-out conferences and meetings. Keep the time sheet until you perceive definite patterns. When you know how your valuable time is wasted, you can more easily plug the leaks.

Avoid writing letters if you can. Have you any idea of what it costs to send a letter from your office? It almost always costs more than a phone call; usually, even more than a phone call from coast to coast. Here is how you can determine the actual cost of sending a letter from your office.

Use a stopwatch to track the amount of time required to think about what you are going to say, to call your secretary in and wait for her to take dictation, to do the actual dictating (along with the time required to spell out unfamiliar words), to read and correct the letters after they are typed, to reread the corrected letters, and finally to sign them.

A minute-by-minute account for even the shortest of letters—say a letter acknowledging receipt of materials—will probably look like this: your time—three minutes at 56¢ per minute ($1.68); your secretary's time—ten minutes at 11.4¢ per minute ($1.14); paper and postage—20¢. Total cost is $3.02, but most letters cost more. One recent survey showed the cost of sending the average length business letter is over $6.

If you make a test like this in your office, you will probably be astonished at the amount of valuable time dribbled away in hesitation over the right word to use, questioning the spelling of words, checking addresses, and the like. From a dollar-and-cents point of view, a telephone call will almost always be less expensive than a letter.

Not only are letters costly. They are the most unsatisfactory way of dealing with people. In a face-to-face or voice-to-voice meeting, you can explain an unclear point. If there is disagreement over terms of a deal, it may be settled at once. When negotiations are conducted by mail, several letters and interminable waiting for replies may be required to reach the same understanding. On the other hand, a phone call, particularly a long-distance call, usually gets immediate attention and decisions can be made at once.

If you must use the mails, do so efficiently. If you dictate letters, wait until all your day's work is finished before you dictate them so that you can go from one to the other without wasting your own or your secretary's time. If you can't avoid frequent interruptions, get a dictating machine so that one of you doesn't have to wait until the other is free. You may find that your most efficient dictating time is at night, when you can think quietly. Dictate into a machine and give the reel to your typist in the morning. Some people use battery-operated machines and dictate while driving.

Use form letters wherever possible. Label the most commonly used letters A, B, C, etc. When one is called for, simply indicate which one your secretary should use. When she types it with the personal salutation, it becomes an individualized letter.

Learn to dictate efficiently. Before you begin talking, have a clear idea of the purpose you want the letter to serve. Get to the point at once and stick to it. Remember that the reader's time is valuable too, and he probably dislikes long-winded oratory as much as you do.

Keep your reader in mind, as you would if you were trying to sell something. By putting yourself in his place, you will find yourself making the points most likely to appeal to him. Avoid literary language. Use natural expressions. Remember that your secretary doesn't know what words are coming next. So get into the habit of stating where you want commas and periods to go and new paragraphs to start. Also spell out unfamiliar names or words. Avoid such cumbersome language as "This will acknowledge receipt of your letter of the 12th inst., for which we thank you." Instead, say, "Thank you for your letter of May 12." Use active instead of passive verbs. "We understood" instead of "it was understood by us" is clearer, more direct, and saves money. Instead of saying "at the present time," say "now"; rather than "we are not in a position," say "we can't"; for "enclosed please find," substitute "enclosed is." Expressions such as "we beg to advise" and "the fact of the matter is" can be dropped entirely. No one will miss them.

If a plain yes or no answer will suffice, give it. You may often be able to scribble your reply on the letter you receive, making it necessary to type only an envelope. If you send out many such letters and need copies for your files, buy or rent a photocopying machine. Copy the original letter with your reply on it and file that.

If your mail volume justifies it, use mechanized equipment. Postage meter machines imprint stamps faster than they can be applied manually, do a neater job, and eliminate stamp loss or wastage. They provide an accurate record of your postal expenditures and, since the stamps are precanceled, they enable your mail to bypass some post office processes.

There are all sizes and kinds of postage meters. Postage meters must be leased and cost anywhere from $15 per month for a small meter to $200 per month for a meter and mailing machine unit capable of handling large volumes of mail. There is also a new kind of postage meter that doesn't have to be brought to the post office to be reset. These remote postage meters can be reset by telephone. You simply dial the number of a data center and your call goes on line to a computer, which issues you a series of code numbers. You key in these code numbers on your meter and the meter is automatically reset. Ever-increasing postage rates make a postage scale a must for most offices, particularly when packages of different sizes are mailed.

Mail early in the day, if possible. A letter deposited in a mailbox in the morning will usually reach its destination sooner than mail taken to the post office in the afternoon. If convenient, mail several times a day.

Use window envelopes when sending out bills. The debtor's name and address shows through the window when the bill is inserted. A second typing, and possible error in the name or address, is eliminated. You also eliminate the chance of bill and envelope having different names.

Keep your files simple. One office management expert maintains that small firms often overfile, placing papers in too many different folders. Often you can put everything connected with one subject in one folder and file it alphabetically. In this way you are certain of having everything in one place. It is easier to find the specific item you want (a letter, for example) in one folder than to try to remember what classification you stored it under. If a document placed in one folder might reasonably be sought in a second, slip a sheet of paper into the second folder stating where it may be found. Leaving a parking lot one day, a real estate agent's car was hit by another car driven by a man named Barnett. He wrote and received letters from Barnett, which he filed under the man's name. In case he might not remember the name when he had to, he placed a sheet in his "Insurance" file stating where the letters could be found.

Renew your files regularly and discard what you no longer need. Some persons maintain "present" and "past" files—the former for all papers within the past year or so, the latter for documents going farther back. If you have the space, this method enables you to throw out everything when it reaches a certain age.

Be sure, however, not to keep unnecessary records. Business owners usually keep too many records, often out of habit and with no current value. One advertising man still keeps a record of the number of resumes he gets each day from job hunters. He started ten years ago to see which way the wind was blowing in his industry. Business looked good to him when the supply of resumes dropped off; but the economy was turning sour when the number of resumes picked up significantly. He still can't stop keeping track of the job market despite the fact that in good times and bad he has been successful.

To beat the paper game, stop keeping all but the most vital records. Start by asking yourself: Will this record do me any good in the future? What will happen to me and my business if I don't keep this record? What is it costing in time to keep this record? Is the record worth the cost?

Set up automatic procedures wherever possible. As a rule, the more chores you do routinely, the less time you need spend on them. Handling receipts should be automatic. Every day, as you go through the mail, set aside cash and checks received. Enter them in your book of accounts, crediting the payer. Rubber-stamp the checks with the legend, "Deposit to the account of ————." Make out a deposit slip, with a carbon copy for your files. If only checks are to be deposited, you might mail them to the bank, a great time saver. If only a small amount of cash is received, it might be held for a weekly deposit. Perhaps the trip to the bank can combine withdrawals for payrolls or petty cash. However, do not keep large amounts of cash in your office overnight or on weekends.

Billing also can be routinized. If you have many slow-paying customers, type the first bill and make two photocopies. File the copies. If the bill is paid, take them out and throw them away. If not, take one file copy, stamp "Please Remit" on it, and send it out. Do the same with the second copy. Then begin your series of collection letters.

Once ordinary procedures are routinized, they are easier for everyone to follow. Moreover, they can be described on paper in

1-2-3 order and given to new or temporary employees, thus saving repeated explanations.

Resist the "tyranny of the telephone." Probably everybody has seen this happen: A business or professional man is "too busy" to see anyone personally. His telephone rings. He may not know who is calling, yet he drops what he is doing to answer. He acts as though some law requires him to do so. So many persons are like him that the ability of the ringing bell to interrupt even the most important activities has been given a name: "the tyranny of the telephone." (As noted above, that is why it is better for *you* to telephone when you can, rather than write.)

Answering phone calls while you are busy at other things takes more time than you may realize. Your train of thought is broken. You may lose time getting to the phone. An employee's time may be wasted while waiting for you to complete the conversation. If you must do something at once as a result of the call, more employee time may be lost. Or you may lose time making a note of what you must do later. Sometimes you realize you will have to spend a long time with your caller and tell him you will phone him later. Hence this particular call accomplishes nothing. More time is lost after you hang up, trying to remember what you were thinking about when the phone rang.

To be sure, phone calls should be answered, but *not necessarily by you.* Efficiency-minded corporation executives have their secretaries screen all calls, and if you have a secretary, you can do the same. Or you can have an answering service or automatic answering device take messages.

Set aside a certain daily period to spend at the phone. Instruct your secretary or answering service to tell callers you can be reached at that time. Plan to return calls then. In this way, interruptions to your other routines are minimized. Think about buying one of the many devices that let you keep hands free while using the phone. A gadget that cradles the receiver on your shoulder is inexpensive. Another device amplifies the other person's voice so that you need not hold the receiver to your ear. While waiting for calls to be completed (or when talking with the long-winded), you can perform routine tasks—signing letters, writing checks, making entries in account books, etc.

Some efficiency experts advise against making telephones too easy for employees to use. The worker with a phone on his desk may be inclined to use it to call his wife, girlfriend, stockbroker, or bookmaker. If he is comfortable while making even business calls, these experts say, he may be tempted to indulge in prolonged chitchat. If he must stand at a phone where others hear him, he won't use it so readily for personal calls or prolonged conversations.

Develop tactful ways of ending calls and interviews. One man who has many visitors tells them when they enter his office that he has another appointment in fifteen minutes; when he gives twenty minutes to them, instead of the thirty they might otherwise take, they feel flattered. Talking on the phone to a long-winded caller, this man cuts the conversation short because a long-distance caller is "waiting on his other line." Another man keeps an alarm clock on his desk. When it rings, he turns it off apologetically, but many visitors get the message. Another instructs his secretary to interrupt after a specified time and ask for a certain file. He rises to get it and doesn't sit again.

Organize your office to eliminate unnecessary steps. Keep within your reach, as you sit at your desk, *everything* you normally need: telephone, phone directory, books frequently consulted. The upper right-hand drawer of your desk is the easiest to reach; keep the things you use most there. The lower left-hand drawer takes the most time to use.

Visualize what distracts you and causes you to kill time—and correct the condition. One man often walked across his office to turn on the radio every hour for the news, then spent five minutes at the water cooler listening to it. He disconnected the radio and put it in a closet. Another man's desk was placed alongside a window. He was constantly distracted by occurrences on the street. He moved the desk and found it easier to concentrate. As long ago as 1911, Walter Scott, one of the first writers on increasing efficiency in business, commented that "the modern businessman is exhausted no more by his actual achievements than by the things which he is compelled to resist doing. . . . It is not the work that is hard; the strain comes in keeping other things at bay while completing the pressing duty."

Keep your desk clear and your wastebasket handy. Deal decisively with paper that comes to you. Otherwise you may pick up letters and memos half a dozen times before disposing of them. Use your wastebasket freely. "It's the most important thing in my office," a market analyst says. "Most stuff crossing my desk is worthless. It goes out at once. Other material I vaguely think I'll read sometime—but I know from experience I never will. That goes too. I keep and file a minimum of material. I think most stuff that people file they never need again."

Learn to change position while you work. Fatigue caused by sitting too long in one position will distract you—send you to the window, the water cooler, or the outer office. Get a chair designed for correct posture seating in which your weight is placed on the bottom of your thighs, not your spine. If you must work at your desk for a long period, remember the need to stand occasionally. You *can* work while standing and can even read while pacing the floor.

Watch the first and last hour of the day. Some persons procrastinate before settling down in the morning. Others wind down near the day's end. Get into the habit of forcing yourself to start. If necessary, continue something you started the day before so that you do not feel it a great effort to start something fresh. Or dispose of minor tasks requiring little effort in a conscious warm-up operation. If you tend to slow down late in the afternoon, schedule activities for then that will not take so much out of you. That may be the time to go over your books, dictate routine letters, or phone people who tried but failed to reach you earlier in the day.

Invest in labor-saving equipment. An electric typewriter can pay for itself in a secretary's time saved. To cut typing costs if you often need copies of bills, documents, etc., get a photocopying machine.

A telephone answering service is indispensable for many self-employed persons. It can insure that your phone will be covered at any hour of the day or night, that you won't miss income-producing opportunities while away from your office during business hours or at nights, on weekends, or during vacations.

Answering services now exist in most communities. Often they are set up by public stenographers seeking additional income. For the value of the service provided, rates are low, often no more than $2 a day for those who need coverage only during business hours. Around-the-clock charges are higher. The telephone company also may charge up to $9 a month plus installation for the connection that enables the answering service to hook into your line.

Calls handled by the answering services can be tailored to particular needs. In a common arrangement, the service operator waits until your phone rings four times. If you don't answer by then, she herself answers to take the caller's message or phone number so that you may call back.

A psychotherapist in Fair Lawn, New Jersey, lets his service answer even when he is in his office. When talking with a patient, he doesn't wish to be disturbed and his answering service answers after two rings. In this way, he knows if anyone is trying to reach him. He then calls back at the end of his fifty-minute appointment.

Another advantage of an answering service even during business hours: it protects you against unwanted calls. Some professional men claim that in this respect it is more effective than a personal secretary because it keeps unwanted callers from you in a way that doesn't offend them.

A host of automatic telephone answering systems are on the market—many for $200 or less. One unit uses cassette cartridges. When switched on, it answers your phone on the first ring, tells the caller you are out and asks him to leave his message. It then records his words. You can listen on an extension phone and cut in at any time to speak personally. This device is said to record up to 120 thirty-second messages that you may play back at your convenience. Distributors advertise it as "a low-cost answer to telephone pests" and says it will keep you from being annoyed by "crank calls at night, nuisance calls from salesmen, creditors, wrong numbers and people you don't wish to speak to."

An intercom system might be worth considering, even if your office is only two rooms. Simple units are available for $100 or less. Some have real time-saving potentialities. One man often had to have letters taken from files in the next office where his secretary sat. Usually he rose from his desk, walked to the next room, waited while she searched for the material, then returned to his seat. He often lost five minutes in the process. With an intercom, he requests the letters without leaving his desk and busies himself at other work until she brings them.

Don't buy labor-saving equipment blindly. A sad story of the recent recession concerned the businessman who bought a computer on an installment plan to help cut his bookkeeping costs. When business became bad and he had to retrench, he still had to pay hundreds of dollars per month for the mostly idle computer. "They told me I could save costs with that thing," he commented. "But they didn't tell me one thing—I couldn't fire it!" Many readers may sympathize with this businessman. Many devices offered to you *may* save labor, but *first* there must be enough labor to save.

How can you tell when equipment will pay for itself? The simplest way is to relate its cost per week to the value of time saved for the same period. Let's say you are thinking of buying a photocopying machine that will cost $2,000. You estimate its life at five years—a cost of $400 a year. (You must also figure what your $2,000 would earn if you didn't buy the machine. At only 12 percent, that's $240 a year in interest.) Your secretary earns $10,400 a year and could keep busy at other things if she no longer had to make copies of letters, reports, bills, etc. Her time is roughly worth 9¢ a minute. Would the copier save seventy-five minutes a week? If so, it might be a good investment. (Recalling the experience of the businessman with the computer, it is wise to *underestimate* the time these so-called labor savers can save.)

Assuming your assistant works a forty-hour week and gets two weeks off with pay each year, Table 1 will help you decide how many minutes per week a device must save in order to be self-paying.

SAVING TIME

I asked dozens of self-employers—professional men, real estate operators, insurance agents, professional writers, etc.—if they had developed any principles of their own to save time and increase productivity. Here are some of their answers.

• I never go any place personally if I can achieve the same effect by writing. I never write if I can achieve the same effect by phoning. I never phone if I can achieve the same effect by doing nothing.

• I learned long ago that most business conferences don't break up until they have to. One that starts at 10:00 A.M. *will* wind up when someone gets up to keep a luncheon appointment at noon, and so will the conference that starts at 11:00. So I schedule them as close to lunch or closing time as possible. I try to avoid drawn-out business lunches. If I *must* go to one, I schedule it as late as possible. It will break up when I or someone else has to keep an afternoon appointment.

Table 1

| Annual cost of equipment* | Minutes that must be saved per week if assistant's weekly salary is: | | | |
	$140	$160	$180	$200
$100	34	30	25	22
125	42.5	37.5	30.5	27
150	51	45	36.5	32.5
175	59.5	52.5	43	37.5
200	68	60	48	43
225	76.5	67.5	54	48
250	85	75	60	53.5
275	93.5	82.5	66	59
300	102	90	72	64
325	105	97	78	70
350	122	105	84	75

* Total cost divided by the number of years you expect labor saver to work efficiently.

• I always take on more work than I think I can handle. This way I am forced to think of ways to save my time. The work always gets done.

• I have a phone jack in my office. When I want to be alone I remove the phone from the jack. My answering service takes the message. When I have the time, I call back.

• If someone insists he must see me at once, I tell him I have other appointments later. I will say something like this: "Can it wait until tomorrow? I'll have more time then." Most people with problems prefer twenty minutes of today's time to an hour of tomorrow's.

• I schedule my "quiet working time" from about 11:30 to 2:30. Few people phone then, and my secretary tells those who do that I am out to lunch. I get more work done in those three hours than in the other five.

• I make many calls on businessmen and often must wait in their offices before seeing them. I always carry business reading matter with me, things I deliberately don't read when I could do something else. I also carry pad and paper with me and often use the time to write reports.

• I avoid like the plague mixing alcohol with business.

Chapter 8

The Art of Collecting
Overdue Bills

ALMOST every self-employer encounters problems in trying to collect money due him for goods sold or services performed. In every business operation you will find customers and clients who are inordinately slow in paying or don't intend to pay at all. Most experienced self-employers, in figuring their charges for goods or services, allow for the probability that a certain amount, in some cases up to 10 percent, of the bills they render will never be paid.

Collecting overdue accounts is perhaps a greater problem for the self-employed than for larger enterprises. Professional people—doctors, dentists, accountants, lawyers—are often last in line when bills are paid. Accounts of other small businessmen are also often neglected, even by corporate customers with plenty of money in the bank. Self-employed persons often lack the power to punish deadbeat customers. Unlike the electric utility, which can cut off power to the delinquent payer, or the telephone company, which can curtail his phone service, the self-employer usually provides goods or services that can be dispensed with, or that a competitor can offer just as readily. When interest rates are high and the debtor reasons he can use his cash more effectively elsewhere, the temptation to keep small creditors waiting is impossible for many to resist.

In self-defense, you must develop skills in getting your tardy customers to pay. Which approach will prove most effective, not only in getting the money owed you but also in helping you achieve your main commercial objectives, depends on five factors:

• *Size of amount owed.* A small sum, $5 or $6, is hardly worth the expense, time, and trouble of collecting it. The cost of a series of form letters or a telephone call is probably all you can afford. As the amount of the debt increases, so does the effort worth making to obtain payment. A $25 debt might warrant several phone calls, a $100 account a personal visit. An overdue account of several hundred dollars almost always warrants hiring a lawyer when you yourself fail to obtain payment.

• *Whether you want or need the customer's business.* When general business falls off, many self-employed persons report pronounced increases in the time customers take to pay bills. During a recessionary period, one woman who prepared a quarterly sales letter for a real estate management firm reported that whereas she used to be paid at once, she now was paid four months after doing the work. She relied on the firm's business and didn't want to jeopardize it, so she never complained. On the other hand, there is the case of a dentist with more patients than he wanted to handle. If a patient failed to pay within two months for services performed, he sent a firm letter requesting immediate payment. If another month passed without some payment, or an explanation why payment was not possible, he turned the bill over to a collection agency and refused to make new appointments for the delinquent.

• *Your power to enforce payment.* An independent contractor laid floor tile for the kitchens and playrooms of six houses in a development. When the builder withheld payment, the contractor obtained a "mechanic's lien." This made it impossible for the builder to transfer title to the houses until the bill was paid. The tile man had his money within two weeks. If a substantial sum is involved, you should consult your lawyer to find out whether there may be a similarly easy way to collect what is due you.

• *The effect on you—or him—of legal action.* The owner of a large travel agency with many branches is a notorious nonpayer of bills. All approaches fail but one, threatened legal action. He apparently feels that he can't afford publicity arising from a suit alleging failure to pay lawfully contracted obligations. Many who deal with him know that they won't get their money until their lawyer writes him a letter. Those who know him well follow their first bill to him by the lawyer's letter within a few weeks.

Once you sue a customer, however, you are unlikely to get the debtor's business again. (Of course, you may not want any of his business.) Delinquent bills usually reach this stage only if the customer is dissatisfied with the goods or services purchased or is in such financial straits that even a court order can't force him to pay. In any event, he may spread tales about you and your business to your present or prospective customers.

• *Alternate possibilities of collection.* If your debtor has goods or services that you want, consider accepting payment in trade. An architect drew plans for a clubhouse for a privately owned country club. When the job was completed, he collected all but $2,000 of the fee due him. The club owner said his cash was low and that the architect would have to wait a year for the rest. The latter decided to take up golf and deducted the membership fees from his bill. "Taking it out in trade" may be worth less to you than a cash payment, but it may be worth more than a full cash payment *less* cost of collecting it. An advertising agent vainly waited five months for a used car dealer to pay a $4,000 bill. Finally the agent agreed to take a used car as full payment. He went to another dealer on the other side of town and sold the car for $3,500. He estimated that the time, trouble, and legal expense of collecting the full amount would eat up more than the $500 loss he actually took.

Collection Techniques

Depending on the circumstances, these are the usual ways of getting customers to pay:

Collection letters. You may be able to buy a set of form letters, custom-tailored to the needs of your profession or trade, from your professional or trade association. Some private firms also sell "general purpose" collection letters that you may use. A typical professionally devised bill collection program consists of four letters, spaced three or four weeks apart, and always including a stamped or postage-paid envelope to encourage a prompt reply. The first letter is a gentle reminder that the bill is past due and that the creditor is sure that payment has slipped the debtor's mind. ("If the enclosed bill is incorrect, please let us know. In any event, may we hear from you soon?") The second letter suggests that the first one may have been misplaced but that the debtor will want to keep his credit standing high by paying at once. The third letter will convey the impression that you are losing your patience, and that soon, much as you regret it, you will have to take sterner measures to enforce payment. If this letter produces no results, you may want to send a fourth letter indicating your intention to turn the matter over to either your lawyer or a collection agency. A word of warning, however: It is illegal to threaten legal action unless you actually do plan to file suit if the customer doesn't pay.

Probably no collection letter should be sent out without considering how the recipient will react to it. So-called humorous approaches, unless handled in an expert way, may do more harm than good. Good results are rarely achieved by insults ("If I knew you were a deadbeat, I'd never have done business with you") or threats ("I'll make sure everybody knows about this"). Even if the customer pays, he may harbor resentments and refuse to deal with you later when you need his business.

You may be sued yourself if you try to collect too aggressively. You could be the defendant in a libel action, for example, if you "publish" accusations against the debtor's character or behavior. Such "publishing" might be using a postal card, sending a telegram, or engaging others to prepare dunning letters when they can read the accusation you are making. Likewise, telling others that your debtor is a "crook" is a slanderous statement and could lead to a damage action against you.

If you know your debtor personally and the sum is large enough, a personalized letter of the "Dear Jim" type may bring in the money. According to the professional collectors, the most effective letter apologizes for bringing the matter up, reassures the recipient that you believe he has overlooked the payment, and appeals to his sense of fair play by reminding him that you too have expenses that you can pay only if you are paid. If this letter produces no answer, a second one might suggest that the debtor phone you to discuss the matter personally. If the amount warrants it, you might phone him.

Phone Calls. The Small Business Administration, in a booklet discussing procedures to use in getting action on past-due accounts says that the telephone, when properly used, is the most convenient, the most practical, and the most inexpensive method of reaching a debtor. "In a matter of seconds," it says, "with a minimum of effort, personal contact can be made with the person you are calling. In many cases, the call will result in payment of the account. In many others, the call will be the opening wedge for successful collection." It continues:

> Talk as though the person were sitting just across the desk from you. Remember that when you talk to a person face to face, every word, gesture and change of expression helps to tell your story. In using a telephone, you must depend on your voice alone to express your personality and to accomplish the purpose of the call. Therefore, you should have a picture of the debtor in your mind before you make the call. Try to have enough information in front of you so you can form a mental picture of the person on the other end of the line. "Knowing" the person you're talking to improves the chances of doing a selling job.

The SBA says three important objectives may be accomplished by use of the telephone:

1. Immediate payment in full. The debtor may have honestly overlooked the bill and, upon being reminded, will pay immediately. Also, the psychology of a telephone call may result in immediate payment. However, don't press your demands too severely, for the debtor can easily hang up at any time.

2. Arrange for a personal interview. Getting the debtor into your office for a personal interview is often necessary and is not too difficult to accomplish on the phone. You are not making an unreasonable demand, for in your conversation you can explain (if appropriate) that you are hoping to help him solve his financial problems.

3. Follow up on accounts. Unfulfilled promises, missed pay-

ments, and other follow-ups are easily handled by phone. Just reminding the debtor will do the trick in many cases, for he will realize that you are carefully watching his account.

Here are other key points regarding telephone collecting:

A person will react favorably if you create a feeling of friendliness and goodwill.

If a debtor happens to be unreasonable or abusive, try to keep calm and relaxed. Try to keep your temper. An angry person can never deliver a sound argument.

Make certain that the person you are talking to is the one you intended to call. Have him identify himself. This can be done gracefully by merely saying "Is this George Doe of 122 Blank Street?" If he answers yes, try to get further identification to make certain that you are talking to the right member of the family. Then approach the heart of the matter.

Organize your thinking before picking up the telephone and plan what you want to say. Never create the impression that you don't know all the facts concerning the account.

Strive to get the debtor, on the phone, to agree to one of the following objectives:

• Immediate Payment. Many debtors are prepared to pay in full but try to hold out for easier terms. Some are experienced at this sort of thing and, unless you are firm, they may put you off. Partial payments are costly and should be avoided whenever possible. At the beginning of the call, make clear that you seek payment in *full*. Stick to your guns until it is obvious that another alternative must be accepted.

• Payment by Loan. If you become convinced that you cannot collect in full and the sum involved is large enough, discuss obtaining a loan for the debtor. With a loan, he can combine his obligations and reduce multiple accounts by making one payment only to the loan company.

• Payment by Installments. If you cannot do better, try to arrange for installment payments based on a promissory note. Most debtors will cooperate with an installment program. You should emphasize that this agreement must be carried out faithfully so as to avoid costly follow-ups later.

Before hanging up, be sure that your call has been completed in every respect, preferably with his commitment to pay at a certain time. If possible, avoid the necessity of calling back. This may irritate him and create an impression of inefficiency.

Conclude your conversation as soon as its purpose has been accomplished. An innocent remark at this stage may irritate him and undo the good you previously accomplished.

Face-to-face interviews. In most cases, if a phone call fails to produce results, you will probably decide that you can't afford to spend more time on the account and you will turn it over to a collection agency. In rare cases, however, the amount involved may be large enough to justify your trying to save the collection fee. Your next step would be to confront your debtor face to face.

According to the SBA, the personal interview is the most effective method of collecting past-due accounts. There are two types of personal interviews: the interview at your office and the interview at the debtor's home or office. The interview in your office has three advantages:

• When the debtor visits your office, he takes a first step toward payment. His presence means he is conscious of his obligation.

• You are on your own ground. You have all the information regarding the account on hand.

• It is less costly than an outside interview in both your time and your money.

When a debtor enters your office, he should be greeted in a friendly but businesslike manner. The typical debtor expects to be threatened and even humiliated. He often is grateful when treated in a courteous fashion.

The interview with him should be conducted in privacy, where it is easier to get him to concentrate on what you have to say about his problem. Payment in full should be your first objective here, too. Consider alternates only as a last resort.

If you can't persuade the debtor to come to your office, you may have to go to his office or home.

Just as you are in a stronger position when you interview him in your office because you are on home ground, he is on familiar ground at his home, so you will have stronger objections to overcome. If you talk to him at his place of business, he may be ill at ease and embarrassed and may try to conceal the real reason for your visit. Conduct the interview as quietly as you can. State your business quickly and try to bring the interview to a quick and successful conclusion.

Collection Services. As a rule, collection services are used after personal attempts to collect have failed but before you call in an attorney. Most collection offices charge a percentage of what they collect. Fees charged may range from 10 to 60 percent but often fall in the range of 33-1/3 to 50 percent. An agency may charge a certain fee for one account and a different fee for another. For instance, one agency charges 35 percent for accounts under six months old and over $50, and 50 percent for accounts over six months old and under $50.

Other agencies charge on a sliding scale based on the size of the account. The commercial collection division of Dun & Bradstreet, Inc., charges subscribers 24 percent of the first $2,000 and 20 percent of the outstanding balance above $2,000. Another firm, North American Commercial Credit Corp., for nonlitigation accounts, charges 50 percent of amounts of $75 and under and a flat fee of $37.50 for amounts between $75 and $150. For accounts above $150 it charges 25 percent of the first $2,000, 20 percent of the next $2,000, and 15 percent of any excess over $4,000.

Some agencies demand a minimum fee whether they collect any money or not. Others hold partial payments until an account is fully paid. Therefore, you may not get any money unless the account is paid in full. So, before hiring a service, find out about *all* its charges and practices.

You should also clarify your own attitude toward your debtors. Are they deadbeats you want nothing more to do with? Are some simply unable to pay without great sacrifice? Is your list of delinquents made up of some persons you might want to serve in the future? The collector works on a commission. Consequently, his sole interest is to collect. But the agency you choose should be willing to let you decide how tough or lenient to be with individual customers.

Sometimes collectors use bullying methods to collect and this may leave lasting resentment directed not against the collection service but *against the person who hired it.* Your image in the community won't be helped by such tactics and you may find the bad customers discouraging good ones from entering your doors.

Legal help. As soon as it becomes apparent that your own efforts won't succeed, and if the amount owed justifies the expense, ask your lawyer's advice about your next step. A competent lawyer will consider all feasible alternatives and will use the least expensive approach that promises to get results. He will be able to cite what various steps will cost. He may tell you flatly that to pursue the matter further will cost more than it is worth.

The lawyer will want to assure himself, by reviewing contracts, bills of sale, etc., that you have a sustainable claim. He will want to determine whether the debtor has made a false financial statement for the purpose of getting credit. If so, he may be prosecuted, even if the statement was made not to you directly but to a recognized credit agency. Your lawyer also will consider whether you are entitled to repossess an item sold. You may attach the debtor's property if it is in your state and he lives in another, if he has left the state and can't be found, or if there is strong evidence that he plans to flee, taking the unpaid property with him.

As this brief statement of possibilities indicates, the legal aspects can become highly complex. In all probability, unless you are a lawyer yourself, they are outside your range of competence. You can't be expected to make yourself an expert in questions that, one hopes, will arise only a few times during your career. If matters reach the point where you must consult a lawyer, let him proceed in the way he thinks best and do what he suggests.

HOW TO AVOID DELINQUENCIES

One of the best ways of avoiding delinquent accounts is to explain *fully* what your charges will be before you perform *any* services. It is always better to state the total amount of your charges at once, including all the services you intend to provide, rather than to quote separate amounts for separate services. Specifically ask your customer, client, or patient whether he has any questions about what your fee will be and whether he agrees to it. If the sum is large, discuss how you expect it to be paid, so much per month, for example. Later send him a letter, restating your fees and requesting that he get in touch with you if he understands otherwise. Many bills go unpaid because the debtor claims he was overcharged or did not agree to the amount billed. This procedure prevents such misunderstandings.

Chapter 9

Tax Specifics for Self-Employers

As LONG as you engage in more than "an isolated transaction" or a hobby, you can get income tax benefits for all expenses related to the operation of your profession, trade, or business. You need not *show* a profit, or even obtain an income, from your activities. All that is required is that you carry them on with the *intention* of getting an income or profit from them. (Despite a common belief, you can continue to show losses in your business indefinitely as long as you are running a bona fide operation. Certain activities which could also be hobbies, like farming and breeding cattle, are presumed to be engaged in "not for profit" if they show a loss for four out of any five consecutive years.)

With some exceptions, the same income tax *rules* apply whether you are a sole owner or yours is a partnership or corporation. Different tax *rates* apply, however. If you are a sole proprietor or member of a partnership, you pay the rates applicable to individuals. Corporation income ordinarily is taxed as corporation earnings. You pay a personal tax on your salary from the corporation as an employee, but your corporation deducts the salary on its own return. When its earnings are distributed to shareholders, they are taxed as dividends.

A *fundamental principle* is that payments you make for goods or services in connection with your business activities are *deductible. Not always, however.* If the services are "abnormal," or the outlays "excessive," the payments may be challenged.

According to the Internal Revenue Service, the burden of proof rests on you to show that "salaries, wages and other compensation or any other business expense, are ordinary and necessary expenditures directly connected with or pertaining to your trade or business." In determining whether compensation is reasonable, the relevant factors are the ability and achievements of the person performing the service, the importance of the work and amount of time required, and the rates prevailing in your community for similar services.

"The rule of reason prevails," a spokesman for the Treasury Department told me. "We don't pass judgment every time a self-employed person pays out money. These rules exist because some people try to beat the tax laws by making business expenditures for personal reasons." For example, a Missouri publicity man deducted $4,700 in one year for "special services" performed by his widowed, seventy-three-year-old aunt who, apart from Social Security, had no other source of income. Upon being questioned, the publicist said that her services consisted of secretarial work and occasional chores such as stuffing envelopes with publicity releases to be mailed to newspapers. Her lack of previous secretarial experience and the small amount of material mailed led IRS officials to conclude that the payments were gifts masquerading as wages. They knocked off $3,500 from his deduction.

THE BEST "TAX YEAR"

A new taxpayer may adopt either a calendar or a fiscal year for income tax purposes. Most persons compute income and expenses on a January 1–December 31 basis. Some use a year of fifty-two to fifty-three weeks; that is, a year that always ends on the same day of the week, such as the last Saturday of December. A fiscal year may begin and end at any time.

In any case, once you begin reporting income on a certain basis, you must continue to use that basis unless the IRS specifically allows you to change. Getting this permission involves making an application in triplicate and showing that you have a substantial business purpose for the change and won't gain significant tax advantage from it.

CASH RECEIPTS AND DISBURSEMENT METHOD

Although you are entitled to compute your taxable income under several different methods of accounting, individuals in business for themselves generally use the "cash receipts and disbursements" method. Under this method, you include in gross income all items of income you receive, or could receive, during the year. (That "could receive" phrase is discussed below.) With certain exceptions, you deduct your expenses in the year in which you pay them.

The rules are intended to prevent you from pushing income and expenses from one year to another for tax advantages. Let's say you have an exceptionally profitable year. You doubt that the next year will be equally successful. In the circumstances, you might try to spread your actual income over the two-year period; at the same time, you might incur and pay certain expenses to offset your high income and thus reduce your tax liability.

To try to prevent you from doing this, at least to some extent, the rules say you must report the income you *could* receive, or what is known as "constructive income." The IRS describes constructive income as "an amount credited to your account or set apart for you (even though it is not actually in your possession) so that it is subject to your control and you may draw upon it at any time. The amount must be available to you without any substantial limitation or restriction as to the time or manner of payment." One example of this form of income is a savings account with interest constantly accruing. From March to December you make no deposits or withdrawals and no interest payments are entered in your passbook for that period. Nevertheless, you *could* have taken the interest. Hence the interest is reportable in the year's income. Or suppose you receive checks this December paying for services rendered. You *may not* hold off depositing them until January in order to reduce your gross income for the preceding year.

On the other hand, if you can't put your hands on income— even potentially—during the year, you needn't include it. You may have no effective control over when your customers or clients pay, even though they owe you in December; this income is *not* reportable until you get it. For this reason, many creditors become unusually patient around the end of the year. They would just as soon you didn't pay them until January. They may even delay sending out bills so as to discourage payment until the next tax year.

A marketing consultant agreed to make a study for a record manufacturer to determine whether college-age youngsters would buy certain musical albums. The agreement called for him to be paid $10,000 in advance to defray research and travel expenses. The agreement was signed in November but stated, at the consultant's request, that the initial payment would not be made until January. Such agreements are acceptable to the IRS. Written into some book contracts is a proviso that, if the work becomes a bestseller, the author will receive no more than a certain amount in royalties in any given year. The idea is to spread income over a long period so as to reduce overall income tax payable.

As a rule, you are expected to deduct as expenses those attributable to the year in question. Suppose you take out a three-year insurance policy in April, effective May 1. You pay the entire premium in advance. For the first calendar year, you may deduct only 8/36 of the amount paid, because the insurance is in effect only eight months. The next year, you may deduct 12/36 of the amount, even though you make no actual cash outlay. Rent paid in advance on property used for business purposes is deductible only to the extent that it pays for occupancy for the tax year.

Many expenses *can* be moved from year to year to suit your convenience. For example, the cost of incidental supplies and materials for which no record of consumption is kept can be deducted in the year incurred. You find your stationery depleted; you can buy letterheads, envelopes, and other forms this year or next. Professional dues and subscriptions for business and professional journals can be paid in December or January and deducted in either year. Your office needs repainting; have it done and paid for late in one year or early in the next, depending on which gives you the maximum tax advantage. If you have a loan or other debts, you may deduct interest paid in advance for a period not longer than twelve months following the end of the current tax year, provided the deduction "does not give rise to a material distortion of income." Suppose you must pay state and federal income taxes; pay your state tax for the year in December instead of waiting until April; then deduct the payment from your federal tax return for the same year.

ACCRUAL METHOD

More complicated for the typical self-employer is the accrual method of accounting under which *all income is credited to the year in which it is earned* (*not* in which it is *paid for*). A doctor treats a patient in November and bills him in December but does not get paid until February. He doesn't receive payment during the year in which he renders service but nevertheless includes it as income. Similarly, if he buys office supplies in December but isn't billed until January, he includes the expense in the year in which he ordered the goods, not the year in which he paid for them.

OTHER METHODS

Special methods of accounting, such as one using the cash receipts and disbursements method and the accrual method for different business and personal activities, may be permitted if they accurately reflect income and outgo for the year. You probably shouldn't venture into these deep waters without the guidance of an accountant thoroughly familiar with the intricacies of the tax law.

BAD DEBTS

Most businesses, and self-employed business and professional men are no exception, must allow for the fact that they won't be paid in full for all the services they perform or goods they sell. Nevertheless, bad debts, accounts, and notes receivable that become partially or totally worthless may be deducted from gross income *only* if they have previously been included in income. If you use the cash method of accounting, you won't be entitled to a deduction for bad business debts because you will not have reported income from such goods or services. However, you are entitled to deduct the out-of-pocket expenses you have incurred in providing the goods and services for which you haven't been paid. In general, the writing off of bad debts primarily concerns businessmen using the accrual method. They may take a deduction for specific debts that become fully or partially worthless within the tax year; or they may be permitted to set up a reasonable reserve for bad debts based on the experience of themselves or others in their trade or business.

TAX ADVANTAGES OF WORKING AT HOME

One of the pluses many self-employers enjoy is the opportunity to make their office in their home. Savings in time alone can be tremendous. Someone who ordinarily works an eight-hour day away from home and spends two hours a day getting ready for work and commuting to and from it must realistically consider his full work day as ten hours. On the other hand, if you have a twenty-second walk from your living room to your home office, you save that travel time and increase your effective work day by 25 percent.

You also gain some tax advantage by working at home, provided you meet certain conditions. If you use your home office exclusively and regularly as your principal place of business, *or* maintain an office in your home where you regularly meet or deal with customers, clients, or patients in the ordinary course of business, you are entitled to take substantial deductions on your tax return. (Incidentally, the term *home* can apply to your actual dwelling place or a nearby structure such as a barn or guest house used as an office.)

The important thing to remember is that you must use your home office *exclusively* and *regularly* for business purposes: that means you can't use the room for any other purpose. A woman I know does medical typing in her home. She works every day from 9:00 A.M. to 2:00 P.M. in a corner of her dining room. She is not entitled to claim a business deduction for the use of this space, however, because she also uses the room to serve family dinners in the evenings and to entertain guests on weekends.

The room you use as your home office should be furnished with a desk, filing cabinets, typewriter, business phone, and any other equipment necessary for your work. Anything such as a sewing machine, couch, television, etc., that is kept in the room and is not essential for your business can cause the space to be disqualified as a home office should the IRS choose to investigate.

If your home office does qualify for a tax break, you then may deduct, on a proportionate basis, such items as interest on your mortgage, taxes, rent, utilities, and depreciation, as well as expenses directly related to your business. *However, your deductible expenses may not exceed your gross income from work in your home office and the expenses must be deducted from your income in the order prescribed by the IRS.* This is the order in which your expenses must be deducted:

1. Taxes, interest, and casualty losses (if any) allocable to the business portion of your home are deducted first. (These expenses would be deductible whether you have a business in your home or not.)

2. From the remaining balance of your income you then subtract business-related expenses. These expenses include a percentage of the operating expenses of your house (utilities, insurance, cleaning expenses, etc.) plus any expenses such as business phone and office supplies directly atributable to your business. You may also deduct certain other expenses on a pro rata basis. These deductible items are the cost of painting the outside of the house or repairing the roof and similar repairs that benefit the portion of your home used for income-producing purposes. You may deduct the full cost of painting and repairs to rooms used exclusively for business purposes, but you may not deduct costs of painting and repairs elsewhere. Nor may you deduct any part of the "purely personal expenses" of running a family household. Specifically ruled out as deductible items, too, are expenditures for lawn care, landscaping, etc.

3. Finally, a depreciation deduction for your home office may

then be subtracted from any balance of income that still remains.

You should maintain records that will provide the data necessary to compute properly the amount of the deduction. You should keep canceled checks, receipts, and other evidence of the expenses paid to substantiate the deductions claimed.

The following example shows how to figure your home office deduction.

Say you use one room in your home as your principal place of business and the room takes up one-fifth of the total area of the house. You can allocate 20 percent of your mortgage, interest, property taxes, and casualty losses to your business. Suppose your gross income that results from your use of this space amounts to $15,000, and interest and taxes that you pay on your home come to $3,000. You must subtract $600 (that is, 20 percent of $3,000) from $15,000. The resulting $14,400 is the ceiling on office-related expenses you can deduct.

If the operating expense of your home comes to $2,600, the portion attributable to your business will be $520 (20 percent of $2,600). To this figure, you add any expenses directly related to your business. Suppose these expenses amount to $800. Your total office-related expense is $1,320, which you subtract from $14,400. This reduces your income to $13,080. From this amount you then may subtract an amount for depreciation of the business portion of your home.

On the other hand, suppose you have an office downtown and use an office in your home to meet customers or clients at night. Say you can show that business income resulting from such meetings is $1,000. You still subtract $600, representing 20 percent of the taxes and interest. This leaves $400 as the ceiling on office-related business expenses you can deduct. If your office expenses come to $1,320, you may subtract only $400 of it.

Instead of determining the ratio of "business space" to total space by the number of rooms in your home, you may compare the square footage used in income-producing activities to total square footage in your home. You then allocate expenses accordingly.

What if you rent the house or apartment in which your home office is located? You don't make the first computation, which reduces the amount of your income by the amount a home owner deducts anyway for interest, taxes, etc., on his entire structure. You can deduct for home office-related expenses the entire amount of income generated by your office-at-home activities.

What constitutes *regular* work at home? If you produce income as a self-employer and have no other place of business, it is generally taken for granted that you use your home for that purpose. Additional evidence are a home phone connection in your business name, use of your home address in sending out and receiving business mail, or physical calls made at your home for business reasons. The fact that the office is the only one you have is generally sufficient proof, even if you spend most of your working hours away from it. A sales agent living outside Boston leaves home Monday morning and spends the week making calls in the New England and Middle Atlantic states. In one room of his home he keeps desk, files, reference materials, etc. He uses the room on weekends writing sales reports. His deduction has never been questioned.

You may be able to deduct home office costs even if you are self-employed only part-time. (You run a small operation in addition to working for someone else.) However, in order to do so you must be able to prove that you use the office regularly. Although the room is used for no other purpose, the IRS won't allow a deduction for "the incidental or occasional" trade or business use.

Even if you maintain an office elsewhere, you may still take a deduction for space used at home if you meet customers, patients, or clients there regularly. A psychologist who lives in Westchester County maintains an office in New York City. She regularly meets suburban patients in her home office. The IRS has never challenged her home office deduction.

Depreciation. (This subject will be dealt with in greater detail later in this chapter.) You may also take a *depreciation allowance* on that part of your home used professionally. First, you determine the fair market value of your home (exclusive of land) at the time you begin using your residence for such purposes. Next estimate "salvage value," the amount you think you would realize if you sold your home or otherwise disposed of it *when you*

expect to discontinue using it for business. Say you began your
self-employment using one-fourth of your home for business on
October 1, 1980. Your home less land had a realistic market value
of $60,000. You are now forty years old and intend to retire at
fifty-five, when comparable value you estimate will be $40,000.
Straight-line depreciation thus works out to $1,333 per year
(fifteen years divided into $20,000). Your annual depreciation
allowance is one-fourth of this, or $333.

Of course, if you later sell your house, for tax purposes you
must consider your cost as the price paid less the amounts
deducted for depreciation. If the price you get exceeds your cost,
you may face a tax liability at that time.

LOCAL TRAVEL EXPENSES

All your local travel expenses, with one exception, are deductible when incurred in connection with your self-employed activities. These deductible costs embrace all expenses of operating and
maintaining your automobile and also train, bus, taxicab, and
airplane fares. The one use you can't make a deduction for is that
of traveling between your home and regular place of business. A
management consultant living in Brewster, New York, rents office
space in New York City, thirty miles away, where he receives his
business mail and has a telephone answering service. He can't
deduct the cost of cabs from his home to the railroad station, of
his monthly commutation ticket, or of cab fares from the New
York station to his office. During the day, however, he often uses
taxis to visit clients; these costs can be deducted.

If you use your automobile solely for business purposes, all
out-of-pocket expenses for its operation, and also a depreciation
allowance, may be deducted. Pro rata deductions must be taken if
you use your car partly for business and partly for pleasure. Thus
you must determine the total cost of your car for the year and the
mileage percentage of business use. Dr. David Wise, a pediatrician I know, keeps a small daily record book in the glove com-
partment of his car. He notes the mileage when he begins and
ends his professional calls for the day. At the end of the year, he
thus has a record of business mileage to compare with the total

car mileage. Of the 30,000 miles he drives each year, roughly 20,000 are devoted to his medical practice. Hence he is entitled to deduct two-thirds of all operating costs.

Depreciation. Since Dr. Wise uses his car for business purposes all year long, he also may deduct two-thirds of the depreciation cost for the year. The covering rule here is that a depreciation deduction must be based on the number of months the car is available for business use (even if it is not used for that purpose) and the ratio between the business and total mileage during the period. Let's say you use your car for business ten months of the year. During July and August, your wife uses it at your summer home, and you use buses or taxis when you make professional calls. You would be allowed a business depreciation allowance on your car for only ten-twelfths, or five-sixths, of the year. On the other hand, suppose you become ill and are hospitalized for the same two months. If you were well, you would use the car; hence it is "available for business use." You take the full business percentage of depreciation for the full year.

Standard Deduction. Many self-employers find it simpler and often to their financial advantage to take a *standard deduction* for the number of miles driven for business purposes, rather than to compute actual expenses and depreciation. Presently, you are permitted a standard rate of 20¢ a mile for the first 15,000 miles of business usage during your tax year and 11¢ for each additional business mile. This rate applies to panel and pickup trucks as well as to automobiles. To use the standard mileage rate, you must use only one car at one time (you can change your car) for business purposes; own the car and not rent it out to anyone; not operate a fleet of two or more cars in your business; not have claimed depreciation using any method other than the straight-line method; and not have claimed additional first-year depreciation on the car. In practice, some small, low-priced cars cost less than 20¢ per mile to operate, particularly when driven more than 15,000 miles a year. You may take the full deduction even though it is greater than your actual cost. In addition, you may deduct all parking fees and tolls incurred during business use.

If you use more than one car for business purposes on an "alternate" basis (for example, car A most of the time but car B on occasion), you may add the total mileage driven for business purposes on the cars and deduct the standard mileage rate. Ed Pollack, an appraiser in the Baltimore-Washington area, generally drives a small sports car when making business calls. Sometimes, he must drive several persons to conferences. Then he uses the family's five-passenger car. At the end of one year, he drove his small car 12,000 miles and his large car 4,000. He was entitled to deduct $3,110 (15,000 miles at 20¢ per mile and 1,000 miles at 11¢)—the amount he would have driven one car the same number of miles.

You are not permitted to use the standard mileage rate if in a previous year or years you used the declining balance method in depreciating your car, a method that allows you to deduct a larger sum during the early part of the car's life.

But suppose that within one tax year you sell car A, on which you may not now take the standard mileage rate, and buy car B? You may compute your deduction for car A on the old basis and car B on the new basis, but you subtract car A's mileage for the year from the 15,000 miles for which you can deduct 20¢ a mile. Let's assume you sell your old car in April, having driven 6,000 miles in connection with your business. You drive your new car 18,000 miles on business. Your standard mileage deduction for the second car is $2,790; $1,800 for 9,000 miles (15,000 less 6,000) at 20¢ a mile and $990 for the remaining 9,000 (18,000 less 9,000) miles at 11¢ a mile.

Interest, Taxes. If you use your car partly for personal travel and itemize your deductions, you must list on Schedule A of Form 1040 only that part of the interest, taxes, etc., in connection with the car that is not claimed elsewhere on your return. However, if you use the standard mileage rate to compute the cost of operating your car and you itemize your deductions, you may still deduct on Schedule A the cost of interest and taxes paid in connection with the purchase of the car.

ENTERTAINMENT

Sums you spend on "entertaining for business purposes" are deductible, *provided* you adhere to certain principles. First, the expenses must be substantiated, you must keep adequate records, and you must be able to prove you actually incurred them. Second, what you spend must be "directly related to" or "associated with" the running of your business as those terms are defined by the IRS.

Deductions for business entertaining are one of the most often-contested items on the income tax returns of self-employed persons. "This is one area where we find a great deal of padding," a revenue agent told me. "But we try to be reasonable. It's usually only the excessive deductions that we disallow."

Whether or not your deductions for entertaining are legitimate depends to a large extent on your business. For example, a retail sales representative for a greeting card company, whose usual sale rarely exceeds $30, could hardly claim a deduction for entertaining prospects at a nightclub where the bill amounts to $100 each. On the other hand, as an advertising consultant seeking a $10,000 assignment, you would probably have no trouble defending $200 spent entertaining the man who could give you such a job. A New York woman, an investment counselor, deducts almost all her entertainment expenses for theaters and dinners; she has successfully proved that virtually every one is or could be a client. Generally, she spends no more than $25 on any individual, however, if she tried to deduct $100 spent to land an account paying only that much in fees, the claim probably would be disallowed.

IRS regulations state that entertainment includes "any activity generally considered to constitute entertainment, amusement, or recreation." This covers paying for guests at places such as theaters, sporting events, restaurants, and nightclubs, and on hunting or fishing trips. Depending on the specifics, it may include entertaining at country clubs and on yachts, or paying for a vacation. Says the IRS: "It may also include satisfying the personal, living, or family needs of any individual, the cost of which would otherwise be a business expense to you, such as the furnishing of food and beverage, a hotel suite, or an automobile to a business customer or his family."

In addition to proving that the person or persons you entertain *could* provide a "specific business benefit" to justify your expenditure, you must be able to show that the expense was incurred to advance your professional interests and that you "did engage in business during the entertainment period with the person being entertained," or that a substantial and bona fide business discussion took place immediately preceding or following the entertainment.

Of course, the IRS doesn't monitor conversations between you and your existing or expected prospects. As a practical matter, it is satisfied if business *could* be discussed during the entertainment session. Hence the IRS mainly wants to know whether the person you entertain *could* help enough in business to justify the expenditure. Meals bought for persons whose goodwill is professionally important to you are rarely disallowed as a legitimate business expense.

The person being entertained need not be a potentially direct source of income. He could be a source of information that benefits you. For example, in doing research for this chapter, I bought several lunches for experts on insurance, accounting, law, and taxes. They gave me much information and were particularly helpful in interpreting various aspects of self-employers' problems. They will not provide income to me directly, but without this expert assistance it would have been extremely difficult, if not impossible, to write this chapter with assurance. Since I obtained a "specific business benefit," the sums spent on lunches in this case are certainly deductible.

Nor need the effort to advance your business interests be successful. An architect, hearing that an acquaintance planned an addition to his store, invited the man to lunch with hopes of drawing the plans. At lunch, the prospective client announced that he had already given the job to his wife's nephew. Nevertheless, the architect had a legitimate deduction. I have often entertained persons in hopes of obtaining information that could be used in books or magazine articles. Sometimes the information proved useful and sometimes not, but the IRS hasn't questioned that my intention was to further my business interests.

How does one determine whether business will be considered the main purpose of the entertaining? This, too, is a question about which hard and fast rules have proved difficult to draw.

Officially, the IRS states only that more time need not be devoted to business than to entertainment, but that the "business discussion" must be more than incidental. In practice, *where* the entertaining occurs may determine whether the deduction for expenses will be allowed.

Some places are considered "clear business settings." A commercial artist worked almost exclusively for beauty shop operators. When they held a convention at a local hotel, he rented a "hospitality room" with a well-stocked bar where he displayed some of his work. His deductions for this expense have never been questioned. The IRS cites the case of a Californian who invited local celebrities—the community's congressman, assemblyman, and other political leaders; local clergymen and prominent businessmen—to a cocktail party to mark the opening of his art gallery. He had never personally met most of his guests before and was unlikely to receive their patronage in the future. Yet he clearly stood to gain by sponsoring the event. By creating publicity, he attracted the attention of potential patrons.

Revenue men put nighttime entertaining in a neutral zone. It could be a business setting; then again, maybe not. A package designer took a customer to a nightclub featuring loud and continuous rock music. His deduction was disallowed on the grounds (which he sheepishly admitted upon questioning) that it was impossible to discuss business matters seriously under such circumstances. The IRS also takes the position, when entertaining is done in certain settings, that the burden rests on the taxpayer of proving business was the primary purpose. In this category are hunting and fishing expeditions, trips on yachts and similar pleasure boats, and other situations where, an IRS official told me, "it's difficult to visualize persons carrying on a meaningful business discussion." On this basis, deductions for entertaining at theaters, sporting events such as football games, and cocktail lounges are often disallowed. While admitting that opportunities exist for long business conversations on the golf course, the IRS may also insist on some evidence that business was in fact discussed.

Entertainment expenses "associated" with the operation of your business, even when not "directly related" to it, may be deducted if the entertainment precedes or follows a "substantial and bona fide business discussion." In the general interpretation, entertainment on the same day as the business discussion is considered "associated" with it.

A professional labor negotiator from Arizona came to New York to sign a contract to help a chemical corporation in its contract discussions in the Southwest. His wife accompanied him. After a two-hour discussion in the corporate vice-president's office, the two men and their wives met for dinner and attended a play. The Arizonan paid all expenses and later deducted them. He was within his rights; under such circumstances it would be impractical to entertain the customer without their wives.

A similarly reasonable attitude prevails in determining when deductible entertainment expenses may be tied in with bona fide business discussions. A building contractor and his wife came to New York on a Tuesday evening before catching a plane for Paris the next afternoon. His insurance agent and his wife entertained them Tuesday night, and the two men held a business discussion Wednesday morning. Even though the discussion did not occur on the same day as the entertainment and lasted only five minutes, the agent received authorization to continue certain liability policies for another year, so all entertainment expenses were deductible. In cases such as these, I was told, "All that is required is a reasonable explanation of why the entertaining and business discussion couldn't take place on the same day."

While entertaining the wives of those in a business relationship is generally a deductible item, entertaining other persons may not be. A direct mail consultant for a jewelry manufacturer located in Brooklyn invited the head of the firm and his wife to dinner when they attended a convention in Miami Beach. The customer said he would like to accept the invitation, except that his wife's friend was with them. "Bring her along," the publicist said. The cost of the friend's meal was *not* deductible. Her connection with the business relationship was too remote.

What about entertaining done in your home? You may deduct such expenses if the expenses are commercially and not socially motivated. "Reasonable" deductions for business entertaining at home probably won't be contested, I was told. When the deductions are large there may be a greater requirement to prove that the guests had a business rather than a social connection and that an opportunity existed to achieve a business or professional advantage.

To deduct the cost of a country club membership, you must be able to show that you used the club more than 50 percent of the time for business purposes on a day-to-day basis. If you pass this "primary use test" (the number of days you use the club for business is more than half the total number of days you use the facility), you are entitled to deduct an amount for dues proportionate to the percentage of days you used the club for entertainment "directly related to the active conduct of your business." In other words, if you do goodwill entertaining at your club, you can use the number of days of goodwill entertaining to figure the total number of days of business use. However, you may not use goodwill entertaining in figuring the proportion of dues that you may deduct.

Suppose you belong to a country club and used the facility a total of one hundred days last year: thirty days for business meals, ten days for other entertainment directly related to the conduct of your business, fifteen days for goodwill entertaining, and forty-five days for personal use. Since you used the club fifty-five days (55 percent of the time) for business, you would be entitled to deduct a portion of your dues as a business expense, but the amount you could deduct would be only 40 percent—the percentage of days when the entertainment was directly related to the active conduct of business.

If you use your club less than 50 percent of the time for business, you can't deduct any part of your dues, but you still can deduct out-of-pocket expenses incurred during business entertaining. Club initiation fees that extend beyond one year are not deductible in either case.

Dues for other social and athletic clubs are deductible on the same percentage-of-use principle. However, membership in certain clubs is accepted as business-connected. Actual use for that purpose need not be proved in order to deduct dues or fees paid to them. These clubs include Kiwanis, Rotary, and similar businessmen's groups, and professional associations that hold regular luncheon meetings.

Business deductions for the cost of maintaining entertainment facilities such as hunting or ski lodges, fishing camps, etc., are no longer allowed. If you entertain at such facilities and can prove that the entertainment is for business purposes, you may take a business deduction only for out-of-pocket expenses for such items as food, drinks, or services. Any interest, tax, or casualty loss on such a facility would be deducted on your personal return under general interest, tax, or loss items.

GIFTS

Business gifts made directly or indirectly to any one person are allowed to the extent that their total yearly cost is $25 or less. Suppose you do some work for a client you know to be a music lover. You wish to give him a Christmas gift. You send him records worth $25. You also send an equivalent amount of records to his wife. Is the second gift deductible? No. For purposes of this regulation, "one person" includes his wife and children unless his wife also has a business relationship with you.

Certain items are not regarded as gifts and may be given in addition to items costing no more than $25. "Promotion items" such as pens, desk sets, attache cases, and books with your name clearly imprinted that you distribute in quantity and that cost you no more than $4 each; and signs, display racks, or other material that will promote your services and are intended to be displayed by the recipient.

If you give a present or prospective customer or client tickets to an event like a baseball game, play, or concert and do *not* accompany him, the tickets *are* considered gifts. However, if you accompany him and discuss business matters with him, you may deduct the cost as entertainment expense. In that case, you may also give him something not exceeding $25 in cost during the year and deduct that expense as well.

You may deduct any amount of bonuses paid to employees if you intend them as additional compensation for services actually rendered. You may pay the bonuses in cash or property (a wristwatch for doing a good job in handling your affairs during your vacation, let's say) as long as the total paid doesn't exceed "what would represent reasonable compensation for services rendered." These are considered as wages, as are cash, gift certificates, and similar items that can easily be converted into cash. Hence you must withhold federal income taxes and deduct Social Security taxes on them.

Regarded as "gifts," the value of which aren't considered salary or wages to your employees, are items of merchandise you distribute on special occasions—the bottle of perfume you give your secretary at Christmas, for instance. The value of such gifts to any one person must be limited to $25 a year to permit you to deduct for them fully as a business expense.

PROMOTION

In order to deduct sums spent on advertising and promotion, you need only show that they are not excessively expensive in terms of what you hope to gain, that they can be reasonably expected to help you professionally, and that they are not intended to promote or defeat legislation. This covers most of the promotional expenses you will probably incur.

Included, of course, are direct advertisements in your local newspaper, in trade or professional journals whose subscribers could use your products or service, and on radio and television. Included is the usual institutional or goodwill advertising intended to keep your name before the public; paying for a program of your local public educational television station that may mention your name only at its beginning and end falls into this category. Also deductible as an advertising expense are amounts paid for ads encouraging contributions to the Red Cross and similar organizations; the only requirement is that the name of the firm under which you do business be mentioned as the sponsor. When the teenage club of his church sponsored a summer dance and solicited advertisements for a souvenir program, a lawyer paid for a full page with the notation "compliments of a friend." In view of his anonymity, he could not claim the $60 outlay as an advertisement. However, he could claim a gift deduction.

You may deduct the full amount of reasonable outlays for publicity, even if the publicity you pay for never materializes. A woman who started a small roommate-matching agency in New York hired as her publicity agent a friend who promised to place stories about the shop in *The New York Times* and the New York *Daily News*. Despite several attempts, not a line about the shop was published anywhere. Nevertheless the $600 paid by the matchmaker was an allowance expense. It was paid in good faith; there was a reasonable expectation of success; and had a story appeared in either newspaper, the value to the owner probably would have been greater than the cost.

INSURANCE PREMIUMS

You are entitled to deduct as a business expense premiums paid on all insurance bought to protect you against business-related hazards.

Deductible premiums include premiums paid on fire, theft, flood, and other casualty insurance; merchandise and inventory insurance premiums; credit insurance premiums paid on insurance to protect you against losses resulting from nonpayment of debts owed your business; liability insurance to protect you in the event of accidents to your employees or customers for which you may be held responsible; group hospitalization and medical insurance premiums you pay for your employees.

You also may take deductions for state unemployment insurance fund contributions for employees; for premiums paid on "employee performance bonds" to protect you against theft, embezzlement, or similar offenses by persons working for you; and for premiums paid for insurance covering damages from accidents involving automobiles and other vehicles. When the automobile is operated partly for business, you are entitled to deduct the portion of your premiums attributable to the business use.

Amounts paid on policies that will reimburse you for loss of income resulting from sickness or disability are *not* deductible; nor are the proceeds from such policies regarded as income. However, you may deduct premiums paid on policies that will reimburse you for business overhead expenses incurred during prolonged periods of disability due to injury or sickness.

Premiums paid on your own life insurance policies are considered personal expenses and are *not* deductible. In the case of partnership and keyman insurance, you may *not* deduct premiums if you are directly or indirectly a beneficiary under the policy.

Fringe benefits to employees, as we have seen, are generally deductible as business expenses as long as they stay within "the test of reason." Hence you may deduct premiums paid on life insurance policies for employees, provided you are not the direct or indirect beneficiary. Also deductible are group hospitalization and medical care premiums for employees; Medicare premiums; payments made under wage continuation, accident, or health plans that make payments to your employees while they are away from work due to sickness or injury; and amounts paid to employees directly because of sickness or injuries beyond the amounts compensated for by insurance or otherwise. When you work for your own corporation, you are considered its employee, and thus you are entitled to all the fringe benefits other employees get.

EDUCATION EXPENSES

If you would like to improve your education or the education of your employees, you can go about it in a couple of ways that also give you tax benefits. The two basic systems approved by the Internal Revenue Service differ in several respects. Each has its advantages and disadvantages. By examining both systems, you can find which one best meets your needs.

One system—which has had IRS approval longer—limits deductible education expenses to expenditures made to maintain or improve business skills. It is available to you or to anyone in your employ without the need for a formal education plan for all your employees.

The other system—available since 1979—doesn't limit deductible education expenses to courses connected with a person's present business. However, it does require you to offer educational assistance to all your employees without discrimination.

If you don't have a formal educational plan for your employees, you can deduct education expenses for yourself and any employees you choose to aid under the older system. In this case, tax rules covering amounts spent to educate yourself in a trade or profession make a subtle distinction. You may not deduct educational expenses incurred to meet the minimum requirements of your trade, business, or profession, or to qualify for a new trade, business, or profession. Once established in a profession, however, you may deduct expenses for education designed to maintain or improve your skills.

Some permitted deductions can be substantial. The IRS cites the case of a psychiatrist in private practice who wishes to practice psychoanalysis. He begins a lengthy program of study and training at an accredited psychoanalytic institute. The study and training "maintain or improve skills required in his profession and do not qualify him for a new one." Hence he is entitled to deduct the $10,000 or so such a program costs. In another case, a self-employed accountant decides it would be advantageous to acquire more expertise in federal taxation. He enrolls in university courses in taxation and tax accounting and incurs a deductible expense. On the other hand, a young college graduate, dissatisfied with the income from a tree surgery service he has established, begins to study law at night. *No* deduction is allowed; a different profession is involved.

Only expenses related to your *current employment* are deductible. Example: A registered nurse who works in the homes of patients on specific assignments quits her practice after her first child is born. When the child enters high school, she decides to resume her professional career. However, many changes have taken place in nursing practice in fourteen years and she decides to take several refresher courses before accepting new assignments. The official ruling would be that her expenses are not deductible if incurred before she reenters her profession; they would be if she resumed her practice first.

You do not lose your right to deduct educational expenses if you take only a "temporary" leave. (The IRS will accept a leave of absence as "temporary" leave if it can be established that the worker fully intended to return to work after a specified period at the time at which his or her self-employment ceased.) If the nurse in the example above had returned to work within a year or so after her child's birth, she could have deducted for the refresher courses even if they were taken before she accepted new assignments.

Also nondeductible are expenses necessary to *enter* a business. You may not deduct bar examination fees and incidental expenses in securing admission to the bar, medical and dental license fees paid to obtain a first license; accounting certificate fees paid to obtain the right to practice accounting.

Under the newer system, if you are an employer and have a formal employee education plan, the education needn't be job-related to be deductible. Moreover, benefits an employee receives aren't included in his gross income. Hence they are always tax-free. But the new system does impose certain restrictions on the employer.

If you want to offer an educational assistance program to your employees, you must put the plan into writing and notify all eligible employees about its availability and terms. The plan can't be part of a cafeteria-style benefit program that would allow an employee who doesn't want educational assistance to select, say, a dental plan instead.

And the plan can't discriminate in favor of some employees. Owners, officers of the company, and highly paid employees and their dependents must not receive preferred treatment. Indeed, no more than 5 percent of the educational assistance funds can be paid or incurred for the benefit of anyone who, on any one day of the year, owns more than 5 percent of the stock, capital, or profits interest in the company.

That 5 percent rule applies to assistance paid or incurred, not merely available. It is not enough to offer the assistance to all your employees. A good many of them must use it if the top members of the company also hope to do so.

A plan won't be considered discriminatory if you pay more for one type of education than for another or if one class of employees takes advantage of the educational assistance more than another class. It's OK to pay more for a college education than for a course in barbering, and it's OK if more office workers than factory workers use the educational assistance. As long as you offer the plan to your employees on equal terms and you follow the 5 percent rule for owners, officers, and stockholders, the plan will pass the IRS test.

Nor will it be deemed discriminatory if you pay the educational expenses only if the employee completes a particular course successfully. Just make sure you tell your employees about that provision in the written notification you give them.

You don't need advance approval from the IRS for an educational assistance plan. Nor does the IRS require that your plan be funded.

What about your own education? If your business is incorporated, you are considered an employee of your company even if you are the president or some other officer. As an employee, you are eligible to take advantage of the employee educational assistance program. But make sure you observe the 5-percent nondiscrimination rule. If you are self-employed, you are also considered an employee, for purposes of this program and you can set up and take advantage of an employee educational assistance plan.

What is covered. Educational assistance payments are deductible for tuition, fees, books, supplies, equipment, and similar items. It doesn't matter whether you reimburse the employee before or after he completes the course or whether you pay the educational institution directly. The employee doesn't even have to attend a formal institution. He can get his education from a tutor or even from you or an employee you direct to instruct him. In any case, the educational expenses are deductible.

An employee education plan doesn't allow you to take some deductions that are available when you simply deduct job-related education costs as ordinary and necessary business expenses.

For example, an educational assistance plan doesn't cover meals, lodging, or transportation expenses, even though they are incurred in the pursuit of an education. Nor does the plan allow you to deduct costs of any tools or supplies the student-employee can keep after he completes the course.

Finally, you can't deduct the costs of any education involving sports, games, or hobbies. You can't take a course to learn how to ski and then deduct its cost—unless you can show that skiing is part of your business and that the ability to ski is necessary. If you own a ski lodge, you can take a deduction for skiing lessons, but if you own a horse ranch far from any mountains, skiing lessons aren't deductible.

Educational assistance deductions are available only to the employer. The employee may not take any deductions.

For the purposes of this program, the owner of a sole proprietorship is considered the employer and an employee. That may sound schizophrenic, but it satisfies the IRS and makes it possible for the self-employed to qualify for the program. The same schizophrenic aspect applies to partnerships: a partnership is considered the employer of the partners, and the partners are considered employees of the partnership.

To claim the deductions under an educational assistance plan, you need only include the costs as ordinary and necessary business expenses. You are saved the bother of including the expenditures in your employees' W-2 forms, since the reimbursements are not considered wages and are not taxable.

Naturally, the tax-free aspect of educational assistance benefits appeals greatly to employees who want to take courses that don't meet the rigid deductibility rules of the old system. If that employee is you, the appeal is immediately apparent.

Another point: if you want to take advantage of an employee educational assistance plan, do it soon. The plan, which became effective for the tax year beginning after 1978, is temporary. Unless present law is extended, it will go out of existence at the end of 1983.

All expenses necessary or desirable to help you keep up to date on developments in your profession, trade, or business qualify as deductible items. These include memberships in professional societies (the American Medical Association, the Society of Real Estate Appraisers); memberships in civic or community groups from which obvious business or professional benefits can be derived; subscriptions to professional journals (the *Journal of Accountancy*); subscriptions to business or trade publications (the *Financial Analysts Journal*); books, (such as this one) intended to help you achieve greater expertise in your craft; and professional equipment, such as date and ledger books, that can be used less than one year. You may not deduct the full cost of equipment such as typewriters, adding machines, or other specialized machinery used in your occupation with a useful life of more than a year. This cost must be depreciated; only a certain amount may be deducted each year until the value of the equipment is written off, less salvage value.

LONG DISTANCE TRAVEL

You are permitted to deduct "ordinary and necessary" expenses of travel away from your place of business overnight, whether in the United States or abroad, if you can establish that the purpose was to advance your business interests. A basic consideration: such expenses shouldn't be lavish or extravagant relative to the benefits you expect.

Travel expenses include virtually all ordinary outlays of travelers away from home: airplane, railroad, and bus fares; charges for extra baggage; costs of shipping sample cases, display materials, or similar items; meals and lodging en route and at your destination; the cost of transportation from the airport or station to your hotel, from your hotel to the airport or station, from one place of business to another; cleaning and laundry, telephone and telegraph expenses; cost of a public stenographer or other person needed to help you in your business affairs; tips related to any of the above expenses.

A vital point is that many travel expenses are allowable *only* if you travel from your "tax home"—the entire city or general area in which your principal place of business is located, regardless of where your family residence is. (If you have more than one office, your principal place of business is the one at which you spend more time and/or from which you get more income than any of the others.) On occasion, a self-employed person may deduct travel expenses for overnight lodgings even though he is close to his family residence. An artists' representative lives in Norwalk, Connecticut, but maintains his "tax home," or main place of business, in New York City. Sometimes he stays overnight in Hartford, two hours from his office but less than an hour from his home. These overnight expenses are deductible. The IRS position is that "you are away from home overnight if your business activities require you to be away from your tax home substantially longer than for an ordinary day's work and it is reasonable for you to need and get sleep or rest during released time while away in order to meet the requirements of your business. You need not be away from your tax home for an entire twenty-four-hour day or from dusk to dawn, as long as your relief from duty during your absence is of sufficient period of time to get necessary sleep or rest."

The main point in deciding if an expense is deductible is that it should be related to your business. If your trip is primarily for pleasure, you can't deduct your travel expenses, even if you do see a client while you are away. Similarly, travel expenses connected with your attendance at a convention can't be deducted unless you can show that it was intended to advance business interests.

What if you combine pleasure with business on your trip? If the trip is primarily for pleasure (such as sight-seeing or enjoying warm weather), the cost of traveling to and from your destination may not be allowed. You may deduct only expenses incurred at your destination that are properly attributable to your trade or business.

But if your trip is primarily related to your business and you make a few side trips for pleasure, travel costs and other living expenses *are* deductible; not deductible are expenses related to the nonbusiness activities.

Expenses incurred in attending conventions pertinent to your profession are generally deductible. The agenda of the convention is what is important: if it is related to your career and its responsibilities, the IRS will accept your statement that you attended for business purposes. However, you can't deduct for incidental personal expenses at the convention city, such as those for sight-seeing, social visiting, etc.

The IRS cites as a nondeductible item the attendance at a meeting of the International Law Association by a lawyer from Akron, Ohio, whose practice is confined to domestic law. Although the lawyer was appointed a delegate to the convention and was interested in international affairs for several years, his deduction was disallowed because he does not practice this branch of law and the meeting's agenda offers nothing to contribute to his proficiency as an Akron lawyer.

If you want to deduct your wife's expenses while attending a convention, she must serve a bona fide business purpose. A man who writes and distributes an investment newsletter went to a meeting of bankers at Coral Gables, Florida, and set up an entertainment suite at a hotel where he sought to enroll subscribers. His wife ran various errands and served drinks when the suite became crowded. A deduction for her travel and lodging expenses was disallowed because she did not perform a "substantial" service.

In another case, a lawyer went from Richmond, Virginia, to

San Francisco to negotiate a contract for the purchase of a large frozen food locker. His wife, who had had previous secretarial experience, made business appointments for him, took notes during the discussions, typed the final contract, and witnessed the signing. Despite the fact that this couple spent a weekend and their evenings sight-seeing, the lawyer successfully deducted the wife's travel expenses.

When you travel on business and your wife goes along as an associate not required for business reasons, it often is financially advisable to drive your automobile rather than use public transportation. You may deduct the *total* cost of operating your automobile to and from your destination, but only *your own* airplane, train, or bus fare. Only *your* costs for meals are deductible, of course. However, you may deduct the cost of a single room, which is generally much more than half the cost of a double room. A room for two might cost $96 while a comparable room for one costs $72. You deduct the $72; the nondeductible part of the bill amounts to only $24.

Rules governing deductible travel outside the states and the District of Columbia are somewhat stricter. In addition to proving that the trip was made primarily for business, you must establish *one* of these five things:

• A personal vacation wasn't your main reason for going.
• You had no substantial control over arranging the trip. For example, a client asked you to represent him at a convention; contract negotiations had to be carried out; a prospective customer asked that you visit him to discuss a large order. Because you could decide *when* to go does not indicate control; the basic question is whether business prudence dictated that you make the trip.
• You were outside the United States for a week or less. You do not count the day of your departure as a day, but the day of return is counted.
• You spent less than 25 percent of your total time outside the United States on nonbusiness activities. Let's say you flew from Denver to Hong Kong. You spent twenty-one "business days" in Hong Kong and took a three-day sight-seeing vacation in Japan. You are permitted to deduct the travel expenses you would have incurred if you had not engaged in any personal activity. Thus

you may deduct plane fare to and from Hong Kong and costs of meals and lodgings, etc. Since the stopover was incidental to the Hong Kong trip and didn't involve additional plane fare, the only nondeductible items are those for your day-to-day living expenses in Japan and those associated with your private activities.

• Your employee who traveled outside the United States was not related to you and was not a managing executive.

What is a "business day?" The ruling is that it is any day you must be in a certain place for a bona fide business purpose, even if no business is transacted due to circumstances beyond your control. Example: You travel to London to see a client. When you arrive, he is too busy to see you for a few days. The days spent waiting are "business days," even though you use your time visiting the London Museum, Shakespeare's birthplace, and the alleged home of Sherlock Holmes. Similarly, costs of meals and lodgings on weekends between bona fide "business days" are deductible.

If your foreign travel does not meet at least one of the above conditions, you will probably have to allocate your travel expenses between business and nonbusiness activities.

In this case, the portion of travel expense you may take as a business deduction is figured by making a ratio of the number of business days to the total days outside the country and multiplying the cost of travel to your business destination by this ratio. Both the day you leave the country and the day you return are figured as days out of the country for purposes of allocating expenses.

For instance, suppose you live in New York and fly to Paris to conduct business. Your round-trip travel expense to Paris is $2,500 and you spend five days there on business matters. Then you fly to England for a vacation and nine days later return to the United States. The portion of your travel expense to Paris that would be allocable as a business deduction would be 5/14 times $2,500, or $892.86. The cost of meals, lodging, and other business expenses while in Paris is also a deductible business expense provided it is not lavish or extravagant.

If your foreign travel is primarily for the purpose of a vacation and any business activity is incidental to the vacation, you are not allowed a deduction for travel expenses.

When you travel for business—in this country or abroad—the IRS insists that you keep detailed records of your travel expenses. If you estimate or approximate expenses, the IRS can disallow your travel expense deductions, even if you were traveling for valid business reasons.

While you are traveling, keep a diary or account book and list your expenses, properly categorized, each day. Also keep receipts and similar documents. It is essential that you have a receipt or paid bill for every expenditure of $25 or more, except local transportation costs.

If you are audited, you must be able to prove the following elements about your travel expenses:

• Amount of each separate expenditure for transportation, lodging and meals. You may group together incidental expenses such as taxis and telephone calls.

• Dates of departure and return for each trip and the number of days attributed to business activities.

• Destination by name of city or other appropriate name.

• Business reason for your travel or the nature of the business benefit derived or expected to be derived. Travel expenses incurred for the purpose of seeking a new location for your business or for a new plant or branch aren't deductible as travel expenses. The IRS instructs you to capitalize them and add them to the cost of the new plant. Again, it's a matter of definition.

MOVING EXPENSES

If you move to a new residence because you transfer your place of work, you may be able to deduct your moving costs. To qualify for these deductions, you must meet two tests.

First, your new place of work must be at least thirty-five miles farther from your former home than was your former place of work, "the place where you spend most of your working time." Say your former business address was three miles from your old home. Your new business address must be at least thirty-eight miles from your old home. The distance between the two points, says the IRS, is measured by the "shortest of the more commonly traveled routes between the points."

This minimum distance requirement doesn't apply to the location of your new residence (unless, of course, you work at home). It does not matter if your new residence is less than 35 miles from your old residence.

There is also a time test. As a self-employed person, you may deduct moving expenses if, during the twenty-four-month period immediately following your arrival at the new principal place of work, you perform services on a full-time basis during at least seventy-eight weeks. Moreover, at least thirty-nine of those weeks must occur within twelve months after you arrive at the new place of work. The IRS defines a self-employed person as "one who performs personal services as the owner of an entire interest in an unincorporated trade or business, or as a partner in a partnership carrying on a trade or business." It says that "whether a self-employed person performs services full-time depends upon the customary practices of his occupation." This full-time work requirement can be waived only if the taxpayer can't satisfy it because of death, disability, or "involuntary separation from work."

Here are the deductible moving expenses if you pass the distance and time tests:

• Travel expenses (including meals and lodging) for yourself and your family while en route from your old to new residence. (Your family includes members of your household who had your residence as their principal place of abode before the move. A servant, governess, chauffeur, nurse, valet, or personal attendant is *not* a member of your family.)

• Cost of moving household goods and personal effects of both you and members of your family. This includes actual transportation or hauling from your old residence to your new one, cost of packing and crating, in-transit storage, and insurance. You may deduct expenses of moving household goods and personal effects from a place other than your old residence only if they don't exceed what it would have cost to move them from your old residence.

• Cost of shipping your automobile to your new residence.

• Cost of premove househunting trips (travel, meals, and lodging) and the cost of temporary quarters (both meals and lodging) for up to thirty consecutive days, but *only* if you have already made substantial arrangements" to begin work at a new location (signed a lease for an office, say).

If you use your automobile to transport yourself, family, or goods to your new home, you may compute expenses by deducting actual out-of-pocket expenses such as gasoline, oil, repairs, etc. (but not depreciation), if you keep an accurate record of each expenditure; or you may deduct 9¢ per mile plus tolls and parking fees instead of the actual costs if you verify the mileage traveled.

"Expenses must be reasonable," the IRS warns. "Expenses in excess of a reasonable amount (determined by the circumstances of the particular move) may not be deducted. In general, the cost of traveling from your old residence to your new one should be by the shortest, most direct route available by conventional means of transportation." The move should be within one year from the time you first begin working at your new place of business. If it doesn't take place within that time, the expenses ordinarily will not be deductible.

The deduction for expenses of househunting trips, temporary quarters, and selling your residence is limited to $3,000 overall, of which no more than $1,500 may be for househunting trips and temporary quarters. Married persons filing separate returns are limited to $1,500 overall and $750 for househunting and temporary quarters on each return.

You may not deduct as moving expenses any loss on the sale of your residence, prepayments of rent, security deposits, fix-up expenses to help you sell your old residence, any real estate taxes, any payments that represent interest, any portion of the purchase price of the new residence, charges for utilities, expenses of refitting rugs or draperies, the cost of auto tags and a driver's license that may be required by the state of your new residence, losses sustained on the disposal of memberships in clubs, tuition fees, and similar indirectly related expenses. (You may be able to deduct some of these items in other places on your return, however.)

CASUALTY LOSSES

Most casualty losses (the complete or partial destruction of property resulting from a sudden, unexpected, or unusual event like an accident, fire, flood, or burglary) are deductible in whole or part. Whereas a casualty loss on property used for personal purposes is deductible only to the extent that it exceeds $100, the loss on property used for business is deductible *in full*.

You must be able to prove (1) that you actually sustained the loss and (2) that the amount lost is what you claim. The IRS may want to know these things: the nature of the casualty and where it happened or when the theft was discovered; proof that you owned the property; what you paid for it (you may have to show receipts or canceled checks for the purchase price and improvements that have raised its value); how much you may have depreciated the property; its worth before the casualty or theft and its worth now; how much will be recovered from your insurance company. Photographs will help in establishing your credibility: photos before the accident (if you have them); photos after the accident showing the extent of damage; photos after repairs have been made, to indicate the extent of work required to restore the property to its previous condition.

What happens if you suffer a casualty or theft loss on property used partly for business and partly for pleasure? You must take into account the percentage of usage for each purpose. For simplicity's sake, say that your car has been demolished and now is worthless. It had a current value of $8,000 and you used it on a fifty-fifty basis. You deduct $4,000 as a business loss and $3,900 (the actual loss minus the $100 deductible) as a personal loss.

CHARITY DEDUCTIONS

While tax advantages aren't the driving force behind charitable contributions, they perhaps encourage people to give more than they would otherwise. Because charitable contributions are usually tax deductible, the government in effect subsidizes part of the contribution, and the higher your tax bracket, the more of each contribution will come from government coffers. If you and your spouse filed a joint return for 1980 showing a taxable income of $20,200, a $100 contribution actually cost you only $72. Put another way, the $100 contribution saved you $24 in federal taxes. If your joint taxable income was $85,600, it cost you only

$46 to give $100. Additionally, state income taxes will further reduce the net cost of the donation.

As a sole proprietor or partner, you may deduct contributions to most charities up to 50 percent of your adjusted gross income. Charities in this category include most organizations exempt as charitable, religious, educational, scientific, or literary organizations; churches or associations of churches; tax-exempt educational organizations with a regular faculty, course of study, and student body attending classes; tax-exempt hospitals; certain organizations engaged in continuous medical research in connection with these hospitals; and publicly supported organizations created to prevent cruelty to children or animals. You may deduct no more than 20 percent of adjusted gross income for contributions to certain other organizations, mainly private foundations, and no more than 30 percent of adjusted gross income if you contribute appreciated securities or other intangible personal property and real estate held long-term.

Specifically included in the 50-percent category are war veterans' organizations, auxiliary units, and trusts or foundations organized in the United States or any of its possessions; nonprofit cemetery companies if the funds are irrevocably dedicated to the perpetual care of the cemetery as a whole; and civil defense organizations created under federal, state, or local law. Organizations qualified to accept deductible contributions also include the Salvation Army, YM(W)CA and YM(W)HA, the Red Cross, United Funds and Community Chests, Boy Scouts and Campfire Girls, Police Boys Clubs, and such organizations as the Heart Association and Multiple Sclerosis Society. When soliciting funds, most qualified organizations will let you know the extent to which you may make a deductible contribution. Local IRS offices also maintain lists of organizations qualified to receive deductible gifts.

If you pay more than the fair market value to a qualified organization for merchandise or other goods, only the amount in excess of value is deductible. A fraternal organization such as the Elks sponsors a dinner party and will send needy boys to summer camp with the net proceeds. Tickets are $30 at a restaurant that normally charges $15 for a similar meal. Only $15 is deductible.

Robert Crasden, a New York accountant who helps many self-employed professionals file their income tax returns, told me that a commonly overlooked deduction is one for *out-of-pocket expenses* incurred when doing work for charitable organizations without pay. Professional men and small businessmen are often asked to give free services to such organizations. A financial consultant is asked to join his church board of trustees and advise on its budget problems. A commercial artist is asked to draw posters and prepare advertisements for the local association for mental health. An interior decorator is asked to decorate a church hall for its annual Christmas party. Although you can't deduct the value of your time or service on your tax return, you can deduct incidental expenses such as expenditures for gas and oil incurred in operation of a car. At the request of the Lighthouse, a charitable organization for the blind, an insurance claims adjuster regularly drives several sightless persons to meetings. He may deduct his automobile expenses in one of two ways; figure actual outlays for gas and oil or take a standard deduction of 9¢ per mile plus tolls and parking fees.

A woman who ran a dancing school was asked to phone a long list of persons in her city to ask if they would solicit from house to house for the Community Chest. She made hundreds of calls before enough persons volunteered. She was not reimbursed for the calls. She could deduct them. Also deductible are the cost and upkeep of uniforms worn while performing donated services but not useful to you at other times.

You can deduct reasonable costs of food and lodging if you travel on behalf of a charity and are too far from home to return at night. A tax deduction is also allowed for the cost of certain items such as stamps, stationery, and other supplies related to volunteer services. Additionally, your expenses in operating your equipment for charity are deductible, but overhead expenses— insurance and depreciation, rental value of the equipment, etc.— aren't allowed.

Long-term gains on real estate and intangible property offer substantial tax benefits to the contributor. When you donate to charity either appreciated real property or intangibles such as securities you have held longer than a year, you can deduct the full market value of the gift and escape taxes on the gain. Let's say that four years ago you bought stock worth $4,000 and now it is worth $12,000. If you give that stock to a qualified charity, you get a $12,000 tax deduction and you don't pay taxes on your $8,000 gain.

Tangible personal property held long-term falls into a different category. The tax law places restrictions on charitable gifts of artwork, jewelry, fixtures, equipment, and other tangible property held over a year. If you donate this kind of property to a philanthropy that plans to use your gift to further its charitable purpose, you can deduct the gift's fair market value. Suppose you donate a painting appraised at $1,000 to a museum. You are entitled to a $1,000 tax deduction. But if the nonprofit organization sells the gift or can't use it to carry out its tax-exempt function, you must reduce your deduction by 40 percent of the appreciation.

From a tax standpoint, therefore, it is prudent to give tangible, appreciated property to organizations that can use it to carry out their charitable work.

You usually must pay income taxes at your ordinary, personal rate on any profits you make when you sell property you have held less than a year. If you give such property to charity, you avoid these taxes but get no deduction for the appreciated amount. If you donate securities you bought six months ago for $2,000 and now worth $5,000, you pay no taxes on the $3,000 gain—but you can take only a $2,000 deduction. When possible, it is advisable to hold appreciated property for a year before contributing it so you can deduct its market value.

The rules on property held short-term also cover other kinds of property that yield ordinary income when sold. These include inventory, farm crops, works of art the donor created, and letters and memoranda the donor prepared. If you donate a statue you sculpted, you can deduct only the cost of the clay, glazing, etc.— not what the statue is worth in the marketplace.

It generally doesn't pay to donate intangible property or real estate that is worth less than you paid for it. You can only deduct the fair market value, and you lose a deduction you could otherwise take on your capital loss. If you bought stock for $8,000 and it is now worth $2,000, you will get only a $2,000 deduction by giving the stock to charity. You are better off selling the stock for $2,000, getting a $6,000 loss deduction, then donating the $2,000 in cash to charity.

But tangible property that has dropped in value, such as used equipment and furniture, won't produce a loss deduction if sold. There is no advantage to selling it if you plan to give the proceeds to charity. You do as well by giving the items directly to a charity that can use them. You will get a deduction for fair market value.

Another way to make a contribution, aside from an outright gift, is to sell property to a charity for less than its fair market value. When you do this, you are entitled to a deduction equaling the difference between the market value and the sale price. Say you bought land for $2,000 that is now worth $8,000. If you sell it to a charity for $2,000, you can take a $6,000 deduction.

However, the law requires you to pay taxes on part of the gain. To figure what this tax will amount to, you divide your cost for the property between the part you sell and the part you donate.

To calculate how much of your cost applies to the sale, divide the sale price by the fair market value and multiply the resulting percentage by the cost of the property. Say you sell a charity that piece of land that cost $2,000 and is now worth $8,000. We arrive at this calculation:

$$\frac{\$2,000}{\$8,000} = 25\% \times \$2,000 = \$500$$

By subtracting your final figure ($500) from the sale price ($2,000) you arrive at your taxable gain, in this case $1,500.

If you sell the same property to charity for $4,000, the equation reads:

$$\frac{\$4,000}{\$8,000} = 50\% \times \$2,000 = \$1,000$$

Since your sale price here is $4,000, your taxable gain is $3,000.

Restrictions on donations of property also apply to bargain sales. Say you bought securities for $6,000 eight months ago; they are now worth $11,000 and you sell them to a charity for $6,000. You get no tax deduction at all because for property held short-term you are allowed to deduct only what it cost you.

If you name a charity as the beneficiary of your life insurance policy, you get a deduction for the current value of the policy. You can also deduct future payments on the policy as you make them. Once you make this move, the charity—not you—is the owner of the policy. You lose the right to change the beneficiary.

NONDEDUCTIBLE ITEMS

You may not deduct fines and penalties levied because you violated federal or state laws. You may not deduct payments that "frustrate public policy." For example, deductions for purposes that violate the law (such as for the purchase, sale, or giving away of alcoholic beverages in communities where it is prohibited) are usually not allowed. And you may not deduct kickback payments if "they violate any state or federal law or regulation or are not otherwise ordinary and necessary business expenses within the meaning of the Internal Revenue laws." In some states, for example, it is unlawful to give, or offer to give, anything of value to an employee without his employer's knowledge and consent with the idea of influencing the employee's action in relation to his employer's affairs. Federal laws prohibit kickbacks to federal employees.

Determining what constitutes ordinary and necessary business expenses under this regulation can involve tortuous reasoning. A businessman paid a kickback to an officer of a bank for the latter's help in obtaining a loan. The payment was "under the table." Top management of the bank neither knew nor approved of the payment. No law was violated and the loan was used for legitimate purposes, yet the Treasury Department ruled that it was not deductible because it was not "ordinary"; that is, it was not normal, usual, or customary. (If *everyone* kicked back to the loan officer, it apparently would be deductible!)

While you may not deduct for kickback payments under the circumstances described, the law states that you must file an Information Return with the federal government on anyone to whom you paid $600 or more during your tax year.

Reciprocal entertaining, whereby one person entertains one or several others, and the latter then entertain him, for the purpose of claiming a business deduction, is not a deductible expense in the eyes of the IRS. "In a business relationship, generally one person is the client of the other," an official of the Service told me. "When two or more persons take turns entertaining each other, it strongly suggests the absence of the customer-client relationship and the lack of strong business reasons for the expense involved."

You may not deduct expenses involved in the investigation of a new business. Such expenses (perhaps including the cost of traveling to different cities, hiring consultants, paying legal, accounting, and appraisal fees) are *not* deductible because the IRS reasons that you weren't in the trade or business when the expenditures were made. The nondeductibility of these preliminary expenses applies whether you are starting your own business or profession or taking over an established one.

The cost of investigative expenses can be added to the total costs of the business you start or acquire, however. If you later sell the business at a profit, you pay no tax on the amount of investigation expenses recovered. If you sell at a loss, you add these expenses to the rest of your outlays and offer the total against other income, if possible.

Bear in mind a distinction in the rules regarding deductions for clothing. Generally, you may not deduct the cost and maintenance of work clothing if it's something like Levis that are commonly worn on the street. But if your occupation calls for special apparel or equipment (uniforms of doctors, dentists, nurses; theatrical clothing worn by professional musicians and entertainers only at work), you may subtract their expense from your income. Costs of special protective clothing (safety shoes, helmets, work gloves) also are deductible.

THREE COMMON WAYS TO COMPUTE DEPRECIATION

In order to determine how much to deduct to compensate you for the declining value of your "plant and equipment," you must know how to depreciate them. Any method of computing depreciation that is reasonable and applied consistently may be used. Three common methods are straight line (the simplest), declining balance, and sum of the years-digits.

Under the straight line method, you deduct the cost or other basis of the property, less its salvage value, in equal annual amounts over the period of its estimated useful life.

Under the declining balance method, you take a larger depreciation deduction for the first year you own the property and a gradually smaller deduction each succeeding year until it's written off to its salvage value. The depreciation you take each year is deducted from the cost or other basis before computing the next year's depreciation. The rate of depreciation remains the same, but the amount of depreciation decreases.

Within limits, the depreciation rate used under this method may be twice or one and a half times as great as the rate used under the straight line method. You may use twice the straight line rate on tangible property having a useful life of three years or more that is bought new or is constructed, reconstructed, or erected by you or on your behalf. Suppose you buy a new machine costing $2,400 with an expected life of ten years. The straight line rate of depreciation is 10 percent. Under the declining balance method, your depreciation allowance for the first year is $480, or 20 percent of $2,400. Next year, your depreciation allowance will be $384 or 20 percent of $1,920—the written-down value of the machine after the first year's allowance is deducted. You may deduct one and a half times the straight line rate on the cost of tangible property having a useful life of three years or more that is bought used.

Under the sum of the years-digits method, you generally apply a different fraction each year to the cost or other basis of each single asset account reduced by the straight line rate. This method may be used only if the property meets the test for the estimated salvage value. The lower part of the fraction is the total value of the digits representing the estimated useful life of the property. Say that you buy a machine estimated to last six years. The sums of these years—one, two, three, four, five, and six—give the total of twenty-one. (Another way to determine this figure is to square the useful life, in this case 36 [six times six]. Next add the years of useful life, another six [forty-two], and divide by two. Result: twenty-one.) The upper part of the fraction represents the useful years left for the property at the start of the year for which the computation is made. On your machine, these useful years would be six for the first year, five for the second, four for the third, and so on. Hence, for the first year you could deduct 6/21 of the value of your machine, less its salvage value; for the second year, 5/21 of the depreciated value less salvage value, and so on.

Depreciation rates vary, and income tax regulations are subject to change. Hence you should consult your accountant before making a major purchase of equipment so as to gain the maximum tax benefit. Under certain circumstances, you may change from the declining balance method to the straight-line method (or back to the declining balance method), with written approval of the IRS. The procedures are complicated and had best be left for your accountant to handle.

In figuring depreciation on office equipment and other assets used to produce income, you must first determine the estimated useful life of the asset under consideration. You then determine its salvage value—its worth at the end of that period. If the salvage value is estimated to be 10 percent or less of the cost of property with a useful life of three years or more, you can ignore it and base your depreciation on the full purchase price. If the salvage value on such property is more than 10 percent, you may disregard up to 10 percent of the salvage value in computing the cost basis on which you depreciate the asset.

The decline in value of the asset represents the *amount* you will be able to deduct on your tax return. The useful lifetime of the asset represents the *number of years* over which the deductions must be taken. To some extent you can estimate the useful lifetime of your asset to further your own tax interests— shortening it if you wish quick deductions, lengthening it if deductions against high tax brackets in later years will produce greater tax savings.

The Treasury Department publishes guidelines that give the useful lives of different categories of property eligible for depreciation. These guidelines need not be followed exactly. But they give you a good idea of the useful lifetimes the Treasury Department considers "realistic."

In the opinion of many business owners, the guidelines understate life expectancies to begin with. According to the Treasury, the usual useful lifetime of an automobile is only three years. If you choose, you may write it off in as little as two and a half years or as long as three and a half years. Office furniture, fixtures, and equipment like desks and files are assigned a normal "useful life" of ten to twelve years. Typewriters, calculators, adding and accounting machines, photocopiers, and similar equipment are estimated to last six years, give or take a year. Light trucks (such as delivery vehicles) may be depreciated over lifetimes of three to five years (the guideline figure is four). Heavy trucks with an unloaded weight of 13,000 pounds or more are allowed a rapid depreciation period of five years, a slow one of seven, and a normal one of six.

If your own experiences differ from the average in the use of any business property, you may make your own estimate of its useful life and depreciate it on that basis. A manufacturer's representative, touring the western states, ran up 90,000 miles on his car each year and figured its useful life at only one and one-half years instead of the commonly allowed three years. A physician who used his car solely to make infrequent house calls in a large city, might estimate its useful life at eight years.

The IRS gives broad leeway to the taxpayer. In estimating useful life you are expected to consider your own experiences with similar equipment, how often you use it, your maintenance and repair policy, special weather conditions that may affect its performance, and similar factors. You will have no problems getting the IRS to accept estimates falling within its depreciation guidelines. When the amounts involved are substantial, you may have to submit evidence to support estimates that fall outside normal limits.

A simpler way of reaching an agreement with the IRS over the expected useful life of your property entails the "Class Life System." It enables you to lump your purchases and give them a blanket treatment. You must use the Treasury's Asset Depreciation Range, but you may choose a useful life for each group of assets between the lower and upper limits permitted.

You may elect the Class Life method for any tax year. You do so by filing Form 4832 along with tax return for the year in question. You must include all eligible property you have placed into service during the year. Each year, you must also file a report showing any changes in the account—property sold, etc.—that would affect your depreciation deduction. For tax purposes you treat all assets in the account as part of the whole and ordinarily don't claim a gain or loss on sale or disposal of any individual item until the account is closed out.

With the Class Life system, you must compute depreciation on the straight-line, declining balance, or sum of the years-digits methods. These are the methods most commonly used by business owners. Other methods that are allowed when regular depreciation procedures are followed—such as one that permits twice the straight-line rate under certain circumstances—may not be used. Once you set up a Class Life account for a year's property acquisitions—a "vintage year"—you may make limited changes in your use of methods. You may move from the declining balance to the sum of the years-digits methods. But once you begin depreciating by the straight-line method, you must adhere to it.

Note that when you elect to use the Class Life system for a tax year, you must include all eligible property placed into service during that year. If you wish, you may disregard the Class Life system in setting up depreciation formulas in succeeding years.

To reduce the possibility of disagreements with taxpayers, the IRS publishes depreciation ranges for various industries. Assets used in the printing, publishing, and allied industries (typesetting equipment, presses, etc.) are assigned a normal useful lifetime of eleven years. Taxpayers in this group may assign as few as nine or as many as thirteen years for such assets. Equipment in most manufacturing fields is assigned a normal lifetime of about twelve years. Equipment in cement manufacturing is estimated to last twenty years; that used in the production of motor vehicles, with their frequent model changes, is given a life of only three years.

What happens if property is fully depreciated down to its salvage value but still has plenty of useful life? Of course, you are no longer entitled to depreciation deductions. If you sell the item for more than the stated salvage value you have estimated for it, you report the excess received as income. In effect, this is money you have already deducted on your tax return.

Estimating how long your business property will last is just that—a guess. While you are guessing, you might as well guess in the direction that does you the most good. The IRS stresses, however, that estimates must be "reasonable."

It may often be unwise to assign too short a life to your depreciable assets. If you choose a depreciation period of less than three years for any property, you won't be able to claim accelerated depreciation—taking a larger percentage of the deduction in the early years. Useful life must also be at least three years to qualify an asset for the 10 percent reduction in estimated salvage value.

To get an additional first-year depreciation when you acquire personal property to be used for income-producing activities, the useful life of the property has to be at least six years. This additional first-year depreciation allows you to deduct 20 percent of the cost of the property in addition to the regular depreciation. It is figured on the basis of total cost (you don't subtract salvage value), and it may be taken on tangible new or used personal property such as furniture. (Gifts, inheritances, and property acquired from certain related parties don't qualify. A purchase of property from your husband or your wife doesn't qualify; property bought from your brother or sister does qualify.) This additional first-year depreciation allowance is limited to property costing $10,000 on an individual return or $20,000 on a joint return. Say you refurbish your office and buy a new photocopier, tabulating equipment, mimeographing machine, typewriters, etc. In addition, you buy a car to be used exclusively for business. Total cost: $30,000. You may deduct $2,000 (20 percent of $10,000) on a separate return, $4,000 (20 percent of $20,000) on a joint return, and $2,000 (20 percent again) if you file as a corporation.

You must keep records that identify each item of property for which you take the additional first-year depreciation and show how you acquired it and the price paid.

Finally, a shortened useful life can cause you to lose investment tax credits. Only one-third of the investment in qualifying property with a useful life of at least three but less than five years is subject to the credit. Two-thirds of the amount invested is subject to the credit if the property has a useful life of at least five but less than seven years. Property must have a useful life of seven years or more to qualify for the full credit.

EXPENSE RECORDS

Under the law, the IRS may disallow your claims of business expense unless you substantiate them in some way. If you seek to deduct traveling expenses, including meals and lodging, you are expected to have a record of the amount involved; time and place of the travel, entertainment, amusement, recreation, or use of the facility, or date and description of the gift; business purpose of the expense; and business relationship to you of the persons benefiting from the expense. The items should be exact. The IRS says no deductions will be allowed for approximations or estimates or for expenses too lavish or extravagant for the results you hope to achieve.

On travel items, you must prove the amount of each major expenditure for traveling away from home, such as the cost of your transportation and hotel room. You may lump together your expenses for breakfast, lunch, and dinner under the category of meals. Expenses for gasoline, oil, and similar items (tips, phone calls, etc.) may also be lumped together in a miscellaneous category. You must also show the dates of your departure and return home for each trip; the number of days spent on business away from home; name of the city, town, or other place you went to; and the reason for your travel, such as the business benefit you expected to achieve.

On entertainment, you must prove the amount of each major expenditure such as the total restaurant check with waiters' tips. Incidental expenses (taxicab fares, phone calls, tips to hat check girls and washroom attendants) may be aggregated on a daily basis. Your records also should show the date of the entertainment; place; nature of entertainment; persons entertained and their occupation, title, etc., so as to establish their business relationship to you; and your reason or reasons for entertaining. If more than ordinary business meals are involved, you are also expected to describe the nature of any business activity or discussion that took place. If the entertainment is "associated" with business and precedes or follows a business discussion, you must also show the date, location, nature, and duration of the business discussion, and what you hoped to gain from it. You also must record that the persons entertained were those involved in the business talk.

On business gifts, you must describe the gift and show your cost; when you presented it; the name of the person you gave it to, including his title or other designation that will establish your business relationship; what you hope to gain by giving it. "To build goodwill" is generally considered an acceptable reason.

The IRS will accept—in fact, recommends—records of travel, entertainment, and business gift expenditures that are maintained in an account or expense book sold at most stationery stores. You are also expected to keep receipts, canceled checks, etc., that will verify major expenditures claimed. Entries in your record book should be made as soon as possible after the expense is incurred.

Here are other points to remember:

• Documentary evidence (a receipt, paid bill) is required to support all expenditures for lodging away from home and for other expenditures of $25 or more, except that if the evidence for transportation charges is not readily available it won't be required. Documentary evidence will ordinarily be considered adequate if it discloses the amount, date, place, and essential character of the expenditure. To establish your claim for a deduction for lodgings, your hotel receipt should show its name and location, date or dates you stayed there, and separate amounts for charges such as room, meals, and telephone. A restaurant receipt should show its name and location, date and amount of the expenditure, and a breakdown of charges for items other than meals and beverages.

• A canceled check will usually be accepted as proving that you paid what you claimed to pay, but you will still need other evidence such as a bill listing date, nature of expense, and name and address where the expense was incurred.

• If you entertain a large group of persons, it may not be necessary to list all of them if you can establish that they could help you in business. A management consultant making a study of a large Cincinnati firm took the treasurer and five men from the business office to lunch. He didn't recall all their names afterward, but the deduction was legitimate because they could conceivably provide information he needed in his work.

• Small gifts need not be recorded separately so long as you don't seek to exceed the $25 a year you can deduct for gifts to one person. An auctioneer sent $15 bottles of whiskey to nineteen of his best customers. His general description of the gift and the recipients was accepted as sufficient documentation.

• As a self-employer, if you incur expenses on behalf of a client, you must also substantiate your records to the satisfaction of the IRS even if your client reimburses you without demanding proof. A "missionary" representing a pharmaceutical house as an independent contractor attended a meeting of doctors in Chicago. He claimed to have done a great deal of entertaining for the purpose of telling the physicians about the value of his client's products so that they would prescribe them for their patients. His bill for $1,700, citing his expenses in broad terms, was paid by the client. The bill was deemed insufficient evidence when the IRS audited his return, however. So $900 was added to his income upon which a tax was imposed.

• Deductions for business entertaining at home aren't difficult to take and make stick, provided your records back you. Let's say you have a Fourth of July lawn party at your home, a catered affair with forty business associates as your guests. You have a list of the forty and their business relationships ("Bill Brown, client" is about all you need say) along with bills from the catering service, liquor store, butcher, and grocer, and your canceled checks as proof of payment. Your total bill comes to $400. The deduction is completely legitimate—*provided* you reasonably could expect more than $400 in benefits to result from the party.

SELLING YOUR BUSINESS

When you sell as a going concern a business or profession you have operated as a sole owner, the IRS states that instead of disposing of your entire business as an entity, you are selling its individual assets. The IRS makes this distinction to determine whether gains or losses realized on the sale of these components are capital or ordinary gains or losses for tax purposes.

You must classify the assets in your business in three categories:

(1) capital assets; (2) real property and depreciable property used in your business and held more than six months; (3) property such as stock-in-trade, inventory, or property used in your business and held six months or less.

These are the applicable categories for the most common assets in sole proprietorships:

Merchandise inventories: 3.

Building, machinery, furniture, and fixtures held more than six months: 2; held six months or less: 3.

Installment notes and accounts receivable related to services or the sale of stock in trade: 3.

Copyrights that are depreciable property used in your business and held more than six months: 2; held six months or less: 3. If you sell a copyright created through your personal efforts, you classify it in category 3 regardless of the length of time held.

Patents that are depreciable property used in your business and held more than six months: 2; held six months or less: 3. If you are the inventor and sell your patent (or all substantial rights to it): 1.

In the sale of many sole proprietorships, goodwill—in effect, steady customers—is assigned a certain value. Goodwill is a capital asset and hence belongs in category 1. Usually, the buyer of the business wants some assurance that the seller won't set up a competitive operation and take his customers with him; hence a covenant not to compete often accompanies the transfer of goodwill. If you are paid a certain amount to agree not to compete, this covenant belongs with goodwill in category 1.

The extent to which the amount received from sale of a professional practice is attributable to goodwill depends on the facts in each case. If the seller retains a right to fees collected for services he performed before the sale, or sells his right to these fees, the amount he receives is ordinary income, and not goodwill. If the seller retains a right to fees or revenue for services performed after the sale, or the purchaser agrees to pay these fees or revenue, these earnings constitute ordinary income. Suppose you are a member of a professional firm and you sell your interest but let the buyer continue to use the firm name and your name as a member of the firm. "No part of the consideration received for the transfer will be regarded as a sale of goodwill."

The selling price, including consideration for goodwill, must reflect in proportion the fair market value of each asset. After you categorize each asset sold and allocate the selling price, you must make a separate computation of the gain or loss for each asset sold. Then treat it according to its classification. Profits or losses made on categories 1 and 2 are capital gains or losses. Gains or losses in category 3 are ordinary income or losses.

Aside from the value of goodwill and the noncompete agreement when you are selling an unincorporated business, several key areas of apportionment can generate controversy—especially when you try to value inventory, land, and leaseholds.

The bulk sale of inventory as part of the sale of a business produces straight income for the seller as surely as if it had been sold separately at retail or wholesale. The cost of inventory is a solid write-off for the buyer, so he is going to push for the highest value he can get. As the seller, you want to keep its value to the minimum in relation to the total price you want for your business.

Land helps the seller's tax profile: any profit here is capital gains. The buyer, however, cannot depreciate land and he gets no tax advantage until he sells it. Since a leasehold expense is a valid depreciation, under some circumstances you might consider a sale and leaseback to sweeten the deal for a prospective buyer.

In selling a corporation, the form of the sale can be as important as the assets involved. Say you want to sell your corporation. Do you want to sell stock and assets or do you want to liquidate the corporation first and sell just the assets?

Liquidation offers tax advantages but may also bring on problems. Selling just the stock in the company creates a straight capital-gain situation. The cheapest transaction on a true basis is to merge or consolidate or take stock for stock, thus deferring taxes until you sell the new stock. Before deciding what form your sale should take, you should review your particular circumstances with a tax expert.

Many people don't want to sever all ties with the business they may have started and built over many years. They really want to free the money they have locked into the business for other investment opportunities. If this is your goal, clever ways exist to keep your cake and eat it.

One interesting—but tricky—technique is to sell the assets and retain the stock yourself. You create a tax loss for yourself by selling the assets—inventory, machinery, buildings, etc.—for less than their book value, taking the payment in cash. (You can also, if you wish, negotiate a solid employment contract with all the fringe benefits you have.) Then use the cash to convert the stock company into an investment/personal-holding company.

This assumes you have a successful, well-managed business; otherwise you won't find a buyer. The advantage for him is that he gets a good business at a bargain price with competent management in place.

This arrangement has a few tax pitfalls. A personal holding company must disburse earnings annually and faces double taxation (unless it is heavily invested in tax-free bonds).

Similar results can be obtained through more traditional mergers or consolidations—provided not all the transfer payments are taken in stock. To come out ahead of the IRS, when you take cash out of one of these trade-offs, you will need detailed advice from accountants and lawyers who know your situation.

A seller often doesn't want, or can't get, all the cash at once. For one thing, you are limited in the amount of long-range capital gains you can write off in any given year (another reason you may yield a bit on the noncompete covenant). Also, you may find a buyer with everything it takes to assume and run the business except the cash to buy it. The best solution is often to sell the business under an installment contract, which also provides some significant tax advantages.

Formerly the law governing deferred taxation on installment sales was confusing and mined with booby traps. Under the old regulations the amount you collected during the first year could total no more than 30 percent of the full price. If you failed to take into account the amount of a deposit, the effect of a mortgage, or the sale of corporate bonds at a discount from face value, you might inadvertently collect more than 30 percent during the first year and be ineligible for deferred taxation.

The Installment Sales Revision Act of 1980 changed many of these regulations and makes it much easier for the ordinary taxpayer to qualify for installment sales tax reporting.

Under the new regulations you are allowed to accept any amount of partial payment during the first year of the deal; the sale does not have to meet a minimum amount, and there is no provision on the number of installments that must be paid or the time over which they must be spread out.

The new law also changes the regulations governing corporate liquidations. Now, if you are a shareholder in a corporation that is undergoing a twelve-month liquidation and whose assets include installment obligations, you are not allowed to postpone reporting any gain until you actually receive it.

While the Installment Sales Revision Act makes it easier for casual (nondealer) sellers of realty or personal property to qualify for deferred taxes, it also imposes new restrictions on related-party sales. If you sell to a related party (either a person or a corporation) and they resell within two years, you become liable for the full amount of the taxes in the year of the resale. If the property consists of marketable securities and the resale occurs at any time during the intsallment period, you become immediately liable for the remaining tax. Also, in a sale of depreciable property between husband and wife the gain is taxable in the year of the sale even if a deferred payment plan has been worked out. The only exceptions are if the sale is part of a separation or divorce proceeding or if there are no significant tax benefits to be gained by deferral.

Some authorities prefer corporate redemption—buying back the stock—to installment payments. Under this arrangement, assuming your corporation has the cash, you accept whatever cash the buyer has, then have the corporation pay you in cash for stock the buyer couldn't cover. This avoids problems with dividend or interest income and converts the whole transaction into capital gains.

PROFESSIONAL HELP

Your federal and state tax returns should be prepared by a professional, of course. The same man should prepare both returns. Preferably, your regular accountant, the one who has worked on your books all year and has made certain that the records needed to justify deductions have been kept up to date all along, should also be your tax accountant. Figures on your federal and state returns should coincide. If they don't, you may face a lengthy, needless investigation. The IRS now puts tax return information on tapes and a majority of the states run the data through their own computers to be sure they get the taxes due them. Many state tax offices also feed information to the federal government.

Unfortunately, there is no way to make sure you will never be audited. The IRS sometimes examines a return not because it has found something wrong but because it wants to check up on something subject to varying interpretations. The higher your tax bracket, the more complicated your return is likely to be and, therefore, the more subject it will be to different interpretations. Or your business may be one that always prompts the IRS to scrutinize a return—one, say, involving cash transactions. You may even have an enemy who has supplied information that causes the IRS to audit your return.

If you can't absolutely prevent an IRS audit, you can reduce chances that your tax return will be pulled out for special attention by following these suggestions:

• *Double-check your arithmetic.* The IRS computers are programmed to screen tax returns for mathematical errors. Once a computer sets a return aside, an IRS agent takes over—and he may look for more than mistakes in addition. To avoid calling attention to yourself, make sure your arithmetic is 100-percent correct.

• *Avoid duplicate deductions.* If you made a political contribution, for example, you can deduct that contribution either on page 2 of the 1040 personal tax return or on Schedule A. But don't deduct the contribution in both places. If you do, the IRS computer will spot the duplication and pull out your return.

• *File on time.* Even if you have IRS permission to file late, your late return will be something out of the ordinary and therefore subject to special attention—just what you don't want. And remember that the injunction to file on time applies to your quarterly reports and payments of estimated taxes as well as to the yearly return.

• *File all the required forms and schedules.* For instance, if you neglect to send in a 5505 form, giving information about your

Keogh deduction, you are calling attention to your return. And failure to submit a detailed statement about your employees' business expenses raises an IRS agent's eyebrows even more. So be sure you supply every form called for and all the information called for on each form. If, for example, you deduct employee expenses for travel away from home, you have to file form 2106, Statement of Employee Business Expenses (a statement that lists the number of days on business away from home during the year, total expenses for meals and lodging during those business trips, and total expenses for travel and entertainment).

• *Attach explanations.* The IRS becomes suspicious when your income doesn't seem to be large enough to support your exemptions and deductions, when your income seems inappropriately low for someone doing the amount of business you do, when your income and deductions have changed a great deal in the past year or two, when you list a high gross income but a low net income, when your investment profit is less than if you had deposited the invested money in a savings account, and when any indicated refund is out of line with your gross income and exemptions. Rather than explain these things in an audit session, explain them in writing when you send in your return. Don't write an essay; just list the appropriate facts and figures in a tabulation.

You may have substantial casualty or theft losses, for instance. If so, attach a statement and possibly copies of appropriate documents to show how you figured the deduction.

Or you may have a bad-debt deduction. If so, attach a statement listing the amount of the debt, the debtor's name, his relationship to you, when the debt was made and when it was due, what efforts you made to collect it, and why you consider it a loss this year and not some other year. If you lent money to a relative, attach strong evidence to show that it really was a loan and not a gift. Send copies of your evidence, not originals.

Or you may exceed the guidelines the IRS has established for certain deductions. For instance, if you claim on your personal return that you have paid out more in sales taxes than the IRS allows in its guidelines, you must be ready to support your figures with documentary evidence. If you can't, you will be better off to list the IRS figures in order to avoid excessive scrutiny.

Let your judgment guide you in deciding what to tell the IRS—

and what not to tell it. You are expected to attach schedules and provide explanations for many items on your business return—for repairs, amortization, depreciation, etc. But most tax experts agree it is generally a mistake (in filing a return or in an audit session itself) to tell the IRS more than necessary. A reasonable deduction for advertising and promotion will often be allowed without going into details, for example. If you list all the items you consider as advertising and promotion, an auditor may decide some of them aren't deductible.

• *Be specific.* If you list big round numbers, you excite IRS suspicion. Rather than list a deduction for $10,000, for instance, put a figure of $9,873 or even $11,265. The odd number conveys the impression that you have the evidence to support such a figure; the big round number looks like a guess.

Be specific in the labels you attach to your deductions. For instance, you shouldn't bracket all religious contributions under "Church." Instead, list the names of all the religious institutions and charities to which you gave money, allotting a dollar figure to each one.

SOME GENERAL TAX GUIDELINES

• *Keep up to date.* You or your accountant—preferably both—should be aware of recent Revenue Rulings and Tax Court decisions that may affect you.

• *Allocate expenses.* Say you use your personal car for business purposes. You must make a reasonable allocation of the expenses that can be deducted from your business return. You can't deduct all your car expenses if you or your spouse use it for personal transportation; you must determine how much time, mileage, and expenses are truly related to business matters and then make the appropriate deduction. Here again, an explanatory statement may be called for when you file your return.

• *Don't repeat past mistakes.* If you have ever been audited or if the IRS has notified you that you owe more money, be especially careful about the things the IRS caught or questioned you about in the past. In those areas, you should attach explanations and documents lest you seem to be claiming excessively high deductions it has already disallowed. You may be liable for heavy penalties if you seek a deduction for expenses you have already been told you may not take.

Your tax man should be ready to accompany you to the tax office if your return is flagged for an audit. Of course, *you* are responsible for the figures over your signature. If penalties are imposed, *you* must pay the fine or, in extreme cases, go to jail. Nevertheless, the assumption is that your accountant knows more about this subject than you, and if serious discrepancies are found in the return, you should have him at your side to explain them. He is likely to be more experienced in IRS auditing procedures and can make sure that you have whatever records you need to prove your case.

Other points:

If given a choice, opt for a review at the IRS offices—not your own. It's too easy for an examiner to ask for all your records and start fishing. Your own office routine may be upset if he calls at your place. He may see signs of affluence not in keeping with your reported income—and ask questions he never intended to raise.

Be matter of fact in dealing with him. He has received the "hail fellow" treatment too often to be impressed. Naturally, he will resent an approach that regards him as an enemy. Above all, don't talk down to him. Antagonize him, and he may demand to see proof for every item on your return. You may get the treatment reported by a professional man in *The New York Times:*

> The Internal Revenue agent went down the list of my miscellaneous expenses. I had itemized 42¢ for paper clips. He asked me if I could produce a bill or canceled check to back it up. I had an item of 55¢ for rubber bands. Similar question.
>
> I was asked how many cigarettes I smoked a day. He wanted to know where I got the cash to buy my lunches and when I argued he said he was trying to get to my cost of living.
>
> He insisted on a look at my bank books. I had deposits of odd amounts like $52.40 and $34.75 that were obviously not deposits from my business—since the amounts come in $5 and $10 multiples.
>
> He insisted that I mark down what each deposit was. I said

there was no possible way to do this, but that most were dividend checks. He indicated that, in the future, I should mark down in my bank book what my deposits represented.

My son is a student and I claimed him as a dependent. He wanted to know how much income my son had from stocks and bonds. I said about $500. He insisted on calling my son in Dayton, Ohio, and did so three times before he let him off the hook.

Don't play for sympathy. Most IRS audits are made of returns reporting higher incomes than the examiner earns. So don't expect special treatment. It is better to make your case on the strict grounds of merit. You have a 40 percent chance of avoiding additional tax and one chance in fifteen of leaving the audit with a refund. If the examiner hits you with an additional tax, you can appeal for a "district conference" before an arbiter. If still unsatisfied after that, you may have a hearing before the IRS appellate division and, beyond that, in the federal courts. Once you make a federal case of it, however, you had better have all the professional help you can get.

Chapter 10

Handling Your Paperwork

WHETHER you do them yourself or have someone do them for you, maintaining records and making reports is an essential part of your self-employment operation. You must keep some records in order to keep track of your financial progress. You must keep some to conform to federal and possibly state and local regulations. You also must make some reports to comply with federal, and possibly state and local, tax laws.

You will need records to get a true picture of your expenditures and revenues, to know the exact components of your costs, and the exact sources of your income. Kept up to date, such records help you make month-to-month and year-to-year comparisons and to detect significant changes; to determine, for example, whether certain costs are getting out of hand or certain operations are becoming unprofitable.

You will need a *ledger* in which you specifically classify various items of expense and income. Probably the best source of such account books is your trade or professional association. At least dozens of bookkeeping systems are available, designed for specific professional needs. (The books of an allergist seeing more than a hundred patients a week will be substantially different, say, from those of an attorney with three or four corporate clients.) Most large stationery shops also carry ledgers that can be adapted to your purposes. Your accountant can help you set up an appropriate system.

In general, the only financially sound way to operate your affairs is to keep a running monthly check on income and outgo. On one page, you show the figures for this month, side by side with figures for preceding months in the year. Running down the left side of the page, list income and major classifications of expenses. Then, from left to right, set up columns for the twelve months of the year. In this way you will be able to make comparisons with preceding months of this year and comparable months of other years. You then will determine whether an increase or decrease in a month's income or outgo can be attributed to seasonal factors or whether other, possibly unrecognized, causes are at work. Items for which you might keep month-to-month entries are:

Total charges billed during the month

Value of uncompleted work at end of the month, for which you have not yet billed

Total of the above figures, which will indicate your total productivity during the month

Operating expenses, broken down into:

Payroll (including payroll taxes)

Rent, office maintenance, light, heat

Telephone

Office supplies and postage

Travel costs (transportation, lodging, meals, tips, etc.)

Entertainment and gifts

Automobile costs (including one-twelfth of licensing and car insurance costs and depreciation. In the month in which such bills are paid, include only one-twelfth, not the full amount.)

Taxes and other insurance (also prorated)

Interest on loans connected with your business (one-twelfth of annual cost)

Professional fees, memberships, subscriptions, etc. (annual cost divided by twelve)

Other major expenses (such as laundry of uniforms for medical and dental practitioners) not included above
Petty cash and small miscellaneous items

Such a record, totaled each month, gives an up-to-date account of your costs. You will be able to compare not only overall expenses from month to month and year to year, but also specific expense items. An ordinary example: An interior decorator hired a new secretary to take charge of his office while he was out on assignments. He noticed a steady rise in his bills for local phone calls. A quick investigation revealed that his secretary whiled away her time in the office by phoning her friends all over town. Most self-employers probably would catch a sudden jump in telephone expenses in any event; what might go unnoticed, however, is the small but relentless month-by-month increase. Similarly, it is often necessary to make actual comparisons to determine that entertainment expenses for specific clients are costing more while revenues from the accounts are declining.

Using these figures on a month-to-month basis, you can work out and record the following ratios:

Ratio of uncollected bills to amount collected during the month. Let's say that your receipts two months ago were $17,200 and accounts receivable were $10,600. Last month's figures were $18,000 and $11,600. This month's, $18,800 and $13,200. Looking solely at income, you seem to be doing well. However, when you determine the ratio of collections by dividing receipts into bills outstanding, you find that you are not getting paid on time for more and more work. Two months ago, uncollected debts totaled 61.6 percent of income; last month, 64.4 percent; this month, 70.2 percent.

Ratio of operating costs to total income. This ratio ordinarily increases as employees are added. However, the dollar amount of income should increase more than enough to compensate for the increased cost. (If total income is $80,000 and costs are $40,000, the ratio is 50 percent. If you add another helper and costs go up to $45,000 and income to $86,000, the ratio is 52.5 percent. But income after expenses has increased by $1,000.) Genuine concern is called for when you add no employees but your operating ratio rises. This means that expenses are running ahead of income and productivity is declining.

Ratio of entertainment expenses to total income. "Expense account entertaining" can become a substantial cost item unless watched closely. A month-by-month rise in entertaining costs without a proportionate increase in income constitutes a warning that business lunches and the like may be less productive. Many persons succumb to the temptation to overspend on entertaining because, within reason, such expenses are tax-deductible. They overlook that a substantial part of the cost still comes from their pockets and, more important, that unless their entertaining serves a genuine income-producing purpose, it consumes time that could be used more profitably. As chapter 6 on time management indicates, you may have to pay the restaurant only $40 for a nonproductive two-hour business lunch, but the value of time lost for other purposes might amount to $80 or more.

RECORDS AND TAXES

Two points should be kept in mind regarding keeping records in relationship to paying taxes. First, the IRS has the power to force you to keep permanent books of account; second, you are required to keep adequate records in order to substantiate business-related deductions.

If an IRS examiner finds that your records are not adequate to support the claims made on your return, he will inform you orally that your bookkeeping must be brought up to standard. A few days later, you will get a letter quoting the official regulations to this effect. You will be specifically directed to keep a permanent ledger and all pertinent invoices, bills, vouchers, tapes, and receipts. It may advise you to make all disbursements (except for petty items) by check and to keep the canceled checks as proof of payment.

The letter will also warn of the penalties for your failure to comply. There may be a follow-up investigation the next year, and if your records are still inadequate, you may be hauled into court and charged with willful negligence—a misdemeanor for which you may be fined up to $10,000 and/or imprisoned for a year. You will also be stuck with the costs of prosecution.

If the IRS suspects that your reluctance to maintain adequate records stems from an intent to evade or defeat the tax, it may prosecute for fraud. If convicted, you face a fine of up to $10,000 and/or imprisonment up to five years, *plus* the costs of prosecution, *plus* a civil penalty of 50 percent of the amount you were found guilty of underpaying.

Accurate and complete records, of course, give the IRS no reason to bring you to court on either count.

The second point is a reminder that only with records will you be able to pay as little tax as the law allows. Of course, there is nothing wrong with wanting to reduce your tax in every legitimate way. In 1934, Judge Learned Hand of the United States Court of Appeals for the Second Circuit delivered the classic words on this subject:

> Anyone may so arrange his affairs that his taxes should be as low as possible; he is not bound to choose that pattern which best pays the Treasury. Everyone does it, rich and poor alike, and all do right; for nobody owes any public duty to pay more than the law demands; taxes are enforced exactions and not voluntary contributions. To demand more in the name of morals is mere cant.

Chapter 9 discusses in detail the income tax deductions to which you are entitled as a self-employer, and also the records you must submit if your deductions are challenged.

While the law doesn't insist upon a specific record-keeping method, it requires that you establish your income, expenses, deductions, and other pertinent information in a way that is "permanent, accurate and complete." Keeping all records in a book is generally advisable; keeping them on the back of envelopes or on scraps of paper is not. The records should be precise; approximations, particularly where large individual sums are involved, are considered inadequate.

RECORD PROTECTION

A St. Louis dentist was a most meticulous man. He kept all the records required of him, conforming to every requirement and suggestion of the IRS. One night, the building in which his office was located burned to the ground. All his financial records, X rays, and histories of patients were destroyed. He had great difficulty in collecting insurance even on his equipment, for he now lacked proof of its cost. He could not recollect precisely how much his patients owed him (a total of about $12,000), and he even lacked records of who they were and where they lived.

The moral is plain. You not only need records but you need *safe* records. This means you should have a separate set of papers that will be safe from fire, flood, and—in prone areas—tornados, hurricanes, and earthquakes. Some alert self-employers reproduce their records of accounts payable and receivable every month and store them away from their office, often in a safe deposit vault in a bank and sometimes, on the theory that lightning won't strike two places at once, in a file at home. It is wise to store in a safe depository insurance policies, deeds for property, mortgages, and other important papers you will need only in emergencies: bills of sale for equipment that may be required to support tax deductions or insurance claims.

Ordinarily, records for income tax purposes need not be kept longer than the expiration date of the covering statute of limitations. This date is usually three years after a return is due to be filed. Some records, such as those that establish the cost of property you bought in order to engage in business, should be kept until you dispose of the property and the covering statute of limitations expires. If you change your methods of valuing inventory or make other accounting adjustments, you should keep the related records as long as they may affect your tax returns plus three years. Also retain copies of your tax returns and other official correspondence dealing with your tax status. These may be helpful in filing future returns, in establishing precedents for allowable deductions, and in establishing claims for future refunds. They may also help an executor settle your estate.

As a self-employer, you should be especially careful to place in a safe depository those papers that will make it less confusing and difficult for your heirs to settle your estate. In this safe place should be a copy of your *will*. (A will is an absolute essential for a sole proprietor. It is difficult at best to sort out affairs after a self-employed person's death; if he dies without a will, the business itself may be destroyed before the courts decide who gets what.)

Since banks always seal safe-deposit boxes held only in the name of the deceased, and often seal a jointly held vault on the death of either party, your spouse or other heirs should hold copies of these important papers in their own personal safe-deposit boxes. Also, your lawyer should retain a copy of your will in his files. Each party to a partnership arrangement should store his own copies of important papers: life insurance policies on each other's lives, copies of tax returns, other essential legal documents.

MONEY-HANDLING METHODS

Here are questions, suggested by the Small Business Administration, to test the efficiency and safety of your cash and check handling procedures:

1. Does someone other than your bookkeeper open your mail and check receipts against deposits? Mail containing checks, cash, and money orders should not be opened by those responsible for handling your money. An employee will be less subject to temptation if he knows that money will pass through other hands before being deposited.

2. Do you deposit each day's cash receipts in the bank without delay? It is unsafe to hold considerable sums of cash and bad practice to make cash payments out of cash receipts.

3. Do you use petty cash funds only to pay small expenditures (not exceeding a stated amount) and limit them to the amount needed for a week or two? The best way to set up your petty cash fund is to draw a check on your bank funds and reimburse it the same way. Don't add other funds to the petty cash fund or hold a large amount of cash in the fund.

4. Is your postage metered? You lessen the risk of misuse and loss when you use a meter.

5. Do you maintain a separate bank account for your self-employment activities so as to make record-keeping easier? It is advisable to deposit all your business receipts in this account and make all business withdrawals against it, by check whenever feasible.

6. Do you prenumber your checks? If each check, whether

issued or voided, must be accounted for, your record of payments will be more accurate. You will also reduce the temptation for employee dishonesty. Keep your voided checks on file.

7. Do you avoid drawing checks to "cash" and signing checks in advance? Always draw checks to the order of a company or a responsible employee. Never sign blank checks ahead of time. It is an open invitation to dishonesty.

8. Have you bonded your employee or employees who handle cash and securities? This step will do much to remove temptation from them. The cost is relatively slight, the potential savings great.

9. Do you keep company securities locked, preferably in a safe-deposit vault? Misplaced securities can cause great inconvenience. Carelessly stored documents invite theft.

10. Do you check your accounts payable carefully? Statements from vendors should always be checked against the accounts or vouchers payable records. Handle payroll items with the same care as other payments by check.

PERSONAL AUDITS AND NET WORTH

Many self-employers don't truly know whether they are improving their overall financial condition year by year. This isn't as strange as it may seem. Many factors may obscure the true picture. It is so easy to borrow money (at least up to a point) and to run up installment debts that you can operate in the red without being aware of it. Also, unless you carefully check your actual receipts (and keep after those who owe you money), your outgo may exceed income without your realizing it. If the balance in your checking account fluctuates, it may drop a few thousand dollars before it becomes obvious that you are spending more than you are taking in. Unless you regularly add up the current value of your diversified investments, you may have an overall loss without being aware of it.

Clearly indicated for self-employers is a procedure similar to the periodic balancing of assets against liabilities in which virtually all businesses engage. At least once a year—preferably, once every six months—you should make a personal audit.

This need not take more than one page. On the left side of the page, list all your assets:

- *Cash.* This includes cash on hand, cash in the bank and in places where you could put your hands on it quickly (in savings bonds or Treasury bills, for example).
- *Receivables.* This includes amounts owed to you, *but* deduct those bills you may never collect. (Your own loss experience provides the best guide to how much you should consider uncollectible.) Also include interest and dividends due you as of the audit date but not yet paid.
- *Inventories.* This includes goods needed in the conduct of your enterprise. The value assigned to these can be the amount paid for them or the amount you would now have to pay. Your method of valuing inventory should be consistent from year to year.
- *Prepaid expenses.* All bills, not yet due, that you have already paid. Let's say you are making your audit as of December 31. You have already paid your office rent for January, the bill for your hospital insurance that won't fall due until February, and the annual dues for your professional society for the year beginning March 1. These amounts should be listed as assets since you could have chosen to hold the cash and pay later.
- *Cash surrender value of life insurance.*
- *Contributions to pension plan.* Assume you contribute $2,000 a year to a self-employment pension program for eight years. (See chapter 11 on retirement planning.) In addition, your previous contributions have earned $3,200 in interest. Your total pension contributions, plus total interest earned ($19,200) should be listed.
- *Stocks and bonds.* List all your securities for which an active market exists and that you could sell readily. If stocks and bonds are listed on a national exchange such as the New York or American Exchange, write down the last price actually paid for them on the day of the audit. If they are traded on the Over-the-Counter market, value them at the last price *bid* for them. (This is the highest price you can be sure that one hundred shares can be sold for.)

These items constitute *current* assets—cash plus the amount of cash you might raise in a fairly short time if you had to.

Next list the value of all your property, whether used in producing income or not. (A yearly audit of these items can serve another purpose: it can give you an up-to-date list that, with receipts, bills of sale, and canceled checks, will help you obtain proper compensation from your insurance carrier in case of theft, loss, or destruction.) Estimate the current market value of:

- *Your house* and other real estate.
- *Works of art and other valuable possessions.* For example, are you a stamp or coin collector? The value of your holdings might increase or decrease greatly in a year.
- *Machinery and equipment* used in your office (less depreciation).
- *Automobiles,* whether used for business or personal purposes.
- *Furniture and furnishings.*
- *Jewelry, wearing apparel, and other personal possessions.*

Now list other assets that should be noted to make your audit comparable with those of past or coming years. Say that this year you put $2,000 into a trust fund for your child. You hope it will grow through the years, tax-free, and help pay his college tuition. This is in the nature of a "prepaid expense," and doesn't represent outgo in the strict sense of the word.

Another recordable asset might be the amount of money or value of time spent in developing work for which you will be paid later. Generally, this sum is worth recording only if it is substantial. An artist has received a firm assignment to illustrate a book for children. He will be paid $1,000 when he finishes the work. As of the audit date, he has completed three-fourths of the assignment. It is realistic to consider $750 an asset. Perhaps you are a claimant in a damage suit, which the defendant will settle for $4,000. You think you can get more in additional negotiation. According to conservative bookkeeping standards, you may list $4,000 as an asset, it being the lowest amount you could obtain. On the other hand, if you plan to carry the case to court and would get nothing if you lost your suit, you can't properly consider any potential award as a present asset.

Add all the values assigned to the assets in this table. Next, on the right side of the sheet, list liabilities, amounts owed by you. First, the *current* liabilities:

• *Current bills,* for work already done for you, which you haven't paid. On a personal level, this might include amounts owed for medical or dental services; amounts past due for hospital or life insurance but before the "grace period" when the bill must be paid or the policy will expire. Typical current liabilities in connection with business might include bills for telephone or electric service; for printing or secretarial work already done; or unpaid office rent for a month that has already begun.

• *Interest due on loans.* Say that your audit is as of December and that you have a $5,000 loan outstanding at 16 percent annual interest, payable quarterly. On January 1, you will owe roughly $200 to cover interest for October, November, and December. This is a current liability.

• *Taxes due.* Strictly speaking, you should include your total federal and, if applicable, state and local income tax liability for your tax year to date. (If you pay taxes on a calendar year basis and your audit date is June 30, estimate half your year's tax liability; if your audit date is December 31, put down your total tax liability for the year.)

Other liabilities include your long-term debts:

• *Amounts owed on home mortgage.* When a certain amount per month is paid to reduce a mortgage loan, the lending institution frequently handles real estate tax payments for the home owner and you pay a certain amount to cover taxes every month, along with amortization and interest payments. The lender may accumulate these amounts and hold them in escrow before tax becomes due. This "escrow balance" should be deducted from the amount owed. Say that your loan balance on December 31, is $16,675. Your escrow balance is $600. If you sold your house on that date, the $600 would be returned to you. Hence the net amount owed in connection with your mortgage is $16,075.

• *Other debts.* Include amounts owed to banks or other lenders against collateral such as stocks, bonds, or savings accounts passbooks; loans on life insurance policies; current amounts owed on installment loans, etc.

Add your assets and liabilities, then subtract liabilities from assets. This gives you your *net worth*, the approximate amount that would be left for your heirs were you to die on the audit date. (Death payments from insurance policies would be additional; costs of settling your estate and winding up your business affairs would be subtracted.)

You now have a figure that enables you to observe your progress, or lack of it, during the year. If you have made little or no headway since the year before, you will probably want to examine the figures on your income and outgo to determine why your results aren't as satisfactory as you may have believed them to be.

Another meaningful test is to subtract current liabilities from current assets to show how much cash you could put your hands on quickly if the need arose. In corporate financing, a ratio of $2 in current assets for each $1 in current liabilities is considered "safe." The typical self-employer should have a ratio of six to one. Could you meet this test? If not, have you worked out a strategy to get more cash quickly if necessary? For example, if you have a small amount of long-term debt, you might increase it in order to obtain short-term cash. Typical possibilities: could you readily increase your home mortgage or convert other property—jewelry, artwork—into cash? Your audit may warn that you should consider contingencies to avoid finding yourself strapped for cash and unable to raise some quickly if you have a temporary drop in income.

TAX REPORTS

A "sole proprietor" must follow certain income-reporting procedures. If you have earnings of $500 or more in any given year, you must file three forms with the IRS. You must report your business income on Schedule C (Form 1040), which contains spaces for you to list both income items and business deductions. If you follow a calendar year (January 1 to December 31), this form is due on or before April 15 of the year following the calendar year for which you report. If you follow a fiscal year (in which your business year ends some time other than December 31), your return is due on or before the fifteenth day of the fourth month after the close of the fiscal year. Thus if your fiscal year ends June 30, your return is due October 15.

At the same time, you must file a form and make a payment of self-employment tax that will be credited to your Social Security account. This form (Schedule SE) is attached to Form 1040. If you expect the total of your estimated income and self-employment taxes for the year to exceed by $100 or more any withholding of them by an employer, you must file a declaration of estimated income tax. The declaration is made on or before April 15 on Form 1040-ES, usually provided with Form 1040.

You must pay the "self-employment tax," for which you receive Social Security credit, if you earn $400 or more in a year from your self-employment. The maximum amount of tax payable (and credit allowable) is figured on an annual salary of $29,700 for 1981 with a provision that this base amount—the amount on which you have to pay Social Security taxes—will rise automatically if earning levels rise in future years and if there is a corresponding increase in benefit rates for the same year.

Suppose you are a part-time self-employer and also receive wages or salary on which your employer deducts Social Security payments. If your income as an employee totals more than $29,700 you need not make additional Social Security contributions from your self-employment net earnings. But suppose your wages total $20,000 on which Social Security contributions are made, and you earn $15,000 in self-employment. You then apply $9,700 from your self-employment income to bring the total to $29,700. You must file a self-employment tax return (and pay the contributions) even if you have already begun to receive Social Security retirement benefits.

For Social Security purposes, net earnings for the self-employed are described as "the gross income from your trade or business less all of your allowable business deductions and depreciation." Such net earnings are the *total* from all self-employed activities if you have more than one; for example, if you are a real estate appraiser and also run a motel. If you show a profit from one activity and a loss from another, you may deduct losses from profits in order to determine net earnings.

The first step in computing your self-employment tax is to

determine your net earnings from self-employment. This net earnings figure is what is left after you have taken from your self-employment income all related business deductions allowable for income tax purposes. (The IRS insists that you must take *all* deductions. It states: "You cannot increase your Social Security coverage and ultimate benefits by failing to deduct any allowable items, including depreciation.")

Certain kinds of income and deductions aren't taken into account in computing your self-employment tax, even though they are included in computing your total taxable income. These items are those not related directly to your self-employment activities. They include:

- Dividends and interest from personal investments (unless you deal in securities as a regular business).
- Interest from loans (unless you are in the business of lending money).
- Income from rented real estate (unless you are a real estate dealer or you run a motel, boardinghouse, or similar operation in which you regularly furnish services for the convenience of your tenants).
- Capital gains or losses.
- Gains or losses from the sale of depreciable property or other fixed assets used in your trade or business.
- Wages received as an employee.
- Nonbusiness deductions (such as for taxes on your home or interest paid on your home mortgage).
- Deductions for personal exemptions for yourself, your wife, or dependents.

Here is a typical example showing how you must separate income and expenses for the purposes of determining your self-employment tax:

Arnold Severin of Sarasota, Florida, was an independent sales representative for several California companies that manufacture parts for travel trailers. He worked on a straight commission basis, set his own hours, and paid his own operating expenses. For self-employment tax purposes, his net income was the $46,000 he received from the manufacturers *less* his business costs of travel, lodgings, meals, and other expenses away from home ($5,800), telephone calls ($680), entertainment expense ($1,580), and secretarial and postage expense ($850). He didn't include as income the $340 in interest he received from a savings account nor the $2,900 profit realized from the sale of some stock. Nor in computing this tax did he deduct family exemptions, $840 given to his church, $3,600 in local taxes on his home, nor similar expenses he would incur whether he were in business for himself or not.

The benefits to which these contributions will entitle you are discussed in chapter 11.

If you are subject to the self-employment tax, you must of course have a Social Security number. If you have been employed at any time, have bank or brokerage accounts, or own stocks or bonds on which dividends and interest have been paid, you probably have a Social Security number already. If not, you can obtain an application form SS-5 at any Social Security office. It is important, of course, to keep one number all your life so that you will get full credit for all your contributions.

DEFINITION OF AN EMPLOYEE

You must withhold certain taxes and maintain certain records if you have employees. For legal purposes, you may or may not be an employer. To know what you are, you must know what an employee is.

According to a definition by the IRS, "every individual who performs services subject to the will and control of an employer, *both* as to what shall be done and how it shall be done," is an employee for the purposes of these taxes. The IRS states:

> It does not matter that the employer permits the employee considerable discretion and freedom of action, so long as the employer has the *legal right* to control both the method and the result of the services.
>
> While not always applicable, some of the usual characteristics of an employee are that the employer has the right to discharge him and that the employer furnishes him tools and a place to work.
>
> If the employer-employee relationship exists, the description of the relationship by the parties as anything other than that is

immaterial. It is of no consequence that the employee is designated as a partner, coadventurer, agent, or independent contractor. It does not matter how the payments are measured, how they are paid or what they are called. Nor does it matter whether the individual is employed full or part time.

Here are some examples of self-employed persons who subcontracted some of their work and discovered that, in the eyes of the Internal Revenue Service, they had become employers:

• A mason in New Haven, Connecticut, received a contract to erect a brick facing for a small apartment house being built for his brother-in-law. It was necessary to work on a scaffold most of the time, so he needed a helper to carry the bricks to him and mix mortar. He hired a young college student on his summer vacation. He supplied all the tools for the student, determined his working hours, and had the power to discharge him at any time. Although he paid the youth by the hour and the latter understood that the arrangement would cease when the building was faced, he was deemed an employer, responsible for filing all the appropriate returns, paying the required taxes, and making the required Social Security contributions for his helper.

• A dentist in Detroit, Michigan, decided to reduce office and equipment expenses by arranging with another to share his facilities. He made an agreement whereby a younger dentist would work designated hours, using his equipment. The latter would be guaranteed $300 a week and would receive 50 percent of the proceeds from his work above $500 a week. All appointments and billings would be handled by the first dentist's nurse and secretary. Both men thought the young man was an "independent contractor," but his legal status was that of an employee.

• For forty years a man operated a successful optometry business in Albany, New York. He finally decided to sell out and move to Florida. Unable to make a sale outright on favorable terms, he decided to accept an offer to run the business under a profit-sharing arrangement. The offerer agreed to keep open six days a week from 9:00 A.M. to 6:00 P.M. and to keep a bookkeeping system set up by the owner and examined regularly by the owner's bookkeeper. After all the operating expenses were paid, the two men would share the profits. The retired man reserved the right to end the agreement on two weeks' notice. Even though he permitted the other to make most of the day-to-day operating decisions, he was legally the employer.

The line between employees, on whom Social Security taxes must be paid as well as unemployment insurance and workmen's compensation, and who are entitled to the fringe benefits that accrue to other employees, and "independent contractors," is often extremely narrow.

You will be on safe ground if you do the following:

• Don't dictate their working hours. Obviously, you can determine what territory they are to cover and the prices for your merchandise they are to charge. But don't insist that they work a five-day week, for example, or that they make a specified number of calls per day.

• Don't supply them with an automobile. Let them buy their own and reimburse them for travel expenses. In determining whether a worker is an "employee" or not, the IRS looks at the amount he is required to invest in tools and facilities. Someone who has the basic tools given to him is more likely to be considered an employee.

• Pay them on a commission basis. Paying a fixed amount per week is more likely to have them deemed employees.

• Have each independent contractor sign a statement expressing his understanding that he is to serve as an independent contractor, not an employee. In doubtful cases, the fact that he clearly understood that his status was that of an "independent contractor" and that he was not to be put on a regular payroll has been the clinching factor.

EMPLOYEE INCOME TAXES

You must withhold income tax from payments for work done by an employee if his pay exceeds the allowance for his withholding exemptions for the regular pay period covered. This regular pay period may run from a day to a year; it need only be the usual one for your operation.

The amount of tax to be withheld for each person depends on his exemptions and also, in special cases, on exceptional itemized deductions. When he enters your employ, ask him to fill out a withholding exemption certificate (Form W-4), copies of which you can get from your IRS office. On this form he should list his marital status and number of exemptions claimed. If you lack a filled-out Form W-4 for an employee, you must consider him a single person without exemptions and hence subject to the largest withholding. If his marital status or number of exemptions changes, he may file a new Form W-4. You are expected to notify employees once a year, before December 1, that they are entitled to file a new certificate if their status has changed.

Employees who have large itemized deductions (such as alimony, exceptional medical expenses, real estate taxes, or interest payments) that will result in a substantially lower-than-average tax bill may qualify for reduced withholding payments by claiming an additional withholding allowance. To do this the employee must estimate his wages and deductions for the coming year and then, by using the Tax Credit Table for Figuring Withholding Allowances, find the number of withholding allowances permitted. (This table is part of Form W-4.) These additional allowances are claimed by filing Form W-4). Employees who expect no tax liability should claim an exemption from withholding by filing Form W-4E.

Withholding exemptions and allowances claimed by the employee remain in effect until the employee files a new withholding exemption certificate.

Circular E, available from your local IRS office, gives the amount of one withholding exemption for payroll periods of varying lengths and the rates applicable to taxable wages. These rates change, of course, as the income tax laws change. Circular E also shows the amounts you must withhold to pay the employee's Social Security tax. This is also known as the FICA (Federal Insurance Contributions Act) tax. The amount to be withheld is computed on your employee's gross wages. These are the "stated" wages: those before deductions for pensions, union dues, health insurance, etc. You may make deductions for income taxes under a "percentage" or "wage bracket" method.

Under the "percentage" method, multiply the amount of one withholding exemption by the total number of exemptions claimed by the employee on his Form W-4. Next, subtract that amount from the employee's wage. Then determine, according to tables given in Circular E, the amount to be withheld according to the employee's wage level and marital status.

You *must* use the "percentage" method if you pay on a quarterly, semiannual, or annual basis; you *may* use it if you use any other payroll period. You also may annualize your employee's wages: compute what they will be for the year, determine from Circular E how much income tax must be withheld for the year, then divide the tax by the number of payroll periods in the year.

The "wage bracket" method requires using tables based on wage rates in order to compute the amount to be withheld. Circular E contains tables for weekly, biweekly, semimonthly, monthly, and daily or miscellaneous payroll periods for both married and unmarried workers. These will enable you quickly to find the amount you must withhold for an employee with the appropriate marital status, total wage payments, and number of withholding exemptions.

Some employees have found that the amount withheld from their wages does not add up, at the end of the year, to the total tax due on their income. To avoid having to pay a large lump-sum payment to make up the difference, an employee may authorize you to withhold more tax than is usually required. If you agree, his request should be made in writing and be cancelable by either party.

What if you give your employee a bonus on a special occasion—Christmas, say—or for exceptional services? Add the amount of the bonus to the wages for the regular payroll period or preceding payroll period (if it was within the same calendar year). Compute the tax on the total.

And what if you forget to deduct the tax or deduct too little? The law states that you, as the employer, are required to deduct and withhold taxes from the salaries and wages of your employees. It holds you liable for payment even if you fail to collect them. You are liable for the *full* amounts. If you fail to deduct enough from your employee's wages, *you* must pay the difference.

Since you are responsible for withholdings or deductions from an employee's wages, you must have an employer identification number. You apply for it on Form SS-4, obtainable from any IRS office. When completed, the application must be filed with the IRS office designated in instructions accompanying form.

Employers with one or more employees may become liable for federal unemployment tax, which they—not their employees—must pay, as well as being responsible for the taxes discussed above. This tax amounts to 3.4 percent on the first $6,000 paid each employee during the calendar year. You are not subject to the tax, however, unless you employ one or more persons on at least some portion of one day in each of twenty or more calendar weeks during the taxable year or during the preceding taxable year. The twenty weeks need not be consecutive. An employer may receive credit for state unemployment taxes of up to 2.7 percent of salaries paid; thus the effective federal unemployment tax rate could be as low as .7 percent of taxable wages.

If you are subject to federal unemployment tax, you must figure your tax liability on a quarterly basis. Any amount due must be deposited by the last day of the first month following the close of the quarter, in other words on April 30, July 31, October 31, and January 31. To determine if you must make a deposit for any of the first three quarters of the year, you figure what part of the first $6,000 of annual wages you paid each employee in that quarter and multiply that amount by .007. If the amount subject to deposit (plus any undeposited amounts from previous quarters) is more than $100, you must make a deposit. If the amount is less than $100, you don't have to deposit it, but must add it to the amount subject to deposit in the next quarter.

Suppose you employ five people who each make $6,000 a year. Your liability for the first quarter of the year would be $1,500 (the amount each earned in that quarter) x 5 (employees) x .007, or $52.50. Because the amount is less than $100, you would not have to deposit it. You would have to make a deposit at the end of the second quarter of the year, however, because your total liability at that time would exceed $100. ($52.50 for the second quarter *plus* $52.50 carried over from the first quarter.) Circular E and Form 940 (used in making the deposit) contain instructions on how to determine the tax and also how to compute credits you may be allowed for contributions required for the unemployment fund in your state. More information is available in IRS Publication 539, *Withholding Taxes and Reporting Requirements.*

You must file an annual return on Form 940 on or before January 31, following the close of the calendar year for which the tax is due. The tax due for the last quarter of the preceding year must be paid in full when the return is filed.

If you are required to withhold income tax from wages or are liable for Social Security taxes, you must make a return for each calendar quarter on Form 941 provided by the IRS. As of the second quarter of 1981 an employer must include with Form 941 a copy of the W-4 form for any employee who claims to be exempt from withholding or who claims ten or more withholding allowances and who normally earns more than $200 per week. Form 941 must be filed before the end of the month following the period covered (for example, by April 30 for the January-February-March period).

You must deposit in an authorized bank both the total Social Security taxes you and your employees pay under the Federal Insurance Contributions Act and the total income tax withheld. These deposits must be made weekly, semimonthly, or monthly, depending on the size of your payroll.

The single remittance covering the taxes to be deposited must be accompanied with a filled-in Form 501, "Federal Tax Deposit, Withheld Income and FICA Taxes."

EMPLOYER'S RECORDS AND REPORTS

You are obliged to report to the IRS all wage payments to employees subject to taxes and to keep records for at least four years after the related taxes become due or are paid, whichever is later.

These records can be kept in your own way, but should include the following.

• Amounts and dates of all wage payments subject to these taxes.

• Names, addresses, occupations, and Social Security account numbers of employees to whom payments are made.

• Their tax exemption certificates (Forms W-4) listing their claimed exemptions.

• Periods during which they were in your employ.

• Amounts and weekly rates of payments made to employees while they were absent due to sickness or injuries and the periods for which they were paid.

- Receipts showing deposits of taxes made and duplicate copies of quarterly and annual returns filed.
- Your employer identification number.

You must furnish copies of Form W-2, "Wage and Tax Statement," to each employee from whom income tax has been withheld or would have been withheld if he had claimed no more than one withholding exemption. The form W-2 should show your employer identification number and your employee's Social Security number; total wages and other compensation paid, whether or not they are subject to withholding; amounts deducted for income tax (federal and, where applicable, state or local), and Social Security tax, including hospital insurance, purposes.

If you haven't withheld income tax from an employee's wages but have deducted money for Social Security contributions, you must furnish him with a written statement showing your name and address; name, address, and Social Security account number; the total wages you paid him during the calendar year; and the total amount you deducted for Social Security on his behalf during the year.

These tax statements should be furnished to employees still in your employ as of December 31 in January of the following year. If an employee leaves your employ and isn't expected to return, you must furnish him with the W-2 or Social Security statement not later than thirty days after your last payment of wages to him.

RECORD-KEEPING ASSISTANCE

"There's a bad thing and a good thing about having people on your payroll," a real estate appraiser once told me. "The bad thing is all the paperwork it involves. The good thing? You can get people to do the paperwork."

Many accountants specialize in setting up ledgers, handling the books, making out payrolls with their various deductions, filing the necessary returns, and keeping the necessary records for self-employers. These specialists generally are aware of all the reporting and record-keeping requirements and thus can handle the work without indecision and delay. If you hire someone to keep your books, set up your payrolls and prepare your tax returns, it is no great added expense to get him to handle the tax reporting and record-keeping as well.

Various services regularly advertise that "our computers will remove the headaches from your bill collecting." They claim that you need only provide the raw material (your ledger of accounts) and they handle all the billing, addressing, and mailing. Services range from the simple sending out of bills and recording of receipts to regular updatings of delinquent accounts and sophisticated analyses of income sources when your records contain breakdowns showing how much is charged for what. The purpose of this analysis is to enable you to pinpoint the most profitable phases of your operation.

Obviously, the value of such services depends on the number of bills sent out each month. The professional man with a few clients has no use for it. On the other hand, a practitioner of general medicine has many low-income clients. His fees are small and paid from many sources: Medicare, Medicaid, labor unions, workmen's compensation, etc. Billing services consider him an ideal prospect. Some claim they can save him 50 percent on his billing costs.

What is the track record of such services to date? Reports are mixed. This much is certain: they are not a magic solution. Some have delivered on their promises and relieved self-employers of what some consider their most disturbing operating problem. When billing inside your office takes one person only one week per month to handle, however, chances are that little or nothing is saved. "I was told I could save on employees' salaries by farming out my billing," a West Coast dentist said. "But I still have the same inside overhead plus the added outside costs." Others have reported incredible computer foul-ups. A Maryland psychologist lost a week's work trying to pacify patients who received an extra zero on their bills. Instead of $100, the computer insisted that they owed $1,000.

If you think any of such services may help you, first make sure of these points: (1) that you have enough work to justify turning the job over to specialists; (2) that the service knows enough about your operation to do a good job, for what is good for a plumbing service may not be good for you; and (3) that the service is reputable and can supply references of customers who will recommend it without reservation.

Chapter 11

Planning Your Retirement

UNLIKE wage earners and employees in many corporations who are offered an opportunity to participate in union- or company-sponsored pension plans, self-employed persons generally must devise their own programs to insure an adequate income in their old age.

This burden may not be quite so heavy as it first seems. As a self-employer, you generally enjoy a major advantage over an employee: no one will tell you to stop working simply because you have reached "retirement age." Self-employed persons in all careers can be found going strong at eighty. Indeed, one of the advantages of self-employment is that at any age it gives you the option of doing as much or as little work as you think necessary.

Nevertheless, income from work does decline for most self-employed persons once they reach their sixties. Work weeks become shorter and vacations longer. Costs of living are met from other sources in descending importance:

- Income from savings and investments.
- Capital gains and dividend income from tax-sheltered pension plans, such as the "Keogh plan," which enables the self-

254

employed to set aside up to a tax-deductible $7,500 or 15 percent of earned income a year during their productive career. The theory is that when they draw from capital in later years, it will be taxed at lower rates.

- Social Security retirement benefits (when self-employment activities are substantially decreased).

INVESTMENT RETIREMENT CUSHION

Hundreds of ways exist to build equity that you can draw on in later years. Self-employers probably have used them all. Inasmuch as you must rely on yourself in sickness and in health, it is probably wise to maintain a quick-cash reserve to carry you through possible periods of lowered income. Professional money managers traditionally recommend the equivalent of six months' income in the form of savings accounts, savings bonds, or short-term U.S. Treasury bills, which may be quickly converted to cash if necessary.

Almost all advisers agree, however, that savings accounts should *not* constitute the major part of a retirement program. As long as inflation remains a threat—and few prognosticators foresee when it won't—savings accounts afford inadequate protection against erosion of the purchasing power of the dollar. In recent years, savers suffered actual losses in such accounts. First, they had to pay taxes on earned interest at ordinary (highest) tax rates. After taxes were deducted, what remained did not compensate for the inflation-caused loss in the purchasing value of their dollars.

Even in noninflationary times, savings accounts are less desirable than other ways to build capital over the long term. They return the same number of dollars originally invested, hence afford no opportunity to make capital gains, which are taxed at lower rates than ordinary income. Moreover, interest from savings accounts generally is lower than that obtainable elsewhere: from bonds, debentures, and preferred stock, for example.

Sophisticated investors favor the building of capital at favored tax rates. *Real Estate investments* are popular. Many sophisticated persons believe that some of the best words on investing were spoken by Will Rogers: "Buy land; they're not makin' it anymore." Income-producing properties such as farmland, business and industrial buildings, and apartment houses are widely favored. Historically, land value has increased over the years to keep pace with the rising tide of inflation. United States post offices and many gasoline, supermarket, and nationally based retail chains prefer to lease the property on which they do business. Because they usually take all responsibility for maintenance, the property owners merely give them the keys and need expend no effort in servicing the investment—a feature that appeals to self-employers concerned with other matters.

Investments in buildings have been attractive in the past because their owners have been permitted to deduct large amounts of income for depreciation, thus getting a quick return without immediate taxes. Prospects of large cash flows have also made it appealing for groups of individuals in high tax brackets to form partnerships to buy goods they can *loan:* jet airplanes, railroad equipment, or highway trailers. Other self-employers invest in *mineral research and oil wells.* They are permitted to take depletion allowances out of income so that their capital quickly returns to them and is thus available for other investments.

Huge profits have been made at times by investors in *art.* Over the fifteen years from 1952 to 1967, a study by Sotheby's auction house in London disclosed, prices of works of six leading Impressionist painters increased 1,000 percent. During the same period, prices of prints by Rembrandt van Rijn increased 2,300 percent. Prices of works by some American artists increased forty times in twenty years. Self-employers also have gained from such traditional inflation hedges as *diamonds, stamps and coins, silver, antiques, arms and armor, and rare art objects.*

To profit from such investments calls for *knowledge and continuing alertness* to changing trends. Just as in other forms of investment, ignorance—or bad luck—can produce appalling losses. While the prices of most famous artworks rose in the 1950s and 1960s, those of certain British portrait painters fell to less than half their previous highs.

STOCK PORTFOLIO

A *Survey of Financial Characteristics of Consumers,* prepared for the board of governors of the Federal Reserve System by Dorothy S. Projector and Gertrude S. Weiss, gives a breakdown of a large representative sample of the self-employed in the thirty-five-to-sixty-four-year age bracket. According to this study, the larger your total assets, the more likely that you will favor investments in publicly traded stocks and bonds. The study revealed that in portfolios of from $25,000 to $49,999, 16 percent was in stocks and bonds; from $50,000 to $99,999, 23 percent; $100,000 to $499,999, 31 percent; $500,000 and over, 72 percent.

A study by Robin Barlow, Harvey E. Brazer, and James N. Morgan, *Economic Behavior of the Affluent,* indicates that self-employed persons in the high-income brackets pay more attention than do average individuals to the management of their portfolios. Most high-income individuals included in the survey, Brazer and Morgan said, "seek information from investment advisory publications, stockbrokers, bank officials, and other qualified professionals, but they ordinarily make their own investment decisions. And even when they delegate some authority over day-to-day transactions, they usually give fairly specific instructions about the handling of their portfolios."

Capital gains are preferred over current yield by most high-income individuals as an investment objective, these researchers found. Safety and liquidity are also considered important, even at higher income levels. Only a few consider current yield to be more important than capital gains, and these individuals are generally the less well informed. Those active in the financial sector (banking, insurance, accountancy, etc.) are most likely to belittle the importance of current yield. They are also the most informed and sophisticated about investment management and are the most interested in liquidity.

The researchers found that almost all of the 957 affluent persons they interviewed have some common stock. "Common stock comprises the largest component of the portfolio for half the entire high-income sample," they reported. "The attractiveness of common stock is shown, too, by the fact that past and expected future changes in portfolio composition consist largely of the substitution of common stock for fixed-yield assets. A major exception to this attitude toward stock is evident among those individuals with the very highest incomes, who tend instead to favor tax-exempt municipal bonds and certain other fixed-yield securities when making adjustments in the composition of their portfolios."

Only one-tenth of the persons interviewed reported delegating some or all authority over their investments. Only 2 percent of the entire high-income group said they delegated all authority. This doesn't mean that advice is scorned. Three-fourths of the high-income sample generally consulted stockbrokers, bank officers, and other qualified professionals. A majority also read business magazines or investment advisory publications to try to keep abreast of the market.

That self-employed persons keep a close watch over their investments should not be surprising, inasmuch as the qualities considered necessary for success on one's own in a career are the same as those regarded as valuable for intelligent investing. Almost by definition, the self-employer has great self-assurance, the confidence that he can make a sound decision. Nevertheless, at least several hours a week must be devoted to managing one's own portfolio. If you can't give this much time, you probably should seek competent investment management.

Many brokers downgrade the ability of independent entrepreneurs to manage their own portfolios. The firm of F. I. Dupont Glore states that

> some self-employed have the illusion that, being pretty intelligent in their profession or business, they can manage their financial life with a little finger, but this may turn out to be a grievous error.
>
> Many experienced investment people say the worst-managed money of all is that of professional men. One stockbroker recently remarked: "When a doctor tells me how to beat the stock market, I say 'Fine, I'll buy myself a do-it-yourself appendicitis kit.'"
>
> Successful self-employed persons with surplus income often may be pushovers for what look to be local investment opportunities such as a business building which may produce more headaches than profit, a vacant lot with a "future" (and high taxes and idle-money losses in the meantime), a farm on the

edge of town which may turn out to be just an extravagant hobby, or a personal friend with a get-rich-quick scheme which needs lots of capital.

The self-employed individual may have taken 10 or 15 years to learn his business or profession, but he may try to become an investor with no more investment experience than that of a little boy collecting postage stamps.

INVESTMENT ADVISERS

Although numerous studies have indicated that professional advisers as a group often achieve no better results than the rest of investors, self-employers can obtain reasonably satisfactory returns by following the suggestions of brokers or other advisers or by letting professionals manage their portfolio either directly or through the purchase of shares in mutual funds. But you should exercise cautions in the choice of any adviser.

• *Brokers.* Any stockbroker you deal with should be a member of a national exchange: the New York or American exchanges, for example, or the National Association of Security Dealers. These are self-regulating bodies that strive to maintain high standards of integrity among their members. The firm you deal with should be financially strong. At certain times it will have your money or stocks in its hands and if it runs into financial difficulties you may have trouble recovering. Investor protection insurance may reimburse you ultimately, but your funds might be tied up for a long period.

Selection of a registered representative ("account executive," "customer's man") is crucial. As the person you will deal with directly, he can do much to help or hinder your investment success. First, you should be compatible. If you incline toward careful conservatism, you don't want a representative who will bombard you with tips on "stock that will double in a week." He should respond to your cue as to how you want your account handled. Do you want someone who will simply execute your orders and provide requested information promptly and otherwise leave you alone? Or do you want him to alert you to investment ideas and call regularly to discuss your portfolio? If you choose a brokerage firm because you think it offers superior investment advice, make sure that he transmits the research department's suggestions. (Many representatives disregard the suggestions and cook up their own.) If you depend on him to supply buy recommendations, let him know that you want to be told at once when he thinks it is time to sell. (Failure of brokers to suggest selling the stocks they have recommended is a common complaint of investors.)

• *Mutual funds.* According to a common but erroneous belief, you can simultaneously avoid all responsibility for investments and achieve even average results by casually buying mutual fund shares. This is not so. Some funds consistently achieve results no better than their clients themselves could get by picking stocks from a hat. Other funds do better in some markets than others. Another problem is the number of funds now widely sold. They have greatly different objectives and investment philosophies. Your chances of coming at random upon a fund that suits your particular requirements are mathematically slim.

The general principle underlying mutual funds is that they are a means whereby the individual with a limited knowledge of stocks can benefit from professional management and enjoy the material rewards and security that come from diversification. This principle is valid, of course. But it does *not* mean there are no incompetents among mutual fund managers. You can't just choose *any* fund and come out ahead.

Mutual funds are generally divided into two categories: those sold by salesmen and involving a commission or "load" paid by the buyer, and those available without sales commission, which usually don't seek shareholders as aggressively. Buying a "no load" fund demands investigation and enterprise on the buyer's part. One not disposed to make the effort to search out a fund suitable for his purposes would be well advised to consult an expert in this field whose judgment he trusts. You should apply the same criteria in choosing a fund salesman as in choosing a broker. (Usually a stockbroker also sells mutual funds.)

The intelligent choice of a mutual fund should be based on two factors: its suitability for you and its performance record. Funds come with a wide range of objectives. Some emphasize safety of principal and invest mostly in high-grade bonds and preferred stocks. Some stress balance and include different grades of stocks and bonds in their portfolios. Growth funds may specialize in issues that pay low dividends now but have good prospects. Some funds aim for maximum protection against inflation; many specialize in particular fields, like emerging technologies; some appeal to church groups and refuse to buy stocks of companies making or selling liquor, tobacco, or playing cards. You must decide which is your kind, and your expert (broker, fund salesman, investment counselor, etc.) should find a fund that fits your objectives and preferences.

Performances of funds (meaning the overall return obtained for shareholders) have varied widely over the years. There is no assurance that a fund that has done well will continue to do so. Fund managers die or switch jobs, funds change objectives, and times change. The fund in tune with the 1980s may be out of harmony with the 1990s. Nevertheless, it seems more prudent to select a fund with a good record than one without it. From the mass of funds competing for the attention of shareholders, your adviser can choose one for you that has been successful for investors; hopefully, it will be so in the future.

The best time to buy fund shares is after dividends are paid. Funds generally make capital gains and other declarations at the end of the year. At that time they distribute all or more of the gains realized through sales of portfolio holdings during the year. The stockholder receiving this dividend must pay a capital gains tax at his applicable rate. Assume that you buy shares on December 1 at the asset value of $16.00. The fund then declares a capital gains dividend of $2.00, and your federal and state tax liability is 20 percent. When the dividend is effective, the asset value per share is reduced to $14.00. Since you will have only $1.60 left after the tax payable on the $2.00 you have received, you lose 40¢ per share on the transaction. If you buy a load fund before the dividend is declared, you also pay a commission on the total dividend, another unnecessary expenditure of perhaps 17¢ per share. On the other hand, if you wait until the fund goes ex-dividend, you may get 5 percent more for your money.

Investors whose mutual fund shares may become part of their

estate should also be aware of an IRS ruling that bases the estate tax on the "asked" rather than the "bid" price of fund shares. Even though the owner of fund shares cannot redeem them at more than the bid price, the tax collectors insist that the shares be valued at the higher figure, which includes the sales commission. This ruling could increase one's estate tax by 4 percent or so. In June 1970 the U.S. Supreme Court refused without explanation to hear an appeal that sought to change the ruling.

• *Banks and trust companies.* These probably handle more investment funds than does any other type of investment management. While investment managing as a separate profession is only about fifty years old, trusts in various forms have operated for centuries. Originally, companies were set up specifically to handle trusts. A hundred years ago, banks began to take trust accounts. Today the pure trust company is a rarity. Most commercial banks, whether state or nationally chartered, have trust departments.

An investor can set up several kinds of trust. The most common type, established under the terms of a will, provides for management of the individual's assets after his death. This is known as a *testamentary trust.* Increasing in numbers are *living trusts.* In a common form, investors set them up in the names of heirs who will be their beneficiaries after death. If a trust is irrevocable, either permanently or for a temporary period, investors gain important tax advantages. (Many public figures such as Cabinet officials put their assets in trusts that remain irrevocable as long as they hold office.) Other trusts are revocable. The maker can change them at will and generally can add or subtract from them as he wishes.

Trusts of this kind are useful in estate planning. In some cases they enable you to minimize gift taxes while alive and estate taxes after death. You may give, with your spouse, up to $6,000 a year to each person free of gift tax. If these funds are invested, the earnings accrue to the beneficiary, presumably at a lower tax rate, and, in the case of minor children with no other earnings to report, possibly at no tax at all. If the funds have been placed in an irrevocable trust, they pass directly to the heirs at the time of death without the time-consuming and costly probate procedure. (The gift having been made during the lifetime, there also is no inheritance tax, since the amount involved is not figured as part of the estate.) If you wish to retain control of the funds during your lifetime, you may set up revocable trusts in the names of your beneficiaries. In that case, the money left to them will be figured as part of the total estate, and an estate or inheritance tax may have to be paid.

You need not place your funds in such formal and contractual situations in order to make use of a bank's investment managing services. Different banks offer different arrangements. A common procedure is for a bank's trust department to manage investors' accounts, making decisions to buy or sell without necessarily getting clients' approval, and keeping custody of the securities, having access to the funds, and doing all bookkeeping. To open such an account, some banks require $25,000 and others $100,000. Often there is also a minimum fee. It may be as low as $200 a year; in other cases it may be as large as $1,500 or more. The minimum is offset against a sliding scale of management charges, often starting at 0.5 or 1 percent of the total amount of the portfolio.

Some banks have several account managers who may handle a few very large portfolios or several dozen smaller ones. You usually can choose between a nondiscretionary account, which requires your approval for all transactions, or an arrangement giving the account manager power to buy and sell without consulting you first. You may also elect to take physical possession of securities in your account or leave them with the bank (sometimes at a slightly higher fee). The typical account manager will try to tailor security selection to your requirements. At your request, he may steer clear of issues with a speculative taint or may deal only in issues with strong potentials for capital gains. As a rule, bank investment managers report quarterly on their portfolio and performance, much the same as mutual funds. They hasten to reassure clients, however, that they keep stocks in the portfolios "under constant review."

Because many customers don't have $100,000 to invest at present—and because many who may ultimately have that sum to invest might have as little as $5,000 to begin their investing— many banks are setting up common trust funds, which are like mutual funds. Since 1937, they have been able to pool the assets of many smaller investors (to commingle them) in order to provide whatever measure of safety is involved in holding securities of many different companies. Some banks allow customers to start with an initial investment of $100 and to add to their assets regularly with as little as $25 a month.

As is true of most other fiduciary arrangements, trusts are often handled by persons anxious above all to protect their own jobs and to avoid being accused of recklessness in managing the funds entrusted to them. They may completely avoid growth stocks about which there is a faint speculative aura but that might, on balance, contain a greater potentiality of gain than loss.

Their investment posture is based on a Massachusetts Supreme Court decision in 1830 setting down "the prudent man rule." The Massachusetts General Hospital and Harvard College, which had been named joint beneficiaries of a trust, brought the trustees to court after its assets declined sharply. Judge Samuel Putnam ruled for the defendants, arguing that to hold trustees responsible for all losses would paralyze their judgment and make it virtually impossible for them to function. At the same time, he pointed out, a trustee must exercise reasonable care: "He is to observe how men of prudence, discretion, and intelligence manage their own affairs, not in regard to speculation but in regard to the permanent disposition of their funds, considering the probable income, as well as the probable safety of the capital to be invested."

Most states define a trustee's obligations in similar terms. The District of Columbia publishes a "legal list," which trustees often use as a catalog of permissible investments. Even if the securities on the list decline sharply in value, it is generally believed that the trustees are safely protected against suits—they exercised prudence and therefore are not responsible.

Some trustees, of course, are more venturesome than others and go beyond blue chips, arguing that what constitutes prudence changes with the times and that the 4 percent bond that once was the safest vehicle for widows and orphans has become a highly imprudent investment due to the ravages of inflation. Nevertheless, the main concern of trustees is still to preserve capital, and the individual who expects a gain in assets from a trust may often be disappointed.

• *Investment Counselors.* As indicated above, many professional men find it desirable to place complete reliance on a private professional manager. They empower him to handle their portfolios and make all buy and sell decisions. You cannot simply choose *any* counselor, however, and achieve satisfactory results.

If you hire an investment counselor, you must make certain that he is competent. To conduct a thorough investigation may be difficult, however. Private investment managers often refuse not only to give any indication of the results they can achieve but also fall back on their professional status to keep the lid on their past performances. Standard advice is to ask a professional for references and to check with other clients to find out whether or not they are satisfied.

A more satisfactory way exists of grading an investment manager's work when he also runs a mutual fund. Funds are managed by Eaton & Howard, Loomis-Sayles, T. Rowe Price, Scudder Stevens and Clark, Van Strum & Towne, among others. Their performance can be compared with that of competitive funds by examining fund records published by *Barron's, Forbes,* and other fund-rating guides.

Ideally, an investment counselor should derive his total income from the portfolios he manages. It should not directly affect him financially whether a buy or sell order is executed or by whom. In the past, some brokerage firms that maintained counseling services were accused of churning accounts in their portfolios. They not only collected fees for their advice but allegedly also profited from commissions generated by frequent purchases and sales. To avoid such charges, some brokerage firms with counseling services deduct their brokerage profit from the counseling fee.

Once hired, a professional manager should be consulted regularly. Unless you check up regularly to see what is being done with your money, you may awaken to discover that large, irrecoverable parts of it have gone down the drain.

PENSION PLANS

Until 1962, self-employed persons were at a distinct disadvantage, relative to corporation executives and employees, in making pension arrangements for their old age. While the latter could gain important tax benefits through pension plans, the former could not. That inequality was remedied in 1962, when Congress enacted the Self-Employed Individuals' Tax Retirement Act. This act applies to anyone with self-employment income.

Under what is now known as the Keogh plan, named after the congressman who pushed the act through, a retirement fund may be established by virtually everyone who fits the description of the self-employed. In any year, those who qualify, and who have no employees, may contribute up to 15 percent of their earned self-employment income (their gross income less all deductions for business expenses) up to $7,500. The amount of this contribution can be deducted on your tax return for the year. You need not contribute to the plan in any year you choose not to do so or in which you have no net profit from your self-employment activities.

If you have an employee who works more than twenty hours per week and more than five months per year, you must include him in the plan within three years after you hire him. Your contribution for him must be proportionately the same as your contribution for yourself. He retains his right to his part of the retirement plan if he leaves your employ. If you have employees in the plan, you may contribute another 10 percent of your earned income up to $2,500. The additional contribution itself may *not* be deducted from taxable income. However, all capital gains, interest, or dividends earned on it are exempt from taxes until you retire. Your employee may also make an additional contribution to match the amount you contribute for his benefit.

If you decide the cost of including your employees in a Keogh plan would be too high, you can opt for an Individual Retirement Account (IRA). Under this plan, you can set aside 15 percent of your earnings up to a limit of $1,500.

You can open an IRA if you are not already making contributions for yourself into a qualified benefit plan, and an employer—private or governmental—isn't making contributions for you. Receiving benefits from a pension plan you had previously doesn't disqualify you for an IRA.

A married couple can set up separate IRAs, each with a $1,500 or 15 percent maximum, when both are earning income. If a spouse isn't working outside the home, you can still open two IRAs, or one IRA with two subaccounts, but the maximum deductible amount you can contribute to such accounts is $1,750 or $875 for each spouse. It is advisable to contribute equally to such accounts, because you are allowed to deduct only twice the lower amount.

You don't have to open IRAs for employees just because you have one. But if you want to, you can give this benefit to key employees. You don't have to contribute the same percentage of their salaries as you contribute for yourself. Nor must the percentage be the same for all employees. You can put an amount equal to 4 percent of your plant manager's salary into an IRA, for example, and 2 percent of a foreman's salary. If they choose to, your employees can add to these accounts from their own funds, up to the 15 percent or $1,500 limit.

You can start withdrawing benefits from your IRA when you are 59½. Earlier withdrawals without penalty are allowed only if you become disabled or die.

Between the ages of 59½ and 70½, you can withdraw any amounts you choose, at any intervals. If there is still money in the account when you reach 70½, you must decide whether to withdraw your money in a lump sum or in periodic payments for the rest of your life or life expectancy (or the life or life expectancy of yourself and your spouse). As a rule, all payments are taxed as ordinary income.

An advantage of IRAs is that you can "roll over" assets of one account into another without a tax liability. You must accomplish the rollover within 60 days and meet other IRS requirements. You can, for example, roll over the assets of a regular IRA into an IRA annuity. You can also roll over assets from a terminated Keogh plan into an IRA. Say your Keogh plan called for a lump sum withdrawal at age 65. If it is not financially desirable to take that lump sum, even considering the tax breaks available to you, you can roll the Keogh assets into an IRA without tax liability. You don't pay tax until you start receiving payments, which you will be able to put off until you are 70½.

You can set up your IRA as a trust or custodial account with a bank, other institution, or qualified individual. The IRS has developed a model trust and model custodial account (forms 5305 and 5305-A respectively). If you adhere to these forms, your plan will meet tax code requirements.

Your IRA can also be in the form of an annuity or endowment contract. Or you can choose to purchase special U.S. retirement bonds.

Penalties for premature withdrawals and excess contributions are similar to Keogh penalties.

Premature withdrawals. The penalty for withdrawing funds before you are 59½ or disabled is 10 percent of the withdrawal. Borrowing or using IRA funds as security for a loan is considered a premature withdrawal. The amount involved is subject to the same 10 percent penalty, and your IRA will no longer be tax-exempt.

Distributions that are too little or too late. If you set up a withdrawal schedule after you are age 70½, but you fail to meet it, the deficiency is subject to a hefty 50 percent tax. For example, if you are supposed to take $3,000 in a year and you take only $1,800 the penalty would be $600—50 percent of the $1,200 shortage.

Excess contributions. If you put more into your IRA than is allowed, you will face a 6 percent tax on the average.

You deduct your contributions to your IRA or Keogh plan from your income when you prepare your tax return. Your contributions must be made by the day the return is due. To be eligible to receive deductible contributions in a taxable year, your Keogh plan must be set up before the last day of that year. An IRA can be set up as late as the filing date for the previous year's return.

The IRS requires that an IRA holder file Form 5329 with his annual return. A Keogh holder must choose between three forms: Form 5500 is for plans with 100 or more participants; 5500-C is for plans with less than 100, and in which no owner-employees participate; 5500-K is for plans with less than 100 and which include one or more owner-employees. Check with the IRS regarding filing dates for these forms and about additional forms they may require.

Your retirement plan must be approved by the IRS. If you use an already approved plan, this is a mere formality. You sign one form for the custodian and another for the IRS. Approved Keogh and IRA plans have been set up by mutual funds and other investment companies, savings banks, insurance companies, and others. Usually these sponsors act as trustee for the plan at little or no charge but reserve the right to apply a fee in the future if the expenses of complying with government rules get out of hand. You could set up a trust of your own, but this is a highly involved procedure and, for almost everyone, more trouble than it is worth.

You may also set up your retirement fund by using special *retirement bonds* the U.S. Treasury offers. You have to buy the bonds in the name of the individual (yourself or your employee) who is covered in the plan.

The bonds carry various interest rates, depending on money conditions at the time of issuance. The interest is compounded semiannually, and their owner cannot cash them until he is 59½ years old. The only exceptions are for death or disability. U.S. government spokesmen say the bonds offer an easy way to set up a plan: "They offer safety, a fixed return, ready availability, elimination of administrative costs, an exemption from state income taxes."

The law specifies the kinds of benefits your plan can provide:

Retirement benefits at the normal retirement age of sixty-five
Delayed retirement benefits
Early retirement (after 59½)
Disability benefits
Benefits for death before retirement
Severance benefits
Death benefits after retirement

• *Delayed retirement benefits* mean that you may postpone your retirement past age 65. But you must begin receiving benefits no later than the taxable year in which you reach 70½. Your employees also may delay their retirement income.

• *Early retirement* permits you or your employees to receive retirement benefits any time after reaching 59½ years of age.

• *Disability benefits* are paid for total and permanent disability regardless of age and service (number of years you or the employees have been in the plan).

• *Death benefits before retirement* are also payable regardless of age and service. Say one of your employees dies at fifty. His survivor must be paid the benefits in the fund for him.

• *Severance benefits* are those an employee is entitled to when he leaves your employ. These benefits will be paid when he becomes 59½. However, if he becomes disabled or dies before 59½, his benefits are paid at the time of disability or death.

If you or your employee dies after retirement, the amount remaining in your fund must be distributed to the beneficiary within five years, or be used within five years to buy an immediate annuity for the beneficiary.

The law provides penalties in the form of extra taxes for the premature distribution of benefits: if you withdraw funds from your plan before you are 59½, the penalty is 10 percent on top of the ordinary income tax that you must pay on premature withdrawals. You are also barred from participating in the plan for five years.

Certain transactions are considered as making premature distributions. If you make loans against the annuities of your retirement fund, the loans count as distributions from the fund. Repayments on loans are regarded as contributions to it.

Certain transactions between you and the trustee of your retirement-plan fund also are prohibited. You may not lend any part of the income or body of the trust. You may not have the trust pay you for personal services you might render to it. You may not receive any services from the trust on a "preferential" basis; for example, if your employees do not get the same services. Nor may you sell or buy any property from the trust.

The primary advantage of the retirement account is that it enables you to deduct money from the top of your taxable income every year. This tax-free amount goes to work, earning capital gains, dividends, or interest, and all the while being sheltered from taxes. Your money thus grows much faster than if you were valuing all your income in the year it was earned. The gains and interest keep compounding until you reach retirement age. At retirement time, when you must pay taxes on it, you probably will have a lower income than now. Consequently, your tax rates will be in a lower bracket.

As an example of the equity-building potentiality of this plan, let's say your taxable income from your profession or business is $50,000 per year. You deposit $7,500 in your tax-qualified account and deduct the full amount on your federal income tax return. In some states, such as New York, you may also deduct the amount from your state income tax return.

Let's assume you are now thirty-five and plan to retire at sixty-five. During these thirty years you may deposit up to $225,000. While you are making new contributions, amounts already deposited are earning money. Assume that you invest in a plan that earns on average only 5 percent a year with all dividends and capital gains compounded on a quarterly basis, not an unreasonable expectation by any means. At the end of the thirty-year period, you will have roughly $531,000—almost two and a half times as much as the actual amount deducted from your self-employment income. When you retire, you can take everything due you in a lump sum or arrange to have it paid to you over a ten-year period.

The kind of plan you choose can have a striking effect on your tax status for the year and the total number of dollars you may be entitled to upon retirement. Under some circumstances (you have few employees, for example, who must be covered under similar conditions) you might be well advised to choose either a Keogh or a corporate plan. If you have a large number of employees and limited profits and income, choosing an IRA for yourself may be indicated.

Before choosing any plan, it is advisable to figure out your potential tax savings and ultimate retirement benefits.

But choosing the kind of plan is only half the problem. How you invest the money the law entitles you to set aside tax-free each year may be a more crucial factor in determining whether you have a relatively worry-free old age or whether your pension will prove inadequate for your daily needs.

The type of pension plan you choose has the same tax features—a deduction for the amount originally deposited, no taxes on interest or capital gains while the fund is in operation, taxes payable only when money is withdrawn. And no matter what plan you choose, if the money is invested unwisely, you may be worse off than if you used your income in your business and sold out at a higher price upon retirement.

The many investment vehicles competing for pension funds offer widely different prospects. Some guarantee that the dollars in your pension fund will grow at a specified rate, year by year. Such guarantees are easy to make. For example, you can invest in securities of the federal government that are regarded as the safest investment anywhere. These securities may pay assured interest rates of, say, 8 percent per year so that every dollar you set aside will double every nine years, subject to no taxes until you make withdrawals.

What is uncertain about this "certain" income, however, is how much those dollars will be worth when you withdraw them. The rate of inflation may have subsided so that you have substantial purchasing power to live on. On the other hand, inflation may have accelerated so much that the dollars with all their tax-free interest that you withdraw at age sixty-five will buy considerably less than the dollars you deposit today.

The preferred haven for investment funds at present is in fixed-interest securities. These are such things as bonds and debentures that promise a specific percentage yield and that, if the issuer is sound, will pay off a specific amount at a specified time. Giant pension funds with their own managers invest in bonds directly, but smaller pension funds are increasingly investing in bond mutual funds, often operated by the same companies that manage common and preferred stock funds.

The motivation for investing in bonds is that it saves the pension trustee from doing any work. Bonds are rated by several rating services, including Moody's and Standard and Poor's. While a pension fund trustee may be held personally responsible if he fails to make "prudent investments," he is almost certain to get off the hook by going into bonds the rating services declare are fully safe. (Investors in New York City bonds and elsewhere have found, however, that a bond rated "fully safe" when it is issued may be considerably downgraded or even perilously close to unsafe when the time approaches to pay it off. Persons in a position of trust who bought such bonds when issued probably cannot be considered "imprudent" if the investments turn sour.)

Another advantage of bonds—for the fund manager, if not for the individual whose future is at stake—is that the retired worker will probably get all the dollars he has been promised. The ability to have dollars ready to pay pensioners is a great advantage to employers, because they need not dig into profits to make up for deficits in their pension funds. The fact that the purchasing power of the dollars held in an employee's name may be less when he retires than they are today will not be held against pension fund managers. Legally, they probably can be held accountable only if there are fewer dollars on hand than there should be. Hence fund managers who invest in top-grade bonds at least assure themselves that they won't be held responsible regardless of what happens to the economy.

In recent years, one of the increasingly popular places in which to invest pension fund assets has been the "money market" type of mutual fund. These funds invest in short-term U.S. government bills and notes, bank certificates of deposit, large loans issued by corporations, and similar instruments that can be converted into cash very quickly. Such funds provide investors with higher rates of interest than savings institutions can pay, yet are about as safe as possible.

Since the first money market fund was launched in November 1971, almost fifty have come on the scene. Their total assets now top the four-billion mark, and share sales have recently been running more than a half-billion dollars a month. Twice as much now goes into money market funds as into conventional stock or bond funds. The standard management fee runs about 1 percent of total assets per year. This includes operating expenses. The investments generally return well over 2 percent more than is obtainable from most savings banks and similar institutions with equal safety. Many money market funds are operated by large management companies, and shareholders often can switch to other funds if they think stock or bond prices are due for a rise.

Savings institutions are very much in the running in the battle for pension fund accounts. It is possible to earn as much as a guaranteed 8 percent and more on deposits. As this is written, in New York state, a seven-year time deposit account pays an annual rate of 7.75 percent. With interest reinvested over the seven-year period, the earnings amount to 8.17 percent yearly. Each account is insured by the Federal Deposit Insurance Corporation to a maximum of $100,000. Over a long span of time, stocks have returned about 9 percent a year. Hence the person who puts pension funds in a savings institution may do as well as one who invests it in the volatile stock market, after commissions, etc., are deducted.

In dollar terms, a regular contribution into a bank savings plan can produce spectacular results—at least before inflation is taken into consideration. If you contribute $1,500 a year under a savings plan that yields 8.17 percent annually, your total savings plus interest after five years would be $9,552. Without the tax advantages, the amount would be only $6,016. After thirty-five years of regular contributions of $1,500 a year, your account would be worth $290,641, as opposed to $181,374 if the pension tax exemption were not applied. As I write, $300,000 would enable the average pensioner to live comfortably for the rest of his life. By the year 2010, however, the buying power of $300,000 may be considerably less.

Insurance Companies Compete

Insurance companies are also actively promoting plans that have received approval of the Internal Revenue Service for use in Independent Retirement Accounts or Keogh plans. In most cases, HR 10 (Keogh) plans include some life insurance—an inclusion permitted within certain limits by the Treasury.

Insurance companies like John Hancock are promoting "fully guaranteed plans"—previously approved by the IRS—that provide life insurance prior to retirement as well as a guaranteed amount of monthly income for life during retirement. If you don't qualify for or need life insurance, you can obtain retirement annuities without it.

The insurance companies also offer plans based fully or partly on stock or bond investments. Under these plans the annual contributions can be invested entirely in variable annuities or mutual funds, or they can be split, with part going to buy life insurance policies and the rest invested in variable annuities or mutual funds.

Under the typical insurance company investment plan, you can make withdrawals on a regular basis of so much per year, with the income taxed only as it is received. Or you can receive your entire interest in a lump sum. This amount received can be income-averaged so that your tax bracket will be lowered.

According to *Forbes,* the financial magazine, pension fund managers are plunging into real estate funds. It estimates that they have been investing $2 billion a year in such things as apartment houses and commercial properties.

Some of these investments are being made by the same banks and financial institutions that launched or supported real estate investment trusts—one of the most disastrous investment vehicles in thirty years.

Real estate investment managers claim they can deliver long-term returns of 9 to 10 percent. On its face, such a return would meet the requirements of all but the most demanding pension funds. But the promised return—if delivered—doesn't reflect actual income from rentals. It also is based on estimates of appreciation in the value of the properties held—an iffy situation at best, made more iffy because the estimates are by "experts" who gain by making higher evaluations rather than lower ones and also because no one can guarantee that real estate will increase in value over the years.

In discussing real estate as a pension fund medium, *Forbes* commented: "Watch your step, boys!"

Basic Question for Stock Investors

The late J. P. Morgan, when asked to forecast the future of stock prices, would say only that they would fluctuate. In order to give pension fund managers the two things they most desire— assurance that the number of invested dollars will at least remain constant and a chance of capital appreciation to keep pace with inflation—many mutual fund groups now offer insurance on their shares. The investor pays an annual premium of about .6 percent per year for a ten-year policy, or about .4 percent for a fifteen-year policy. He is then guaranteed the full value of the amounts originally invested, sales commission, and the cost of the insurance itself. For instance, over a ten-year period, the insurance guarantees that $10,000 invested in the fund will bring at least $10,720 (the premium charge plus a fixed fee of $12 a year). Appreciation in the fund, over and above the original investment, naturally is credited to the pension fund.

More and more mutual fund managements are offering these shares, but they are not without defects. The insurance is only as good as the insurers. An unanswered question is whether these insurers will have enough cash to cover gigantic stock market losses such as occurred in 1929 and even 1970.

Another question revolves around the purchasing power of the payment the insurance company will make if the price of the fund shares declines. The typical plan requires that investors reinvest all dividends so that money earned during the ten-year period is not counted in the amount the insurance company must make good. A $10,000 investment that dropped to $9,000 in actual share value but that paid $2,000 in dividends during the period could leave the investor worse off with the insurance than he would have been without it.

Achieving Maximum Flexibility

Investing pension money in mutual funds appeals to some business owners with a risk-taking mentality. The flexibility of dealing with a fund company with a variety of funds also has an appealing aspect. For instance, if you believe the stock market is due for a rise, you can specify that your pension assets be placed in a fund that concentrates on common shares of growth-oriented issues. If you think it is time to switch to fixed income securities like bonds, you can instruct the management company to transfer your assets to a bond fund. When you think the stock market is due for another rise, you can switch your assets again. Usually only a small fee is charged when the same manager transfers assets from one fund to another.

Anyone now investing in a bond or "money market" fund managed by a diversified management company can also avail himself of the option of switching out of bonds at any time, and for a small fee go into any other fund managed by the company. (It is important that the pension money, once invested, be in your hands at no time. Such a situation could disqualify the pension. You would be considered to have made a premature withdrawal, even though you fully intended to invest the money elsewhere.)

"Do-It-Yourself" Investing

Many mutual fund managements aggressively seek small pension fund investments. However, their performance record in recent years is nothing to cheer about. Studies have shown that the typical fund does no better than the stock market as a whole, and the fact that your money is handled by a professional is no guarantee that it won't fall as far or as fast as the market itself. From 1970 to 1980, for example, the assets of many fund-managed pension plans dropped 50 percent. This means that persons seeking to withdraw their funds in 1980 would have much less to take out than they expected. If retiring persons were guaranteed a certain amount per month, the employer must pay it to them, regardless of the investment performance, and cut into his own profits to do so.

While they are often unhappy about the professional management of their funds, most owners of small firms don't have time to make their own investment decisions. They have a business to manage and cannot be bothered. Another disadvantage of doing it yourself is that the small pension fund usually lacks sufficient assets to diversify and thus minimize risk. For example, it is generally not feasible to invest in some government or corporate bonds in amounts of $100,000 or less. As a practical matter most business owners entrust others with the management of the pension fund.

Making the Right Decision

Unfortunately, the only sure way of putting your pension funds in the best place is to arm yourself with a crystal ball. As in the case of life insurance itself, you will know whether you made the right decision only after the game is over.

Making the best choice depends on two factors—the extent to

which you will need withdrawals from your pension plan to live comfortably in retirement (if, indeed, you retire at all), and the extent to which inflation or deflation will influence the value of your holdings.

If you anticipate retirement at sixty-five, and an adequate return from your pension investments will make the difference between living in comfort and living in penny-pinching circumstances, you probably will be better off (and feel more secure during your working years) if you choose a plan that guarantees a certain return. Taking on speculative securities is not advisable if you would be reduced to dire circumstances if you lost. On the other hand, if the amount you get from your pension will not materially affect your own standard of living—only the amount you will leave your heirs—you can more readily choose a plan, like investments in mutual funds, that has the possibility of greatly appreciating in value but will not create severe hardship if it doesn't.

The extent to which the buying power of the dollar will decline (or increase) in coming years also must be considered. Virtually all economists consider inflation inevitable in the foreseeable future.

In the opinion of many highly regarded investment analysts, a share in a profit-making American business is the best long-term hedge against inflation. As I write this, many of such shares are available at bargain prices. What is lacking is the public's faith that American business can continue to increase profits in the years to come. When and if investors come to believe that again, prices of common stocks in sound companies probably will reflect their true values.

SOCIAL SECURITY RETIREMENT BENEFITS

Ever since the federal system of old-age insurance was born in 1936, Social Security has formed a basic part of most Americans' pension planning. This system combines life insurance on the head of the family and old-age insurance. As a self-employed person, you probably must pay a self-employment tax (see chapter 10) to the Social Security fund. Therefore, you are legally and morally entitled to various payments which the system provides.

Like other insurance, your retirement benefits will depend on the amount of your contributions over the years. This amount depends, in turn, on your earnings and the length of time during which you have made (or have had made for you) contributions to Social Security. The amount of your monthly benefits will also depend on whether you take them at age sixty-two, when a lower income may be obtained, or at age sixty-five or later.

If you intend to work past sixty-five, you should apply for benefits two or three months before reaching that age. You will thus establish your right to Medicare benefits and to monthly benefits when you retire. You will not jeopardize your right to continue working later if you decide to do so.

If you wish, you may begin to take retirement benefits at sixty-two. The amount will be reduced, of course; the closer you are to sixty-five when you begin receiving payments, the less the reduction. If you return to work after sixty-two, the benefits you will receive later will be adjusted upward.

According to law, if you are under the age of seventy-two (seventy starting in 1982), you are allowed to make no more than $5,000 if you are over sixty-five, or $3,720 if you are under sixty-five, without losing some of your Social Security benefits. If your earnings go over the annual amount, $1 in benefits is withheld for each $2 of earning above the limit. However, you will be granted retirement benefits even if you continue to receive large sums (in the form of royalties, for example) for work completed before you retired.

To obtain Social Security retirement payments, you must have credit for contributions for a number of calendar quarters. You get credit for four calendar quarters for each taxable year in which your net profit from self-employment covered by the law is $400 or more. A net profit of less than $400 for any year does not count for Social Security.

Most self-employed persons are covered. An oddity is that clergymen, even those working as employees, are regarded as self-employed. Their earnings as clergymen are covered unless a cleric files a statement that he is conscientiously opposed, or "opposed by reason of religious principles," to making contributions and receiving benefits.

If you have any doubts about your own status, your local Social Security office will tell you whether your work is covered. If covered, you must pay Social Security contributions regardless of your age and even if you are now receiving benefits. You get credit for these contributions no matter how old you are.

As a self-employer, you report your own net earnings after the end of each taxable year in which your net income totaled at least $400. This report is part of your individual federal income tax return and is labeled "computation of Social Security self-employment tax." You must pay this tax even if you need not pay a federal income tax.

One credit is allowed for each "quarter of coverage." The number of credits you will need for retirement benefits is shown in Table 2. Credits earned at any time after 1936 may be counted.

Table 2

Year you are 65	Quarters of coverage needed for retirement benefits		Quarters of coverage needed for hospital insurance	
	Men	Women	Men	Women
1971	20	17	12	12
1972	21	18	15	15
1973	22	19	18	18
1974	23	20	21	20
1975	24	21	24	21
1976	24	22	24	22
1977	24	23	24	23
1978	24	24	24	24
1982	28	28	28	28
1986	32	32	32	32
1990	36	36	36	36
1994 or later	40	40	40	40

Table 3 shows maximum benefits payable for different categories. In figuring average earnings, take the highest earnings for the number of years you are required to count. Say you were born in 1921 and retire in 1981. You need count only the 27 years in which your Social Security contributions were highest.

The exact amount of the monthly retirement payment you will receive can't be figured accurately until you apply for benefits. The reason, of course, is that all earnings until the time of your application must be considered. However, Table 3 shows the various benefits in effect as of 1981. From it, you may at least approximate the benefits to which you may be entitled upon retirement.

MEDICARE BENEFITS

In addition to retirement benefits, Social Security provides broad health insurance for those sixty-five and older. Some persons have found this insurance, Medicare, the most valuable part of the Social Security program. One part, hospital insurance, helps pay for hospital care and some follow-up services. The other part, voluntary medical insurance, helps pay bills for physicians and other medical services.

When you reach sixty-five you are eligible for hospital insurance if you are entitled to monthly benefits either as an insured person or dependent. Those not entitled to monthly retirement benefits can buy this protection. To buy hospital insurance, you also have to enroll and pay the monthly premium for medical insurance. You can apply at any Social Security office.

The number of credits needed for *hospital insurance* under Medicare is shown on the extreme right of Table 2. When physical treatment is required, this hospital insurance pays the cost of covered services up to 90 days of inpatient care in a participating hospital in each benefit period. A benefit period ends 60 days after you leave the hospital and during which time you haven't been a patient in another hospital or nursing home. Theoretically, you could be covered for two 90-day and one 65-day period of hospitalization (245 days) in a calendar year. For the first 60 days of any stay, the insurance pays for all except the first $180 for all

Table 3

Monthly retirement benefits for workers who reach 62 in 1979–83

Average yearly earnings	For Workers				For Dependents[1]				Family[2] benefits
	Retirement at 65	at 64	at 63	at 62	Spouse at 65 or child	at 64	at 63	at 62	
$923 or less	121.80	113.70	105.60	97.50	60.90	55.90	50.80	45.70	182.70
1,200	156.70	146.30	135.90	125.40	78.40	71.90	65.40	58.80	235.10
2,600	230.10	214.80	199.50	184.10	115.10	105.50	95.90	86.40	345.20
3,000	251.80	235.10	218.30	201.50	125.90	115.40	104.90	94.50	384.90
3,400	270.00	252.00	234.00	216.00	135.00	123.80	112.50	101.30	434.90
4,000	296.20	276.50	256.80	237.00	148.10	135.70	123.40	111.10	506.20
4,400	317.30	296.20	275.00	253.90	158.70	145.40	132.20	119.10	562.50
4,800	336.00	313.60	291.20	268.80	168.00	153.90	140.00	126.00	612.70
5,200	353.20	329.70	306.20	282.60	176.60	161.80	147.20	132.50	662.70
5,600	370.60	345.90	321.20	296.50	185.30	169.80	154.40	139.00	687.10
6,000	388.20	362.40	336.50	310.60	194.10	177.80	161.70	145.60	712.10

6,400	405.60	378.60	351.60	324.50	202.80	185.80	169.00	152.10	737.10
6,800	424.10	395.90	367.60	339.30	212.10	194.30	176.70	159.10	762.30
7,200	446.00	416.30	386.60	356.80	223.00	204.30	185.80	167.30	788.90
7,600	465.60	434.60	403.60	372.50	232.80	213.30	194.00	174.60	814.70
8,000	482.60	450.50	418.30	386.10	241.30	221.10	201.10	181.00	844.50
8,400	492.90	460.10	427.20	394.40	246.50	225.80	205.40	184.90	862.60
8,800	505.10	471.50	437.80	404.10	252.60	231.40	210.50	189.50	883.80
9,200	516.00	481.60	447.20	412.80	258.00	236.40	215.00	193.50	903.00
9,400	520.40	485.80	451.10	416.40	260.20	238.40	216.80	195.20	910.40
9,600	524.60	489.70	454.70	419.70	262.30	240.30	218.50	196.80	918.00
9,800	530.40	495.10	459.70	424.40	265.20	243.00	221.00	198.90	928.00
10,000	534.70	499.10	463.50	427.80	267.40	245.00	222.80	200.60	935.70

[1] If a person is eligible for both a worker's benefit and a spouse's benefit, the check actually payable is limited to the larger of the two.

[2] The maximum amount payable to a family is generally reached when a worker and two family members are eligible.

covered services. For the remaining 30 days of each stay that qualifies for benefits, it pays for all covered services except for the first $45 a day.

You also are entitled to these benefits:

• A "lifetime reserve" of 60 additional hospital days, which can be used if more than 90 consecutive days of hospital care are required. For each of these additional days, hospital insurance pays for all covered services except for $90 a day. (This provision makes possible one extended hospital stay, paid by insurance as indicated, of 240 days.)

• Up to 100 days of care in each benefit period in a qualified facility when you need continuing skilled nursing care for a condition treated in a hospital. When all conditions are met, the insurance pays for all covered services for the first 20 days and all but $22.50 a day for 80 additional days.

• A maximum of 100 home calls by nurses or other health workers employed by a health agency affiliated with Medicare when ordered by a doctor as an extension of hospital treatment. Payments for these visits can be made for up to twelve months after your most recent discharge from a hospital if your doctor has set up a home health plan for you within fourteen days after your discharge from a hospital or participating skilled nursing facility.

The *medical insurance* part of Medicare is available to almost everyone 65 or older. If you want medical insurance protection, you have to pay a monthly premium for it whether you are eligible for Social Security or not.

If you are receiving Social Security benefits you will be enrolled automatically for medical insurance (unless you don't want it) at the same time you become entitled to hospital insurance. You should receive information about the plan from the Social Security Administration about three months before you are eligible for hospital insurance. If you are not receiving Social Security, you can get information about both plans when you apply for benefits.

Medical insurance has a seven-month initial enrollment period. If you sign up during the three-month period just before the month you reach sixty-five, you will be protected as of your sixty-fifth birthday. When you apply during the month of your birthday or the three months following it, protection starts as of the month you enroll. If you turn down medical insurance, then decide you want it after your initial enrollment period ends, there is a general enrollment period during which you can sign up—January 1 through March 31 each year. By doing this, however, you will pay a higher premium for your protection and the protection won't start until July of the year you enroll.

The medical insurance generally requires that you pay the first $60 each year for physicians' and surgeons' services or other covered medical expenses. Thereafter it pays 80 percent of them. The only requirement is that the charges be "reasonable."

In addition to physicians' and surgeons' fees, these services are covered:

• Outpatient hospital services for diagnosis and treatment, such as care in an emergency room or outpatient clinic of a hospital.

• Up to 100 home health "visits" each calendar year. These are in addition to the 100 visits covered by the hospital insurance.

• Outpatient physical therapy and speech pathology services.

• Diagnostic tests, surgical dressings, splints, casts, braces, rental or purchase of medical equipment and other medical and health services.

• Services of independent physical therapists, limited to a maximum of $80 during any one year.

• Physicians' psychiatric services outside a hospital, limited to a maximum of $250 during any one year.

DEATH OR DISABLEMENT BENEFITS

If you die before you become sixty-two, certain members of your family may be eligible for survivors' benefits. You must have one-quarter of coverage for each year after 1950 and up to the year of death if you were born in 1929 or earlier, or after the year you reached twenty-one and up to the year of death if you were born in 1930 or later. In all cases, your surviving dependent children are entitled to monthly benefits if you worked six quarters in the three years before your death. Widows may also receive benefits if they take care of children entitled to benefits.

Under Social Security law, a worker is considered disabled if a physical or mental condition keeps him from doing any substantial gainful work and is expected to last (or has lasted) at least twelve months or to result in death.

Evidence from a physician or other qualified sources must be presented to prove the severity of your condition and the extent to which it disables you. If you can't do your regular work but can take other gainful jobs, you are not considered disabled.

Among conditions ordinarily considered disabling are: loss of major function of both arms, both legs, or a leg and an arm; acute arthritis that severely limits the ability to get about or use the hands; diseases of heart, lungs, or blood vessels that have caused serious loss of heart or lung reserve; serious loss of kidney function; cancer that is progressive and has not been controlled or cured; severe loss of judgment, intellect, orientation, or memory; mental illness resulting in deterioration in personal habits and seriously impaired ability to get along with other people.

The number of work credits needed for disability benefits depends on your age when you become disabled.

If under twenty-four, you need credit for six quarters of work out of the three-year period immediately preceding the disability.

If twenty-four through thirty, you need credit for half the quarters from the time you reach twenty-one until you become disabled.

If thirty-one or older, you need the amount of credit shown in Table 4. Five years of this credit must have been earned in the ten years ending when you became disabled. The years need not be continuous or in units of full years.

Disability benefits for workers disabled after 1978 and their dependents are based, in part, on earnings that have been adjusted to take into account increases in average wages since they were earned. The adjusted earnings are averaged together and a formula is applied to the adjusted average to figure the benefit rate.

Monthly benefits for workers disabled in 1980 range as of 1980 from $122.00 to $552.40. Monthly benefits to a worker and family range from $183.00 to $966.70.

Table 4

Work credit for disability benefits

Born after 1929, became disabled at age	Born before 1930, become disabled before 62 in	Years of work credit you need
42 or younger	1971	5
44	1973	5½
46	1975	6
48	1977	6½
50	1979	7
51	1980	7¼
52	1981	7½
54	1983	8
56	1985	8½
58	1987	9
60	1989	9½
62 or older	1991 or later	10

Disability benefits are not paid in addition to Social Security retirement benefits. If you could receive more than one monthly benefit at the same time, the amount you receive will ordinarily be the larger one. If you become disabled after you start receiving Social Security benefits, it may be wise to seek disability benefits. If you start receiving retirement benefits at sixty-two and become disabled at sixty-three, your benefit may be higher if you change to disability payments.

Index